William George Searle

Ingulf and the Historia Croylandensis

William George Searle

Ingulf and the Historia Croylandensis

ISBN/EAN: 9783743357259

Manufactured in Europe, USA, Canada, Australia, Japa

Cover: Foto ©ninafisch / pixelio.de

Manufactured and distributed by brebook publishing software (www.brebook.com)

William George Searle

Ingulf and the Historia Croylandensis

INGULF

AND THE

HISTORIA CROYLANDENSIS

AN INVESTIGATION

ATTEMPTED

BY

W. G. SEARLE, M.A.,

LATE FELLOW OF QUEENS' COLLEGE, CAMBRIDGE,
AND LATE VICAR OF HOCKINGTON, CAMBRIDGESHIRE.

Cambridge:

PRINTED FOR THE CAMBRIDGE ANTIQUARIAN SOCIETY.

SOLD BY DEIGHTON, BELL, AND CO., AND
MACMILLAN AND CO.

1894.

Dissertatio Epistolaris
pag. 71.

carnacionb xpi Septingentesimo uno Sextodeci
mo ✠ Ego Æthilbaldus Rex Merciorum
gr Apchiepi naucicam ✠ Ego Wymund
ar consensi ✠ Ego Aldwinur lichesfeld
epo Æthelpeduy Albay de Bandenly multan
aliorb pogani ✠ Ega Comes Lindcolne
co Ego Saxulphur filius Saxulpli com
trupth uocatur audiun ✠
...n Merciorum epo gubernacula ruma
phtacb republicum in p°. encarnacioneq
i sanctab matur ecclesue pplicabuy bs

✝

Sutton Nicholls sculp.

INGULF

AND THE

HISTORIA CROYLANDENSIS

AN INVESTIGATION

ATTEMPTED

BY

W. G. SEARLE, M.A.,

LATE FELLOW OF QUEENS' COLLEGE, CAMBRIDGE,
AND LATE VICAR OF HOCKINGTON, CAMBRIDGESHIRE.

Cambridge:
PRINTED FOR THE CAMBRIDGE ANTIQUARIAN SOCIETY.
SOLD BY DEIGHTON, BELL, AND CO., AND
MACMILLAN AND CO.
1894.

The frontispiece is a photographic copy of the engraving of the lower part of the 'Golden Charter' of King Æthelbald (§ 122).

Cambridge:
PRINTED BY C. J. CLAY, M.A. AND SONS
AT THE UNIVERSITY PRESS.

CONTENTS.

		PAGE
j.	Croyland	1
ij.	The 'Historia Croylandensis' .	1
Part I.	Ingulf's Chronicle	3
iij.	Authorities for the history of the Anglo-Saxon period of England, and their notices of Croyland . .	3
iv.	St Guthlac	25
v.	The name of the place, Croyland or Crowland?	42
vj.	The text of the 'Historia Croylandensis'	44
vij.	The foundation of Croyland Abbey .	54
viij.	The 'Golden Charter' of King Æthelbald	55
ix.	Jews in England in A.S. times	58
x.	The Benefactors of Croyland Abbey during the Mercian period	60
xj.	The Destruction of Croyland Abbey by the Danes in 870	62
xij.	Turketul [Thurcytel] abbat of Croyland, and the Restoration of the Monastery in the year 948 .	69
xiij.	The King's Chancellor in Anglo-Saxon times	79
xiv.	Great Britain. . .	82
xv.	The royal title	85
xvj.	Coronations in A.S. times	87
xvij.	The two charters of 17 July 17 Ric. II. 1393, and of 1 Nov. 1 Hen. IV. 1399	88
xviij.	The Sempects . .	89
xix.	Hereward	93
xx.	Earl Waltheof, the martyr . . .	104

		PAGE
xxj.	Ivo Tailbois	110
xxij.	Alliteration in the Ingulf	113
xxiij.	Discrepant marks of the date of the writer (Ingulf)	114
xxiv.	Chronological and historical mistakes in the Ingulf	115
xxv.	Exaggerations in the Ingulf . .	144
xxvj.	Meteorological observations	148
xxvij.	History of the Ingulf since the 15th century.	149
xxviij.	The Ingulfine charters	153
xxix.	The witnesses to the Ingulfine charters . .	156
xxx.	The anachronisms found in the Ingulfine charters	164
xxxj.	The dating of the Ingulfine charters . . .	185
xxxij.	Formulæ of Subscription in the Ingulfine charters	188
xxxiij.	Norman words and expressions found in the Ingulf	190
xxxiv.	Authors quoted or incorporated by Ingulf . .	192
xxxv.	Abbat Ingulf	194
	The Author's postscript .	206

In the earlier years of Henry VIII.'s reign John Twine (Wood's Ath.) wrote his De rebus Albionicis published in 1590 (8°. Lond.). In this work he refers to a work 'de fundatione Monasteriorum in Anglia' by Henry Crompe (or Crump) a Cistercian monk who flourished temp. Ric. II. (Bale ; Dict. Nat. Biogr.), respecting the restoration of forty monasteries by King Eadgar. From his silence respecting any restoration under Eadred we may perhaps conclude that neither Crompe, whose work does not seem to be known, nor Twine knew anything respecting the restoration of Croyland described by Ingulf.

*** Part II., dealing with Peter of Blois and the three anonymous continuations, is in preparation.

BIBLIOGRAPHY.

Acta Sanctorum ord. S. Bened. fo. Paris, 1668 ff.
„ „ of the Bollandists. fo. Antw. 1643 ff.
Æthelweard, Chronicorum libri iv, in Savile.
Anglo-Saxon Chronicle ed. B. Thorpe. 2 vols. R. S. 1861; ed. J. Earle. 8°. Oxf. 1865.
Art (L') de vérifier les dates. 3 vols. fo. Paris, 1783.
Asser, Annales rerum gest. Ælfredi magni. 8°. Oxf. 1722.
Asserii Annales, see Chronicon.
Bale (Joh.), Illustr. majoris Britanniæ Script. summarium. fo. Basil. 1557–59.
Baronius (Cæs.), Annales Ecclesiastici. 12 vols. fo. Antw. 1670.
Beda, Historia Eccles. gentis Anglorum, ed. J. Smith. fo. Camb. 1712.
Bellarminus (Rob.), De Scriptoribus eccles. 4°. Rom. 1613.
Birch (W. de Gray), Memorials of St Guthlac of Crowland. 8°. Wisbech, 1881.
——— The Chronicles of Croyland by Ingulf. 8°. Wisbech, 1883.
——— Cartularium Saxonicum. 3 vols. 8°. Lond. 1885–1893.
——— Fasti Monastici Ævi Saxonici. 8°. Lond. 1872.
Bowen (Emanuel), Map of Lincolnshire. 1767.
Brompton (J.), Chronicon (588–1189), in Twysden.
Caius (Dr J.), De antiquitate Academiæ Cantabrigiensis. 4°. Lond. 1568, 1574.
Camden (W.), Britannia. 8°. 1586, 1587, 1590.
——— „ 4°. 1594, 1600.
——— „ fo. 1607.
——— Remaines of a greater work concerning Britaine. 8°. Lond. 1605.
——— Anglica, Normannica, etc. fo. Francof. 1603.
Campbell (J. Lord), Lives of the Lord Chancellors. 4th ed. 10 vols. 8°. Lond. 1856-7.
Canisius (Hen.), Thesaurus. fo. Amstel. 1725.
Capgrave (John), Nova legenda Angliæ. 4°. Lond. 1516.
Caxton (W.), Chronicle. fo. Lond. 1480.
Chronicles and Memorials of Great Britain [R. S.]. 8°. Lond. 1858 ff.
Chronicon fani S. Neoti, sive Asserii Annales, in Gale Scriptores xv.
Commelinus (Jer.), Rerum Brit. Scriptores. fo. Heidelb. 1587.
Delisle (Léop.), Rouleaux des morts. 8°. Paris, 1866.
Diceto (Rad. de), Works, in R. S.
Dictionary of Christian Biography. 4 vols. 8°. Lond. 1877 ff.
Domesday Book. 4 vols. fo. Lond. 1783.
Ducange (Ch.), Glossarium. fo. Paris, 1736.
Duchesne (Andr.), Historiæ Normann. Scriptores Antiqui. fo. Paris, 1619.

Dudo of St Quentin, Historia in Duchesne.
Dugdale (Sir W.), History of Embanking. fo. Lond. 1662; fo. 1772.
────── Monasticon Anglicanum. 3 vols. fo. Lond. 1655-61-73.
────── ,, ,, 8 vols. fo. Lond. 1817-27.
Eadmer, Historia novorum in Anglia, ed. J. Selden. fo. Lond. 1623.
Earle (J.), Handbook to the Land charters. 8°. Oxf. 1888.
Ellis (Henry), General Introd. to Domesday. 2 vols. 8". Lond. 1833.
Elton (C. T.), Origins of English History. 2nd ed. 8°. Lond. 1890.
English Historical Society, Publications. 8". Lond.
Fabyan (Rob.), Chronicle. fo. Lond. 1516. 4". Lond. 1811.
Felix the monk, Life of St Guthlac, see Birch.
Florentius Wigornensis, Chronicon, ed. B. Thorpe. 2 vols. 8°. Lond. (E. H. S.) 1848.
Freeman (E. A.), The Norman Conquest. 6 vols. 8". Lond. 1867 ff.
Fuller (Thos.), The Hist. of the Worthies of England. fo. Lond. 1662.
Fulman (W.), Rerum Anglicarum Scriptorum Vet. Tom. I. fo. Oxf. 1684.
Gale (Thos.), Historiæ Brit. Sax. Anglo-Danicæ Script. XV. Vol. I. fo. Oxf. 1691.
────── Historiæ Anglicanæ Scriptores quinque. Vol. II. fo. Oxf. 1687.
Gallia Christiana. fo. Paris, 1715-1786.
Geoffrei Gaimar, L'estorie des Engles, in R. S.
Gibbon (Edw.), Miscellaneous works. 4". Lond. 1815.
Giles (J.), Chronicon Joh. Abb. S. Petri de Burgo. 8". Lond. 1845.
Giraldus Cambrensis, Works, in R. S. 1861-1877.
Goldschmidt (S.), Die Geschichte der Juden in England. Berl. 1886.
Gough (R.), The History and Antiq. of Croyland Abbey. 4". Lond. 1783.
────── Mr Essex's Observations...and other additions. 4". Lond. 1784. (Bibl. Topogr. Brit. nos. XI. XXII.)
────── A Second Appendix to the History of Croyland. 4". Lond. 1797.
Gregorovius (Ferd.), Geschichte der Stadt Athen. 2 vols. 8". Stuttg. 1889.
Gresley (Rev. J. M.), see Stukeley (W.).
Gunton (Symon), Hist. of the church of Peterborough. fo. Lond. 1686.
Guthlac (St), Life by Felix, see Gough, Birch.
────── Anglo Saxon life, ed. C. W. Goodwin. 8°. Lond. 1848.
Hallam (H.), A view of the state of Europe during the Middle Ages. 9th ed. 3 vols. Lond. 1846.
Hamilton (N. E. S. A.), Inquisitio Comit. Cantabr. 4". Lond. 1876.
Hardy (T. Duffus), Descriptive Cat. of MSS. relating to the history of Great Britain and Ireland, in R. S. 1862 ff.
Hardyng (John), Chronicle. 4". Lond. 1812.
Harryson (Wm.), Description of Britain, in Holinshed.
Heeren (A. H. L.), Gesch. des Studiums der class. Lit. 2 vols. 8". Gött. 1797.
Heimskringla, see Snorri Sturluson.
Henry of Huntingdon, Historia Anglorum in R. S. 1879.
Hickes (Geo.), Thesaurus. 2 vols. fo. Oxf. 1705.
Holinshed (R.), Chronicles of England, Scotland and Ireland. fo. Lond. 1577.
Hunter (Jos.), Magnus Rotulus Scaccarii 31 H. 1. 8°. Lond. 1833.
Ingulf, History of Croyland Monastery, see Savile, Scriptores, Fulman, Birch, Riley.
Jehan de Waurin, Recueil des Chroniques...de la Grant Bretaigne, in R. S. 1884 ff.
[John, abbat of Peterborough], Chronicon Angliæ Petriburgense (MS. Cott. Claud. A. v.), ed. Jos. Sparke. fo. Lond. 1723; J. A. Giles. 8". Lond. 1845.
John of Salisbury, Policraticus, in Opp.

Kemble (J.), The Saxons in England. 2 vols. 8º. Lond. 1848, 1876.
Kingsley (Ch.), Hereward. 2 vols. 8º. Lond. 1866.
Lambard (W.), 'Αρχαιονομία. fo. Camb. 1644.
Landnámabók. 8º. Copenh. 1843.
Langebek (J.), Scriptores rerum Danic. medii ævi. 5 vols. fo. Copenh. 1783.
Langtoft (Pierre de), Chronicle, in R. S.
Leland (J.), Itinerary ed. Tho. Hearne. 9 vols. 8º. Oxf. 1744-45.
——— Collectanea. 6 vols. 8º. Oxf. 1770.
——— De Scriptt. Britan. 2 vols. 8º. Oxf. 1709.
Le Prévost (Aug.), see Ordericus Vitalis.
Liber precum publicarum. 4º. Lond. 1560.
Liber vitæ Dunelmiensis ecclesiæ. 8º. Surtees Soc. 1841.
Liebermann (F.), Ostenglische Geschichtsquellen, in Neues Archiv XVII. 1892.
Lingard (John), Hist. of England. 5th ed. 10 vols. 8º. Lond. 1849.
Liturgical Services set forth in the reign of qu. Elizabeth [Parker Soc.]. 8º. Cambridge, 1847.
Major (J.), Historia Majoris Britanniæ. Paris, 1521. 4º. Edinb. 1740.
Marianus Scotus, Chronicon. fo. Francof. 1601.
Maseres (Franc.), Historiæ Anglicanæ...monumenta. 4º. Lond. 1807.
Matthæus Paris, Opera, in R. S.
Ménard (N. H.), Martyrologium Benedictinum. 8º. Paris, 1629.
Michel (Fr.), Chroniques Anglo-Normandes. 3 vols. 8º. Rouen, 1836-1840.
Migne, Patrologia Latina. 8º. Paris, 1844 ff.
Monumenta historica Britannica. Vol. I. fo. Lond. 1848.
MSS. MS. Cott. Claud. A. v. Chron. of abb. John of Peterborough (?).
MS. Cott. Nero C. vij. Annals of Thorney Abbey.
MS. Cott. Otho B. xiij. Historia Croylandensis (XV cent.).
MS. Cott. Vesp. B. xj. Vitæ abbatum Croilandiæ (XV cent.).
MS. Arundel 178. Ingulf's history (XVI cent.).
MS. Harl. Y. 6. Guthlac roll.
MS. Camb. Univ. Libr. Dd. xj. 78. Vita Guthlaci metrice composita.
MS. Trin. Coll. Dublin, B. 2. 7. Vita Guthlaci auctore P. Blesensi.
Patent rolls (Public Record office) 17 July 17 Ric. II. 1393, 1 Nov. 1 Hen. IV. 1399.
Neubauer (A.), Notes on the Jews in Oxford, in Oxf. Hist. Soc. 1890.
Nichols (J. G.), The earldom of Lincoln, in Topogr. and Geneal. 8º. Lond. 1846.
Oliver (G.), Monast. Dioc. Exon. fo. Exeter, 1846.
Ordericus Vitalis, ed. André Duchesne in Hist. Norm. Scriptt.; ed. Aug. Le Prévost. 8 vols. 8º. Paris, 1838-55.
Oudin (Casim.), Commentarius de Scriptt. Eccl. 3 vols. fo. Francof. 1722.
Palgrave (Sir Fr.), On the Sources of A. S. History, in Quart. Rev. 1826.
——— Rise and Progress of the English Commonwealth. 4º. Lond. 1832.
Parker (Abp. Matthew), De antiquitate Britan. Eccl. fo. Lond. 1572.
Pearson (C. H.), Hist. of England. 2 vols. 8º. Lond. 1867.
Pitsius (Joh.), De Angliæ Scriptoribus. 4º. Paris, 1619.
Proclamation concerning the King's Majesties stile [20 Oct. 1604].
Prynne (W.), Short demurrer to the Jews' long discontinued Remitter into England. 4º. Lond. 1656.
Reynerus (Clem.), Apostolatus Benedictinorum in Anglia. fo. Douai, 1626.
Riley (H. T.), Ingulph's Chronicle of the abbey of Croyland translated from the latin. 8º. Lond. (Bohn) 1854.
——— The history and charters of Ingulfus considered, in Archæol. Journal, 1862.

Roger Hoveden, Chronicon Magistri Rog. de Hoveden, in R. S.
Savile (Sir H.), Scriptores post Bedam. fo. Lond. 1596; Francof. 1601.
Schlumberger (Gust.), Sigillographie byzantine. 4°. Paris, 1884.
Selden (John), see Eadmer.
Smith (C. G.), Domesday book for Linc. and Rutland. 1870.
Smith (Thos.), Catalogus libr. MSS. bibl. Cottonianæ. fo. Lond. 1696.
Snorri Sturluson (1178-1241), Heimskringla. 8°. Christiania, 1868.
Sparke (J.), Historiæ Anglicanæ Scriptores Varii. fo. Lond. 1723.
Spelman (Sir H.), Concilia. fo. Lond. 1639 ff.
Stapleton (Tho.), Mag. Rotuli Scacc. Normanniæ, 1180-1203. 2 vols. Lond. 1840-1844.
Stevenson (Jos.), The hist. of Ingulf, in Church Historians of England. 8vo. Lond. Seeleys, 1854.
Stewart (D. J.), Liber Eliensis. Vol. I. 8°. Lond. 1848.
Stubbs (W.), Registrum Sacrum Anglicanum. 8°. Oxf. 1858.
Stukeley (W.), Some account of Croyland Abbey, ed. by Rev. J. M. Gresley. 4°. Ashby de la Zouch, 1856.
Symeon Dunelm., Works, in Twysden; in R. S.
Tanner (Bp. Tho.), Notitia monastica. fo. Lond. 1744.
Teulet (A.), Relations politiques de la France...avec l'Écosse. 8°. Paris, 1862.
Thompson (Pishey), History of Boston. 8°. Boston, 1856.
Thorpe (B.), Ancient Laws and Institutes of England. fo. Lond. 1840.
—— Codex Exoniensis. 8°. Lond. 1842.
—— Diplomatarium Anglicanum Ævi Saxonici. 8°. Lond. 1865.
Topographer (The) and Genealogist. 8°. Lond. 1846 ff.
Turner (Sharon), Hist. of the Anglo-Saxons. (8°. Lond. 1852.)
Twine (J.), De rebus Albionicis...lib. ij. 8°. Lond. 1590.
Twysden (Rog.), Historiæ Anglicanæ Scriptores X. fo. Lond. 1652.
Walcott (M. E. C.), Inventories of Westm. Abbey at the Dissolution, in Publ. of the London and Middlesex Archæol. Soc. 1878.
Warner (R. F.), Hist. of Thorney Abbey. 8°. Wisb. 1879.
Warren (F. G.), The Leofric Missal. 4°. Oxf. 1883.
Wharton (H.), Historia de episc. et dec. Londin. 8vo. Lond. 1695.
Wilkins (D.), Leges Anglo-Saxonum. fo. Lond. 1721.
Willelmus Malmesburiensis, De gestis regum Anglorum, in R. S.
———————————— De gestis Pontificum, in R. S.
Wion (Arn.), Lignum Vitæ. 4°. Ven. 1595.

THE
'HISTORIA CROYLANDENSIS.'

j. Croyland.

CROYLAND is a large village of about 3000 inhabitants, [1] which lies in the south of Lincolnshire, close to the boundaries of Cambridgeshire and Northamptonshire. It is situated in a neighbourhood formerly rich in monastic establishments, being distant from Peterborough about 10 miles, from Thorney 5 miles, from Spalding 8 miles, from Ramsey 15 miles, from Chatteris 18 miles, and from Ely 26 miles.

ij. The 'Historia Croylandensis.'

Our knowledge of the foundation and of the subsequent [2] fate in mediæval times of the monastery of Benedictine monks, which existed for many centuries at Croyland, and the abbat of which was one of the spiritual Lords of Parliament, is derived mainly from the 'Historia Croylandensis,' a series of five separate, but connected, works, all printed by W. Fulman in his 'Rerum Anglicarum Scriptorum Veterum Tom. I.' (fo. Oxon. 1684), pp. 1 – 132, 449 – 593.

St Guthlac, with whom the history of Croyland begins, was [3] a nobleman of the kingdom of Mercia, connected with the royal house of that land. He was born c. 674, as Florence of Worcester (d. 1118) mentions him as renouncing the world in the twenty-fourth year of his age in 697; the same authority brings him to the 'island' of Croyland in 699, where he continued to live as an anchorite until his death 11 Apr. 714; he was then about 41 years of age.

The interest, which attaches to the abbey of Croyland, [4] has been mainly created by the long and curious history of the monastery in its early days, from its foundation in 716 down to c. 1095, the first part of the 'Historia Croylandensis,' which goes by the name of 'Ingulf's chronicle,' professing to be compiled by an abbat of Croyland of that name.

The continuation of the Ingulf, which bears the name of Peter of Blois (Petrus Blesensis), is interesting, to Cambridge men especially, because it contains an often quoted account of certain lectures given c. 1109 on Grammar, Logic, and Rhetoric, in a barn at Cambridge by some monks of Croyland monastery, who went daily from Cottenham, a manor belonging to Croyland and distant from Cambridge about six miles, for that purpose. This second part of the 'Historia Croylandensis' begins in the time of William II., and went on to the accession of king Stephen in 1135, but through mutilation comes down no lower than 1117.

5   These two parts of the 'Historia Croylandensis,' which bear individual names, are followed by three continuations, which are anonymous.

a. The First Anonymous Continuation, the third part of the History, is the work of a Prior of Croyland; it began in 1135 and ends in 1470; but the beginning is lost.

b. The Second Anonymous Continuation, the fourth part of the History, is by a 'Doctor in jure canonico,' 'unus ex consiliariis regis;' it is complete, and extends from 1459 to 1486.

c. The Third Anonymous Continuation, the fifth and last part of the History, was written by a person, of whom no description is given, and who only states concerning himself, that he was present at the death of cardinal Beaufort in 1447. It mentions events of the one year 1486, chiefly the proceedings connected with the transfer of the church of Brynkhurst, otherwise Eston (Bringhurst V. with Great Easton Leic.) to Peterborough monastery. How far this part was continued, cannot now be ascertained, as it breaks off in the middle of a sentence.

6   There is no further continuous history of the abbey of Croyland from 1486 to the Dissolution in 1539. The series of the abbats is nearly all that is known of that period.

A few shorter histories of Croyland exist; the most noticeable is the 'Vitæ abbatum Croilandiæ' (MS. Cott. Vesp. B. xj) from the foundation to 1427, which will be described later.

I. INGULF'S CHRONICLE.

iij. Authorities for the history of the Anglo-Saxon period of England, and their notices of Croyland.

The historical works of undoubted genuineness, which refer to the times of St Guthlac and to the early-mediæval period of the existence of the abbey of Croyland, are:

1. The 'Historia Ecclesiastica gentis Anglorum' by the Venerable Beda, extending from Cæsar's invasion of Britain to the year 731;
2. The Anglo-Saxon Chronicle to the year 1154;
3. The Life of King Ælfred (849 – 901) by Asser, bishop of Sherburn (d. 910);
4. The Chronicle of Æthelweard to the year 975;
5. The Domesday Book of 1086;
6. The 'Chronica ex Chronicis' of Florence of Worcester (d. 1118) to the year 1117, continued to 1141;
7. The 'Historia Ecclesiastica' of Ordericus Vitalis, to about the year 1141;
8. The 'Historia de gestis Anglorum' by Symeon of Durham (d. 1130);
9. The 'Histoire des Angles' to the year 1100, composed in French verse by Geffrei Gaimar;
10. a. The 'De gestis pontificum Anglorum' to the year 1122 by William of Malmesbury;
   b. The 'Gesta regum Anglorum' to the year 1128 also by William of Malmesbury;
11. The 'Historia Anglorum' of Henry of Huntingdon (d. after 1154).

These are mostly to be found, up to 1066, in the solitary Vol. I. (1848) of the Monumenta Historica Britannica.

Besides these works there are two documents, which more particularly relate to St Guthlac:

1. The Life of St Guthlac by the monk Felix, a work of the 8th century;

2. The Harley MS. Y. 6. in the British Museum, a roll of parchment, of the 12th century, containing drawings illustrative of the life of the saint, without any text.

The references to Croyland to be found in the above works will now be mentioned under the heads of the several books.

I. In the 'Historia Ecclesiastica gentis Anglorum' of Beda (d. 735) are no references to St Guthlac (d. 714) or to Croyland itself.

Æthelbald king of Mercia (716 – 755), who is claimed by Ingulf as the founder of Croyland abbey, is indeed mentioned by Beda, but nothing is said of his having founded Croyland, although the building of Medeshamsted (now Peterborough) abbey by bishop Sexwulf in 675 is given in B. iv. c. vi., and the beginning of Ely nunnery by Æthelthryth or Etheldrida about the same time is in B. iv. c. xix., book iv. extending from 665 to 687, and book v. from 687 to 731.

The collection of Jerome Commelin 'Rerum Britannicarum...Scriptores vetustiores ac præcipui' (fo. Heidelb. 1587) contains under the title 'De gestis Anglorum libri tres, incerto auctore,' as an appendix or continuation of Beda's History, what is only a great part of the first three books of Will. Malm. G. R.

II. The Anglo-Saxon Chronicle, edited by Benj. Thorpe [Rolls Series] in 1861 and by prof. Earle in 1865, is known in six MSS., extending from early times to different years between 975 and 1154.

They are marked: A (Winchester) to 975, B (St Augustine's [Earle]) to 977, C (Abingdon) to 1066, D (Worcester) to 1079, E (Peterborough) to 1154, F (Canterbury) to 1058. A seventh G (MS. Cott. Otho B. xj) was mostly burnt in the disastrous fire at Ashburnham House in 1731; it had however been used by Abraham Wheloc in 1644 as the basis of his edition; it extends to the year 1001.

There is, according to Dr Stubbs, 'an error of two or three years in many of the entries' in the 8th and 9th centuries between the death of Beda and the birth of King Ælfred (Registrum Sacrum p. 9: Hoveden [R. S.] i. pp. xc. – xcv.). But see: W. de Coventria [R. S.] ij. p. xciv.³⁻; Haddan and Stubbs, Councils and Eccl. Doc. iij. 397.

The references in the A. S. Chronicle to St Guthlac and to Croyland are but few:

a. 714. St Guthlac dies, the locality not being specified (A etc.).

a. 870. The destruction of Peterborough is recorded, but nothing is said of any destruction of Croyland (Ingulf), except so far as it may be included in the statement, that the Danes 'destroyed all the monasteries, which they came to' (E only).

a. 948. Nothing is said about the restoration of Croyland abbey by Turketul (Ingulf), although an abbat Thurcytel of Bedford is mentioned s. a. 971 (B, C).

a. 1066. The abbey of Croyland is mentioned as having been, before that year, given to Leofric abbat of Peterborough together with the monasteries of Burton, Coventry, and Thorney (E only). This is not alluded to in the Ingulf.

a. 1076 (E) or 1077 (D). The earl Waltheof is beheaded at Winchester; his body is conveyed to Croyland, and is there buried.

The Peterborough Chronicle E (Bodl. MS. Laud. 636) stands alone among the different MSS. of the Chronicle, in that it contains long notices of the local affairs of the monastery of Peterborough in addition to those pertaining to the general history of England. For 75 years after 1079 it is the only copy of the Chronicle; all the others had broken off before that date, D (Worcester) being the last survivor. In 1154 the Peterborough Chronicle itself comes to an end.

It is written in one hand to the end of 1121, having probably been begun after the great fire of 1116 (Earle). The earlier part of E embodies the contents of A (Winchester); from 892 to 991 it is a very meagre chronicle of general history, being for many years wholly blank, but containing an account of the restoration of Peterborough monastery by bishop Æthelwold in 963; from 991 it is continuous to the year 1121. The periods 1121 – 1131, and 1132 – 1154 are continuations by different hands belonging to Peterborough.

Although compiled so near to Croyland, the Peterborough Chronicle contains no mention of the abbey of Croyland or of its abbats, with the exception of the entry of the year 1066 above given. But the Ingulf has many notices of Peterborough after its restoration in 963 (E); the writer mentions abbat Adulph of Peterborough assisting at the funeral of abbat Turketul in 975; he speaks of the oppression of the abbey of Pegeland by the abbats of Peterborough Ælfsige [c. 990 – 1041], Arnwi [1041 – 52], Leofric [1052 – 66], although he seems to have had no exact information respecting the dates of these abbats, since he represents Leofric as abbat before 1048 and even in the time of king Harthacnut 1039 – 41 (Fulm. p. 62). Ingulf mentions further some circumstances connected with the brothers Egelric and Agelwin monks of Peterborough, successively bishops of Durham, and their fate after the Conquest, the burial of Ælfric archbishop of York at Peterborough in 1051, and the doings of Hereward at Peterborough in the times of abbat Brand his uncle and of his successor the Norman Thorold; he speaks of a destruction of Peterborough in 1013, of the burial of Kinsige archbishop of York in that monastery in 1060, of the promotion of Wulfstan a monk of Peterborough to the see of Worcester in 1062, and of the hospitality shewn at Croyland to some monks of Peterborough in 1076.

14 No reference to any destruction of Peterborough Monastery by the Danes c. 1013 as related by Ingulf (Fulm. p. 56) is to be found in E, in Fl. Wig. or in John of Peterborough (MS. Cott. Claud. A. v.). There was indeed a fire at Peterborough 4 Aug. **1116**, by which the church also was destroyed; this is mentioned in E, and by Joh. Petrib., and also by Hugo Candidus (Sparke) in a chapter headed 'De secunda combustione Monasterii,' the first having been that of 870.

15 In 972 King Eadgar granted his charter to Peterborough: the terms of this charter are given in E (s. a. 963) and in Hugo Candidus, and the charter itself is given in Ingulf, though with some variations, and with the date 970. In it the word 'Crulande' occurs as a geographical term only. The names of the witnesses to that charter found in E are also found in Ingulf, but many more are recorded there; in E the King speaks in the first person singular, but in Ingulf in the first person plural. The forms of assent of the witnesses also are quite different in the two documents.

III. Of the life of King Ælfred (b. 849, d. 901) by Asser bishop of Sherburn c. 895 – 909, 'Annales rerum gestarum Ælfredi magni, auctore Asserio Menevensi,' ed. Wise (8vo. Oxf. 1722), a great part is incorporated in Fl. Wig.

The only event, which especially belongs to the neighbourhood of Croyland in Ælfred's time, is the destruction of that monastery; but neither of that, nor of the destruction of Peterborough, is anything to be found in Asser.

There is also another work going under his name, 'Chronicon Fani Sancti Neoti, sive Asserii Annales,' printed in Gale Scriptores, Vol. I (1691) pp. 159 ff.; it belongs however to the latter part of the 12th c., or to about the year 1175 (Th. Duffus Hardy, Descr. Cat. j. 577). It mentions the death of St Guthlac in 714 and that of bishop Sexwulf the founder of Medeshamsted in 705, the martyrdom of Eadmund king of the East Angles in 870, but it says nothing about the destruction of Croyland in that year.

IV. The Chronicle of Æthelweard, 'Patricius Consul Fabius Quæstor Ethelwerdus,' reaches down to the year 975. It was first printed in Savile's Scriptores post Bedam, probably from MS. Cott. Otho. A. x, a MS. unfortunately destroyed by the fire of 1731. It mentions the death of St Guthlac in 714 (lib. ij. c. 12), but says nothing further respecting the foundation (a. 716), destruction (a. 870), or restoration (a. 948) of Croyland.

V. In the Domesday Book of 1086 a full account of the possession of Croyland abbey is given; a few tenants are mentioned by name, and one single benefactor, 'Turoldus vicecomes.'

Ingulf has (Fulm. pp. 80 – 82) an account of the possessions of the monastery, which he professes to have extracted from the Domesday Book of king William I. (1086), as well as from a similar Domesday Book of king Ælfred (871 – 901), a document unknown (apparently) to English antiquaries. Sir Henry Ellis observes (Gen. Introd. to Domesday, Vol. I. p. 10, ed. 1833): 'The formation of such a Survey...in the time of Alfred, may be more than doubted; as we have only a solitary authority for its existence, and the most diligent investigation has not been able to recover, among the Records either of Saxon or of later times, the slightest indication that such a Survey was ever known.' The idea of a Domesday Book of Ælfred seems to have arisen from the existence of a Dom-boc of that king; through confusion of somewhat similar sounds, the Dom-boc was supposed to be synonymous with Domesday Book, and to have been therefore a similar kind of register; whereas it was really the Code of Saxon laws, and as such is noticed in the laws of Eadward the elder and of Æthelstan, (Ellis j. 11, 12).

Gale Scriptores (I., p. 795) thinks, that Ingulf had not actually seen the two volumes now in the Public Record Office, since he speaks of Domesday as a 'rotulus' (Fulm. p. 80) and also of the 'incorporatio Regalium rotulorum' (Fulm. p. 83), as if they had not yet been drawn up in book form. Other monasteries seem to have copied their revenues (Gale, p. 796): 'Abbatiæ fere omnes suos reditus hinc desumpsere, et in libros digesserunt. Croylandensis, Elyensis, Wigornensis liber, in hoc genere, adhuc servantur.' On this Domesday Book of Ælfred, however, Gale (p. 795) remarks: 'Ethelredi frater Rex Alfredus totam suam ditionem descripsit. Hujus descriptionis meminere Gul. Thorne, Rad. Dicetus MS. et Ingulphus, p. 870, et 908.' [Frankfurt reprint of Savile, 1601] 'ubi *Similem multum et talem* fuisse *rotulum* dicit, qualem postea Gulielmus I edidit, et *vulgariter ab Anglicis cognominatum fuisse utrumque rotulum* **Doomesday**. Mox ex priori illa descriptione, quam Alfredus fecit, verba nonnulla citat. *Hæc sedes est Abbatiæ* [*Croyland*] *tempore regis Ethelredi, estque soluta, etc*.' Unfortunately Gale has not specified the passages in Thorne and Rad. de Diceto, which in his opinion referred to Ælfred's Survey.

19   Ingulf professes mostly to have abridged, though sometimes to have expanded the Domesday Book account of the lands of Croyland; but his account is really just as full as the original of 1086 where this can be traced, as well as a man, who did not understand its technicalities and abbreviations.

could do the work. Thus the expression 'm° similiter,' meaning 'it is valued at a like amount now,' is turned into '...monetæ. Similiter...' This is the more strange, that Ingulf has used the 'm° similiter' correctly in some of his own additions interpolated in the text of Domesday.

The word 'Wapentake,' which in Domesday is written WAP̃, has in the Ingulfine additions been on two occasions expanded into 'warp,' and so the wapentake of Ellohe has been corrupted into 'Ellowarp, and the wapentake of Kirketon (Kirton) into 'Kirketona warp.' In all other cases Fulman (1684) has 'wapp,' but the first editor Savile (1596) and the Arundel MS. (Brit. Mus.) 178 have everywhere 'warp.'

'Carucata,' a measure of land, is sometimes confounded with 'Caruca' a plough; 'tailla' the cutwood is changed into 'talba' in Fulm. and 'tulba' in the MS. Arundel 178, 'pet.' (petitionem) into 'pecuniam,' and 'post' into 'usus.'

Ingulf's account ('elucubratiuncla') of the property of the monastery contains the articles from William's Domesday respecting the monastic estates in

        Lincolnshire,   Huntingdonshire,
        Northamptonshire,   and
        Leicestershire,   Cambridgeshire,

but not always in the same order as in Domesday.

He has besides unaccountably made several additions to the property of the monastery not found in Domesday, while yet leaving out some details, that are mentioned there.

Thus he has added:

1. a paragraph at the beginning respecting the site of Croyland;

2. articles respecting Pinchbeck, Sutterton, Halington, Laythorp, and Kirkby Linc., and Optenagreen and Glapthorn Northants, which were recovered by Turketul (Fulm. p. 39) after 948;

3. an article respecting Rippingale taken from the account of the property of Oger the Breton (§ 145) in Domesday, which has also been worked up into a charter of c. 1091 to 'Oger the priest of Repyngale' (Fulm. p. 100);

but he has omitted, though found in Domesday:

1. the statement: 'Hanc terram dedit Turoldus Sancto Guthlaco pro anima sua,' with reference to the estate at Bukenhale (Bucknall, near Horncastle) Linc.; [vicecomes]

2. an article about a rent in eels due from Wisbech Cambridgeshire ;

3. an article respecting three houses, which the Monastery possessed in the town of Leicester ('Ledecestre').

He has inserted, besides, most of the Sokes and Hundreds and all the Wapentakes except one in Leicestershire, the names being sometimes much disfigured. But it must be remembered, that 'Lincolnshire is divided into thirty Wapentakes, or Hundreds, yet there are only about nineteen which bear anything like the same names in Domesday which they do at present' (Ellis j. 34).

In his transcript of Domesday he has left unmentioned the two tenants Gamel and Colegrim, and the one recorded benefactor 'Turoldus vicecomes.'

21   Having given his version of the Domesday of 1086, Ingulf, writing less than ten years after (c. 1095), feels it necessary to give an explanation of some points, which seemed to need elucidation. The points are six in number:

1. The use of the word 'leuca' in the measurement of the site of the abbey; of this word he gives a fantastical derivation; it is used again in the account of Optenagreen; these passages are Ingulfine additions. In Domesday itself the word 'leuca' or 'leuua' very frequently occurs, with its subdivision ($\frac{1}{12}$) of 'quarantena' a furlong, and we find the Ingulfine transcript, 'Marisci duas leucas in longitudine et duas leucas in latitudine' represented by 'Maresc . 11 . lev̆ lg̃. 7 11 . lat.' 'The ordinary mile of England...in former times was more of a traditionary than an ascertained measure. It was nearly a mile and a half of the present standard' (Ellis j. 59). The word 'leuca' is always translated 'mile' by C. G. Smith in his Translation of the Lincolnshire part of Domesday Book

[1870]; Ord. Vit. and Fl. Wig. use the word 'milliaria' for 'miles ;'

2. The situation of the marsh of Alderlound, another Ingulfine addition ;

3. The date of the king Æthelred mentioned in the Ingulfine addition of the site of Croyland, in which also no. 1 occurs ;

4. The omission of any reference to villeins, bordars, or socmen at Croyland, a matter which is mentioned only in the same Ingulfine addition ;

5. A reference to berewicks at Spalding and Algar (in Domesday) ;

6. The description (in Domesday) of the manor of Badby as a possession of Croyland, though at that time it was in the hands of the monks of Evesham ; this manor seems really to have belonged to Evesham (Reg. Evesham [R. S.]; Kemble Codex Dipl. n° 1316), at all events abbat Joffrid tried in vain to get it out of the hands of that society (Fulm. p. 124).

'Ingulphus, or rather the compiler, to whom we owe the rifacciamento which has so long passed current as the production of the venerable abbat, speaks with great complacency, when he records the favour shewn to the Monastery by the Domesday Commissioners. In order that the possessions of the Abbey might be protected against encroachments, they,' [he tells us quoting Fulm. p. 83] 'enlarged the size of the township to double its size. The description, however, to which Ingulphus refers, does not occur in any part of the volume : and the whole passage relating to Domesday, is one of the many which tend to impugn the authenticity of the Croyland History' (Palgrave, English Commonwealth [see § 117] Proofs and Illust. p. ccccxlvij). From the Cartulary of Battle Abbey founded by king William I. in 1067, it would appear that the property of that monastery was occasionally overrated in the Survey (Ellis Introd. j. 30).

Among the additions made by Ingulf to the text of Domesday, the most remarkable one is the introductory statement, that St Guthlac (i.e. the monastery) has woods and marshes four leagues in length and three leagues in breadth, forming the seat of the abbey, free and absolved from all secular services from the time of king Æthelred. This latter remark, made in defiance of his own previous statement, for Æthelbald of Mercia, not any king Æthelred, was the founder of the monastery, Ingulf feels it necessary to explain, saying, that there were three Æthelreds, the first of Mercia 675 – 704, d. 716, the second of Wessex 866 – 871, the third of England 978 – 1016, and that since the time of each of them the abbey had been exempt from secular services (§ 118).

This is the statement, which Gale (§ 18) seems to think due to the Domesday Book of Ælfred.

Mr Riley, without apparently having consulted Domesday Book itself, remarks (Archæol. Journal 1862 p. 125): 'The fabricators...of the history, finding a passage in Domesday to the effect that, "from the time of King Ethelred, the seat of the abbacy has been quit and free of all secular services," have laboured (Fulm. p. 84) to make it incidentally subservient to their purpose.' The passage however is not found in king William's Domesday, where king Æthelred is only once mentioned, and that as the father of the Confessor (Ellis i. 303). Mr Riley seems also to have thought, that the Wapentakes are mentioned in the Survey.

24 The date of Ælfred's Domesday would necessarily lie between 871 and 901. Now, according to Ingulf, after the destruction of Croyland monastery in 870, king Burgred of Mercia seized its estates, and either kept them for himself or divided them among his military chiefs, so that during the whole of Ælfred's reign, and indeed till 948 in the time of his grandson Eadred, there remained to the abbey nothing but the island of Croyland, which had been the site from the foundation (Fulm. p. 25), and so 'Ælfred's Domesday Book' would not, as also Gale seems to recognize, mention any other estates as the property of Croyland Abbey, descriptions of which Ingulf could extract for his account of the possessions of that house.

25 VI. The 'Chronicon ex Chronicis' of Florence of Worcester 'Florentius monachus Wigornensis' extends to the year 1117, the author dying in 1118. He is mentioned in the 'Titulus sanctæ Mariæ Wigornensis ecclesiæ' in the mortuary roll of abbat Vitalis of Savigny (Delisle, Rouleaux des Morts [8vo. Paris 1866] p. 313): 'Orate pro nostris...pro Florentio et Henrico...monachis et omnibus aliis.'

The 'Chronicon ex Chronicis' consists of the Chronicle of Marianus Scotus (b. 1028, d. c. 1086), with insertions relating to England from Beda and from the A. S. Chronicle, and a great part of Asser's life of Ælfred, by Florence, and his additions to 1117, continued by a monk of Worcester named John to 1140.

It has been so printed by Lord William Howard in 1592, and from him (with Matth. Westm.) at Frankfurt in 1601. The additions to the Marianus alone have been edited by Benj. Thorpe in 1848 (E. H. S.), and in the M. H. B.

The Chronicle of Marianus Scotus without the additions of Fl. Wig. is contained in Migne P. L. Vol. 147.

'Although the Chronicle of Marianus Scotus has hardly anything of importance connected with England, yet, as it became the basis of that of Florence of Worcester, our early writers frequently refer to Marianus Scotus, meaning Florence of Worcester, and sometimes the continuation of Florence, as low as the middle of the 12th century, nearly 100 years after the death of Marianus' (Hardy D. C. ij. 47).

The MSS. used by Thorpe are spoken of as 'manuscripts of Marianus embodying Florence.' Some have in addition a Catalogue of the bishops of England, Genealogies of all the A. S. dynasties, and a sketch of the History of the A. S. kingdoms continued down to Henry I. These are printed in Thorpe's edition.

The Catalogue of the bishops has no dates and very rarely anything beyond the names: it must be used with caution.

Fl. Wig. contains several references to St Guthlac and to some persons connected with the history of Croyland abbey, but only very few to the monastery itself.

a. 697. St Guthlac renounces the world in his 24th year, and is received as a member of the monastery of Hrypandun (Repton Derbyshire), the burial place of the Mercian princes, 'sub abbatissa nomine Alfthrytha.' His birth in 973 is not mentioned.

a. 699. St Guthlac reaches 'Cruland' on viij Kal. Sept. or 25 Aug., and begins to lead there a hermit's life. His ordination in 705 is not recorded.

a. 714. St Guthlac dies 11 April. He is described as the brother of St Pegia the virgin; she it was, from whom in later days Peykirk 4½ miles W. of Croyland received its name. St Guthlac is succeeded by Cissa, one of his companions,—'cui Cissa successit'—; this statement is made also by Felix the biographer of the Saint and by Ordericus Vitalis,—'Cissa... post eum sedem ejus possedit.' Ingulf makes no reference to this, and this is the more remarkable, that he has, just before his notice of Cissa (Fulm. p. 5), extracted from Ord. Vit. a long paragraph respecting the nature of the soil at Croyland.

a. 870. Under this date Fl. Wig. gives no hint of the destruction of Croyland, nor even of that of Peterborough, though he of course mentions the martyrdom of St Edmund the king of the East Angles by the heathen Danes.

a. 948. Fl. Wig. is totally silent as to the existence of Turketul and the restoration of Croyland; neither does he however say anything of the restoration of Peterborough in 972 (A.S.Chr. E, Joh. Petrib.).

a. 1066. It is curious that Fl. Wig. puts the battle of Hastings, 'certamen Senlacium' (Ord. Vit.) on Saturday xj. Kal. Nov., 22 Oct., whereas the actual day was the feast of St Calixtus, prid. Id. Oct., 14 Oct.; this day was really a Saturday, but 22 Oct. fell on a Sunday. A.S.Chr. D. and Will. Gemetic. give 14 Oct., A.S.Chr. E gives no date for the battle, and Sym. Dun. follows Fl. Wig. in giving the erroneous date, as do also Roger de Hoveden and Walter Hemingford.

a. 1071. Hereward joins Eadwine and Morkare in the Isle of Ely, no details of his exploits being given. He is stated to have made his escape, the other leaders surrendering to King William.

a. 1074. The nobles conspire against William I.

a. 1075. Earl Waltheof is executed at Winchester, and buried at 'Cruland.'

a. 1083. A riot is caused in the monastery of Glastonbury by the unwise actions of abbat Thurstan, then recently appointed. He is removed back to Normandy. After the death of William I. in 1086, he contrives to return to Glastonbury, and dies some years after. Abbat Wulketul (Ulfcytel) was, according to the Ingulf, placed after his deposition in 1075 in Thurstan's custody.

a. 1085. King William holds his Christmas Court at Gloucester, and on that occasion three of his chaplains 'capellani' are presented to bishoprics, and, according to the latin appendix to A.S.Chr. A, abbat Ulfcytel of Croyland is deposed.

a. 1091. No mention is made of the destruction of Croyland abbey by fire, although the fire (§ 354) is mentioned in the 'Annales de Wintonia' [R. S.], by Ordericus Vitalis, in MS. Cott. Vesp. B. xj, also by Joh. Petrib. (MS. Cott. Claud. A. v.), and in Leland's extracts concerning Croyland. Fl. Wig. mentions some damage done in that year by a thunder-storm at London and elsewhere.

a. 1108. No reference is made to the death of abbat Ingulf, or to the appointment of abbat Joffrid in 1109.

Florence of Worcester's Chronicle was after his death 7 July 1118 continued to the year 1141 by a monk of Worcester named John; a further continuation to 1295 is to be found in Thorpe's edition from MS. C. C. C. C. n°. xcii, but this is only a compilation from the Chronicle of Henry of Huntingdon to 1151, from that of John de Taxster a monk of Bury to 1265, and of John de Everisden also a monk of Bury. [28]

a. 1124. No mention is made of the death of Abbat Joffrid, or of the succession of abbat Waltheof, although the writer speaks of the death of the abbat of Hyde, and in the following year gives a long account of the new abbat of Worcester.

a. 1138. Nothing is said of the deposition of abbat Waltheof at the council held at Westminster 6 Dec. 3 Steph. 1138, although the council itself is mentioned with some detail, and a new abbat of Pershore is spoken of just before. The deposition of Waltheof is mentioned by John of Hexham (Joh. Hagustaldensis) the continuator of Sym. Dun., probably because Waltheof belonged to the family of the old earls of Northumberland.

The passage Fulm. p. 20, in which are incorporated words and expressions from Fl. Wig. a. 868, contains the statement, 'sicut Chronici tradunt.' A similar expression, however, 'secundum Chronicorum fidem' occurs (Fulm. p. 36) in the account of the early life of abbat Turketul, concerning which nothing is known except from the Ingulf. [29]

Fl. Wig. very frequently gives not only the day of the month, but also the day of the week of an event. These latter statements, it is easy to verify by chronological tables (L'art de vérifier les Dates, N. Harris Nicholas, Bond), and though mostly right are at times wrong. [30]

870 A.	xij Kal. Dec.	= 20 Nov. B.	'Sunday'
940 ED.	vj Kal. Nov.	= 27 Oct. F.	'Wednesday'
991 D.	vj Id. Nov.	= 8 Nov. D.	'Tuesday'
1033 G.	xiv Kal. Sept.	= 19 Aug. G.	'Tuesday'
1066 A.	xj Kal. Nov.	= 22 Oct. A.	'Saturday'
1096 FE.	Kal. Jan.	= 1 Jan. A.	'Wednesday'
1099 B.	Id. Jul.	= 15 July G.	'Thursday'
	xj Kal. Aug.	= 22 July G.	'Thursday'
	iv Kal. Aug.	= 29 July G.	'Thursday'
	xix Kal. Sept.	= 14 Aug. B.	'Sunday' (right).
	iij Nov. Dec.	= 3 Dec. A.	'Friday'.

He is sometimes wrong also in the Indiction

870 'Indictione ij,' really iij,
924 'Indictione xv,' really xij,
984 'Indictione ij,' really xij,
1016 'Indictione xv,' really xiv.

Some of these mistakes might be only errors of the transcriber, who omitted the x of the xij and so wrote ij, and who read xii as xu.

In 919 he speaks of the death of Æthelflæd the Lady of the Mercians as happening in xix Kal. Jul. This is an impossible day, as the earliest day before the Kalends of July is xviij Kal. Jul.; but if it be taken to mean the day before xviij Kal. Jul., it is 13 June (Id. Jun.), which agrees with the time named by the A. S. Chr. 'twelve nights before Midsummer.' In this unusual notation Fl. Wig. has been followed by Sym. Dun.

31 In many places Ingulf has incorporated words and sentences from Fl. Wig. :

Fulm. p. 5. ll. 47 – 52	= Fl. Wig.	a. 755
6. ll. 27 – 31	=	a. 794
7. ll. 18 – 41	=	a. 819, 824
17. ll. 42 – 45	=	a. 855 [858]
20 ['14'] ll. 19 – 24	=	a. 868
27. ll. 35 ff.	=	a. 872
54. ll. 20 – 21, 43 – 49	=	a. 975, 1016.
61. ll. 52 – 53	=	a. 1037
64. ll. 39 – 40	=	a. 1048

65. ll. 41 - 45	=	a. 1051
66. ll. 12 - 16, 26 - 28, 41 =		a. 1055, 1058, 1059.
68. ll. 16 - 20	=	a. 1064.
69. ll. 42 - 43	=	a. 1066.
72. ll. 30, 42 - 43	=	a. 1075
79. ll. 42 - 43	=	a. 1086
94. ll. 49 - 51	=	a. 1087

The speech of archbishop Dunstan in Ingulf (Fulm. p. 54. ll. 43 - 49) is nearly the same as in Fl. Wig. a. 1016, but is very different from his speech as reported by Will. Malm. in 'Gesta Regum' [R. S.] ij. 164.

VII. The 'Historia Ecclesiastica' of Ordericus Vitalis, **32** the English born 'Angligena,' contains accounts of St Guthlac, of Croyland Abbey, and of Waltheof the martyr-earl.

Ordericus (Freeman, Norm. Conq. iv. 495 ff.) was the son of Odelerius of Orléans, chaplain of Roger of Montgomery, ('Rogerius de Monte Gomerici,' the French Montgomery being situate in the dep. of the Calvados near Lisieux,) earl of Shrewsbury. Odelerius settled at Shrewsbury, where Ordericus the eldest of his three sons by an English wife was born in 1075. He became a monk at the age of ten years in the monastery of Ouche or Saint-Évroul (in the dep. of the Orne near Argentan) under the monastic name of Vitalis, and died there sometime after the year 1141, the year in which he brought his history to its close.

His work was edited by André Duchesne in his 'Historiæ Normannorum Scriptores' (fo. Paris 1619) pp. 319 - 925, but the most useful edition of it is that by Auguste Le Prévost (5 vols 8º Paris 1838 - 55), where its countless mistakes in persons and dates are carefully corrected in the notes. 'Ordericus...is very confused in his account of earl Ælfgar [Fulm. p. 66.], as he confounds him with his father Leofric, and makes Godgifu (Godiva) the wife, instead of the mother, of Ælfgar' (Freeman ij. Ed. III. 681).

The historical matter relating to Croyland 'Crulandia' is found in Le Prévost ij. pp. 268 - 290; an account of earl Waltheof is given besides in the previous pp. 258 - 267.

Ordericus abridges the life of St Guthlac by Felix the monk **33** on pp. 268 – 279. The biographer he erroneously styles bishop of the East Angles, a mistake corrected on chronological grounds in Pet. Bles. (Fulm. p. 109). This abridgment was made 'rogante venerabili Vulfino priore' of Croyland (Le Prévost ij. 268). He then proceeds to give a compendious history of the monastery, derived 'ex veraci relatione Ansgoti subprioris aliorumque seniorum.' This was done about the year 1115, when he spent five weeks at Croyland, and it is certainly very curious to find men of the same two names appearing as holding the same two offices about the year 1192 in the letter of abbat Henry of Longchamp prefixed to Peter of Blois' continuation (§ 4) of Ingulf's history (Fulm. p. 108).

In his account of St Guthlac Ord. Vit. mentions (from Felix' life) several personages, not spoken of by Ingulf.

34 Ordericus speaks of the founder Æthelbald king of Mercia, referring to a visit paid by him to St Guthlac in which he promised the saint a large tract of land free from all secular burdens, and of the foundation and building of the 'cœnobium,' of which a certain Kenulf was for some time abbat. Then, taking no notice of Kenulf's successors, Ordericus passes on to the time of king Ælfred, and mentions, though without giving any details, the destruction of the abbey by the Danes in 870, and the consequent loss of its estates, that were seized by laymen, though monks continued to dwell at Croyland.

From the destruction of Croyland he passes on to the reign of Eadred 946 – 955, and recounts the restoration of the monastery by Turketel, a clerk 'clericus' of London, who was of royal descent 'de regali progenie,' and related to Archbishop Osketel of York, and of great wealth and large estates. Turketel endowed the monastery with six of his sixty manors 'maneria,' and became abbat of the monastery. He subsequently procured a charter from king Eadgar 959 – 975, and also a document signed by archbishop Dunstan and his suffragans, excommunicating all plunderers of the monastic estates.

Ordericus next gives a brief history of the succeeding abbats to the time of Ulfcytel 'Ulfketelus,' a monk of Burgh or Peterborough, who received the appointment to Croyland from king Eadward, 'jubente Leofrico abbate suo.' In his time it was, that the body of earl Waltheof was brought from Winchester to Croyland for burial. After ruling for 24 years he was deposed by archbishop Lanfranc and sent to Glastonbury, 'Glestoniæ claustro deputatus est.'

Ulfcytel was succeeded 'dono Guillelmi regis' by Ingulf, a **35** monk of Fontenelle or Saint-Wandrille in Normandy (on the Seine near Caudebec), who gives his name to the first part of the 'Historia Croylandensis'. This abbat, who was of English birth, 'natione Anglicus erat', had been secretary 'scriba' to the king, and had afterwards gone to Jerusalem on pilgrimage. In his time part of the church 'pars ecclesiæ', with the offices and vestments and books and many other things, was burnt. He transferred the body of earl Waltheof from the chapter house into the church, and buried it 'prope altare'. This fire is stated in the Ingulf to have been of a much more serious character, and the deposition of abbat Wulfcytel is there placed in 1075, whereas Ord. Vit. puts it 24 years before Ingulf's death in Dec. 1108, and so in 1085, a date fixed also by the latin Appendix to the A. S. Chr. A (Winchester).

Abbat Ingulf was succeeded in 1109 by a French monk, **36** 'francigena', the prior of Ouche or Saint-Évroul in Normandy (§ 32) named Goisfredus, in Pet. Bles. 'Joffridus', who rebuilt the church in a very beautiful style, and sat for 15 years. In his time, c. 1115, Ordericus visited Croyland.

After the death of Goisfredus in 1124 an English monk of Croyland Guallevus (in Pet. Bles. Waldevus) or Waltheof, the brother of Cospatric earl of Northumberland, was abbat till 1139, when he was deposed (Sym. Dun.). Although Ord. Vit. brought down his work to the year 1141, he does not mention this fact; the news possibly had not reached Ouche.

The history of Croyland abbey as told by Ord. Vit. very **37** much resembles that as told by Ingulf, but it also varies from it both by omission and by difference. Thus he knows nothing of the period 716–870, in which time Ingulf puts several abbats and many charters of the Mercian kings; he gives no details of the destruction of the monastery, nor of the personal history of the abbat Turketul; he has also no acquaintance with any history of Croyland written by Ingulf, although he was at the monastery only seven or eight years after Ingulf's death.

Ingulf differs from Ord. Vit. as to the date of the death of Turketul and that of Ulfketel; for the former Ingulf (Fulm. p. 52) gives 3 July, but Ord. Vit. 12 July, for the latter Ingulf (Fulm. p. 79) gives 30 Sept., but Ord. Vit. 7 June.

38 Ingulf has borrowed many expressions and sentences from Ord. Vit. (Le Prévost) ij. 268 – 279:

Fulm. p. 2. ll. 29 ff.	= Ord. Vit. pp. 275, 276, 278
4. ll. 41 – 51 =	p. 268
5. ll. 8 – 9 =	p. 284
41. ll. 48 – 49 =	p. 281
44. ll. 48 – 51 =	p. 282
52. =	p. 283
55. ll. 25 – 47 =	p. 283.
62. ll. 45 – 51 =	p. 284
65. ll. 47 ff. =	pp. 284, 285
67. ll. 4 – 9 =	p. 285
72. l. 38 =	p. 267
73. l. 53 =	p. 285
74. l. 42 =	p. 285
78. l. 50 =	p. 286
102. ll. 9 – 15 =	p. 286.

39 The MSS. of this author are very few in number, and none of early date seem to occur in English libraries. Speaking of Croyland monastery, Camden in the Britannia of 1607 (p. 399) says: 'Privatam huius Monasterij historiolam retexere non libet, cùm ex Ingulpho jam ædito vulgò prostet'. From this it would seem probable, that he had no acquaintance with Ord. Vit., of whom besides there are no traces in the Britannia.

The work of Ord Vit. was known also to the author of the 'Vitæ abbatum Croilandiæ' in MS. Cott. Vesp. B. xj (§ 6).

40 VIII. Symeon of Durham, monk and precentor of the church of St Cuthbert of Durham, is the author and compiler of a 'Historia regum Anglorum et Dacorum', extending to the year 1129; the continuation of John prior of Hexham ('Joh. Hagustaldensis') carries the history on to the year 1153. This work, which exists in one MS. only (C.C.C.C. no. 139) is mainly a compilation from Beda, Asser from 802 to 888, Fl. Wig. from 889 to 1117, his continuator John the monk of Worcester, and Eadmer from 1118 to 1119; from 1119 to 1129 it is an independent authority. Information referring to Northern history is inserted from a Northumbrian chronicle and other sources.

Symeon's works have appeared in Twysden's Scriptores Decem (1652), in the M. H. B. as far as 1066, in the Surtees Society's publications, and in the R. S.

Passages in Ingulf supposed to be derived from Sym. Dun. **41** are all probably taken from Fl. Wig. Mr Riley (Archæol. Journ. 1862, p. 128) seems not to have known, that, for the whole period of Ingulf's history 716 – 1095, Sym. Dun. is a mere copier of Fl. Wig. Speaking of the lines on the comet of 1066, he says: 'These lines are probably borrowed from Simeon of Durham or Henry of Huntingdon, as they are not to be found in Florence of Worcester'. They are in Hen. Hunt. and also in Ord. Vit.

In consequence, Sym. Dun. has no notice of the foundation **42** of the monastery in 716, nor of its destruction in 870, nor of Turketul the chancellor, nor of the restoration of the house in 948 Under the year 745 a notice has been written above the line by a different though contemporary hand: 'Hic temporibus floruit sanctus Anachorita Guthlacus'. The only other reference to Croyland in the index to the R. S. edition is to the deposition of the abbat [Waltheof] and the succession of Godfrey prior of St Albans in 1138, a time when the 'Historia Croylandensis' is defective.

IX. The 'History of the English', 'Lestorie des Engles', **43** to the year 1100, composed c. 1140 in french verse by Geffrei Gaimar, for the A. S. period is mainly derived from the A. S. Chronicle, and for the period 1066 – 1100 much resembles Fl. Wig. It is printed (as far as 1066) in the M. H. B., and completely in the R. S. with a translation.

This history mentions the conspiracy of 1075 and earl Wal- **44** theof's execution at Winchester in 1076 (Freeman), also the burial of the earl at 'Crulande', and the miracles wrought by his body.

There is no other mention of Croyland, so that nothing is

found about the events of 716, 870 and 948; Turketul and Ingulf are not referred to.

The history of Hereward's struggle in the Isle of Ely (vv. 5469 ff.) and of his plundering of Peterborough monastery is told by Gaimar, and a long account is given of his murder by some Norman knights (vv. 5600 – 5700).

45   X. Of William of Malmesbury we have two historical works, the ' Gesta pontificum Anglorum ' and the ' Gesta regum Anglorum ', both in Savile's Scriptores (1596), and in the R. S.

46   a. The ' Gesta pontificum' (G. P.) comes down to the year 1125. It has a long paragraph about ' Croland ', which is very disappointing, as it gives no information worth having.

After speaking of the situation of ' Croland ' in the fens, of St Guthlac's life there for 15 years, and of the miracles which occurred after his death, the author says, that by virtue of St Guthlac's merits, a monastery having been built ' ad ossa ejus ', the ' place ' had suffered no loss amid the turmoil of wars and the changes of the times (' Meritis quoque ejus datur, quod, ad corpus ejus edificato monasterio, inter tot bellorum turbines, inter tot temporum volubilitates, nullam ærumnam vel detrimentum sui locus ille persenserit'), that a fresh guest had come thither, St Neot, whose remains had been transferred from Eynesbury to Croyland in consequence of the invasion of the Danes (see Fulm. p. 55), and that ' the place ', though accessible only by water, yet had many visitors. He then goes on to speak of earl Waltheof ' Waldefus ', his execution, and his burial at Croyland, and of the miracles wrought at his tomb, and he mentions that the prior of ' the place ' had assured him, that he had touched the body of the earl, and had found it undecayed and with the head rejoined to the body, only a red line round the neck bearing witness to his decollation (R. S. pp. 321 – 2).

47   The only passage, where Ingulf seems to have used the language of the 'Gesta pontificum', is in a passage (Fulm. p. 69), where speaking of William's coronation by Ealdred archbishop of York and its reason, he first uses words of Fl. Wig. (s. a. 1066) and then continues his account borrowing words from the 'Gesta pontificum ' (lib. I § 23, [R. S.] p. 35).

b. The 'Gesta regum Anglorum' (G. R.) extends a few years further than the 'Gesta pontificum', coming down to 28 Hen. I. or 1128.

The kings, to whom from a perusal of Ingulf one would naturally turn, are the kings of Mercia (R. S. j. 76 – 96) and the English kings from Eadred onwards; but Croyland is nowhere mentioned.

Many passages, however, borrowed from the 'Gesta regum' are found embodied in the text of Ingulf:

Fulm. p. 1. ll. 29 ff.	=G. R. lib. j. (R. S.)	§ 74
17. ll. 18 ff.	= lib. ij.	§ 114
25. ll. 51 – 53	=	§ 121
26. ll. 6 - 7, 36 – 45	=	§ 121
28. ll. 44 – 54	=	§ 135
29. ll. 14 – 15	=	§ 131
37. ll. 52 – 38. ll. 10, 23 – 24	=	§ 135
41. l. 30	=	§ 146
55. ll. 8 – 11	=	§ 165
62. ll. 7 – 11	=	§ 188
70. l. 2	=	§ 252.
74. ll. 6, 11, 19	=	§ 356, 368.

Some of Ingulf's statements respecting king Ælfred seem to be derived from Will. Malm., as they are not contained in Asser's life. Ingulf gives further the text of the settlement of the Primacy of 1072 with the signataries, as it is found in the G. R. (lib. III. § 298 [R. S.] ij. 349 – 352).

XI. The 'Historia Anglorum' of Henry archdeacon of Huntingdon, coming down to the year 1154, contains very little information respecting the monastery. It was first published in the 'Scriptores post Bedam' of Sir H. Savile and is to be found also in the R. S.

St Guthlac hermit of Croyland is mentioned (R. S. p. 113), and the abbey of 'Crulande' is spoken of as lying in the Fen country (p. 165), but nothing is said of its foundation by Æthelbald, or of its restoration by Eadred, or of Turketul's obtaining a charter from king Eadgar, although Eadgar's ecclesiastical activity elsewhere is gratefully commented on. The monasteries mentioned as having been founded or restored by Eadgar are: Glastonbury, Abingdon, Peterborough and Thorney.

At p. 206 we read of the beheading of earl Waltheof and of his burial at 'Crulande.'

51 Ingulf has possibly derived the name Alexis, which he gives to the emperor Alexius Comnenus (Fuhn. p. 74) from the words of the Hist. Angl. (p. 219): 'Alexi...apud Constantinopolim imperante...', or perhaps from Benedict of Peterborough (R. S.) s. a. 1180.

H. Hunt. is quoted by name by Pet Bles. (Fuhn. p. 127). who is supposed to be writing in c. 1192.

In addition to the writers contained in the M. H. B., a few later ones may be mentioned, as treating of the Ingulfine period of the 'Historia Croylandensis.'

52 XII. The 'Chronica Magistri Rogeri de Hoveden,' published first by Savile in 1596 (Francof. 1601) and also in the R. S., is a continuation of Beda beginning with the year 732 and extending to 1201. It is compiled from Fl. Wig., Sym. Dun., and Hen. Hunt. with northern dates. From 1170 to 1192 it agrees closely with Benedict of Peterborough (R. S.), while from 1192 to 1201 it is original and an authority of the first importance. It is, however, not original during the period covered by Ingulf's portion of the 'Historia Croylandensis.'

53 XIII. The 'Chronicle of John abbat of Peterborough' (Joh. Petrib.), contained in MS. Cott. Claud. A. v., and extending in the same kind of hand to 1368 (§ 140), furnishes Ingulf with many expressions in passages, which may be here noticed:

Fulm. p. 57	= Joh. Petrib. a. 1017
66. ll. 1 - 6, 7 - 11, 33 - 37 =	1059
70. l. 25	= 1069
71. ll. 15 - 16	= 1069
73. ll. 23 - 25	= 1075

It was printed by Jos. Sparke in his 'Scriptores varii' fo. Lond. 1723 and has been reprinted with some corrections by Dr Giles, 8vo. Lond. 1845.

54 XIV. The 'Gesta Herwardi' (see § 203), edited by Francisque Michel in his Chroniques Anglo-Normandes, and in the R. S. edition of Geffrei Gaimar, has perhaps supplied a few expressions:

Fulm. p. 67. ll. 20 - 34 = F. M. ij. 5
  67. ll. 53 - 54 =   86
  68. ll. 6 - 8   =   98.

XV. The Polycraticus of John of Salisbury (d. 1180) 55 contains a passage (§ 312) from which a few words have apparently been borrowed (§ 309 - 10).

iv. St Guthlac.

The life of St Guthlac the hermit of Croyland (§ 8) written 56 by Felix the monk, 'catholicæ congregationis vernaculus,' is a long and minute account in latin of the saint. It describes his parentage, birth and early education, his adoption of a monastic life at Repton, his settlement at 'Crugland,' the miracles that he wrought there, and his death and burial.

Felix the biographer was an English monk of the 8th 57 century. He must not be confounded, as has been done by Ord. Vit. (§ 33), with St Felix bishop of the East Angles in the 7th century, who died in 647 (Fl. Wig.), 27 years before the birth of St Guthlac. The monk Felix flourished in the first half of the 8th century, and enjoyed the friendship of Alfwold king of the East Angles 713 - 749, to whom he dedicated his work. The same mistake is represented in the Pet. Bles. as having been made by abbat Henry de Longchamp (§ 465, Fulm. p. 108).

The Life of St Guthlac was written shortly after the death of the saint, as Felix states, that he had received his information respecting him from several of his companions.

St Guthlac was the son of a noble Mercian named Penwald, 58 a name occurring as that of a moneyer of Offa king of Mercia 757 - 796. He was born about 674; after leading a military life for some years, he renounced the world, and at Repton monastery in Derbyshire received the tonsure in 697 (Lingard A. S. Church, 8vo. Lond. 1845 j. 214). Somewhat later he desired to become a hermit, and left Repton. Connected with him in some way there was at that monastery a bell, for in MS. Cott. Cleop. E. iv. (papers relating to the dissolution of Monasteries) fo. 185 is written : '*Monasterium de Repingdon alias Repton: Superstitio.* Huc fuit peregrinatio ad sanctum

Guthlacum et ad ejus campanam, quam solent capitibus imponere ad restinguendum dolorem capitis.'

59 Coming into the Fenland he heard of the island of 'Crugland,' a place of horrors and fears, and in 699 he made it his dwelling place. A great change must however have taken place in the next five centuries, 'for whereas, as antiently time out of mind, [the fens] were neither accessible for man or beast, affording only deep mud, with sedge and Reeds; and possest by birds (yea much more by Devils, as appeareth in the life of S. Guthlac, who finding it a place of horror and great solitude began to inhabit there) is now changed into delightfull meadows and arable ground: and what thereof doth not produce Corn or Hay, doth abundantly bring forth sedge, turf, and other fuell very usefull to the borderers' [Matth. Paris, Hist. Major s. a. 1256, translated by Dugdale, History of Imbanking 359].

60 Some difficulty exists as to certain days in St Guthlac's life connected with the festival of St Bartholomew as mentioned in Felix. The chief point is, that he is there stated to have arrived for the second time at Croyland 'die viij Kal. Sept. [25 Aug.], quo S. Bartholomæi sollempnitas celebrari solet' (Birch, Memorials of S. Guthlac, p. 19), a day given also by the A. S. translation of Felix, by Fl. Wig. and by Ord. Vit. (ij. 270).

The festival of St Bartholomew is usually ix Kal. Sept. or 24 Aug., and to avoid the difficulty the Bollandists, in their reprint of Felix, alter 'viij Kal. Sept.' into 'nono Kal. Sept.' But the same date of 'viij Kal. Sept.' for the festival of St Bartholomew is given also by Kalendarium Floriacense, Stabulense, Brixianum, Vallumbrosanum (Migne P. L. vol. 138, pp. 1188, 1199, 1274, 1283); and in the Martyrologium poeticum of Beda (Migne, vol. 94, p. 604) are the following lines for August:

'Machabæi Augusti coronantur mensis in ortu [Kal. Aug.]:
Sanctumque et Xystum octavis tenet Idibus almum [viij Id. Aug.].
. . . .
Inde Timotheus undecimas tenet ordine digno,
Atque simul martyr sortitur Symphorianus [xi Kal. Sept.].

Octonas sanctus sortitur Bartholomaeus [viij Kal. Sept.];
Bis binis passus colitur Baptista Joannes [iv Kal. Sept.]'.

In a second case (Birch, p. 18) the Bollandists get out of the difficulty by omitting the passage altogether; the third (Birch, p. 50) they leave untouched. The same date (25 Aug.) is given in the Anglo-Saxon 'Calendarium poeticum' printed from MS. Cott. Tib. B. 1. art. 2 in Hickes Gramm. Anglo-Sax. (pp. 203 - 208) p. 206.

In his lonely life the saint was sore vexed with demons, [61] but received comfort not only from St Bartholomew the Apostle, but also from an angel. At Croyland bishop Headda visited him and ordained him to the priesthood. Æthelbald, a prince of the Mercian house, being outlawed by king Ceolred 709 - 716, came to St Guthlac, and received from him consolation and a prophetic promise of future royal dignity.

In Stukeley's account of Croyland abbey, published from his [62] MSS. by the rev. J. M. Gresley (4⁰ Ashby-de-la-Zouch 1856), is a drawing of a large quatrefoil with a centre panel still existing on the west front over the chief entrance. This contains five scenes from the life of the saint; one represents his arrival at Croyland in a boat, shewing a sow and her little ones lying on the shore under a tree, while the centre panel represents the saint compelling a demon to carry a large object, perhaps a block of stone for the building of his oratory. These scenes are not found in Felix, nor in the Guthlac scroll, nor in the Cambridge MS. Dd. xj. 78; the latter of them however is mentioned in Capgrave. The Cambridge MS. describes also some events in the saint's life which are not otherwise found: the loss of his psalter and its recovery, the arrival of St Bartholomew with his scourge, his temptation by the Devil in the guise of St Pega his sister, and how birds and fishes conversed familiarly with him.

On 11 Apr. 714 St Guthlac died, and being laid in a leaden 'sarcophagus' sent him in his life time by the abbess Ecgburga, daughter of king Adulf [of the East Angles 664 - 693], he was buried in his 'oratorium.' A year afterwards his coffin was by his sister Pega placed 'in memoriale quoddam, quod nunc ab Æthelbaldo rege miris ornamentorum structuris in reverentiam (v. l. venerantiam) divinæ potentiæ ædificatum conspicimus' (Birch, p. 60). Ord. Vit. speaks of the 'mausoleum venerabilis Guthlaci' (ij. 278), this word being used also by Fl. Wig. (a. 850), Æthelweard (a. 874) and by Ingulf (Fulm. p. 7).

63 Mr Freeman's statement, quoting from Ord. Vit. (ed. Duchesne 539 D.), that St Guthlac appeared 'from time to time as the rebuker and adviser of kings,' seems too strong, as neither Felix nor Ord. Vit. (l.c.) mentions any other royal personage than Æthelbald visiting the saint, and he during Guthlac's life time was only an exile. The words of Ord. Vit. are: 'Fama de beato Guthlaco longe lateque celeriter volante, multi ad cum veniunt diversorum ordinum gradus: abbates, monachi, comites, divites, vexati, pauperesque de proximis Merciorum finibus, et de remotis Britanniæ partibus, pro salute corporis aut animæ' (Le Prévost ij. 274). Canon Moore improves upon this, and says, that Felix speaks of kings and bishops being received by St Guthlac, and of their being domiciled in houses upon the island (Journ. Archæol Ass. 1879 p. 134); but Headda is the only bishop mentioned by Felix.

64 A long account of St Guthlac from Felix is given in the Dictionary of Christian Biography (Vol. II. pp. 823 ff.).

This life of St Guthlac by Felix exists also in a shortened A. S. translation (see § 71).

An abridgment of Felix' life is to be found in Ord. Vit. lib. iv. c. xv (ij. 268 – 279), and both the original by Felix and the abridgment by Ord. Vit. were known to Ingulf, who uses expressions extracted from both in his account of the appearance of St Guthlac to Æthelbald the Mercian 'clito' or ætheling, who afterwards founded the abbey, and of the foundation itself.

65 An epitome of the life of St Guthlac compiled by a 'certain monk,' and the life by Felix were found by Leland 'in eodem codice.' His words are: 'Quidam monachus impulsore Wlfwinno Prior redegit libellum de vita D. Guthlaci in epitomen, cuius exemplar fuit in eodem codice quo liber Felicis' (Itin. 8º

Oxon. 1744. iv. 133), while Ord. Vit. says, that he made his abridgment of Felix' life of St Guthlac 'rogante venerabili Vulfino priore.'

The passage in Ingulf (Fulm. p. 2) is as follows:

'Sed interim post aliquanti temporis evolutionem **præfatus-exul-Ethelbaldus** in remotis adhuc latitans regionibus, **audita-sancti-viri-morte,-mœrens** et lugens illuc advenit: **cui-post-lacrymas-et-longam-orationem-in-proxima-casula** vigilanti **sanctus apparuit,** et **eum consolatus** est (the words in thick type being from Ord. Vit.), dicens, "Confide fili, et **noli contristari, quia-Dominus-per meam intercessionem audivit-preces-tuas,** et ante præsentis anni cursum circularem **sceptris-regni-do-mi-naberis** in felicitate longævo dierum spatio fruiturus." **Ille-vero** respondit, "**Domine-quod-signum-mihi-erit,** quod ista **sic-evenient?**" (Felix). Et sanctus "**Crastina die ante horam** diei **tertiam habitantibus in hac** insula Croylandiæ cibaria **insperata d-a-buntur**" (Felix, Ord. Vit.). **Exin-ipse-omnia,-quæsibi-dicta** erant **recordans,** et **indubitata spe futura fore-credebat. Nec-fides-illum-fefellit,** quia cuncta juxta viri Dei vaticinium effectui mancipata perpendit. **Defuncto** igitur et **sepulto** Dei **famulo-Guthlaco,-signa-virtutum-ac-sanitatum per-invocationem intercessionis illius** coruscare frequenter cœperunt (Felix), ut in libro de vita ac miraculis ejus clarius et luculento stylo (prout de memorandis vestris colligere potui) seriatim panduntur. **Rex** autem **Ethelbaldus,-ut-beatum-consolatorem-suum-miraculis-coruscare-comperit,-locum-sepulturæ-ejus-gaudens** et devotus **expetiit,-et-ea-quæ** dicto **viro** Dei adhuc viventi **jam-regnum-adeptus** ante promiserat, plene persolvit. Accersito namque quantocyus quodam famosæ religionis monacho Eveshamensi, nomine Kenulpho, ut ibi cænobium aggregaret, sibi et Deo **servientibus** ibidem **perenniter-concessit,** dedit et confirmavit **et-ab-omni-redditu** et **consuetudine-seculari** totam insulam Croylandiæ omnino **absolvit,-et-inde-chartam** suam **in-præsentia-episcoporum,-procerumque** regni sui securam statuit' (Ord. Vit.).

It is strange, that, while it is quite plain, that the Ingulfine writer had Felix before him, he yet has put into St Guthlac's mouth (Fulm. p. 2, l. 19 f.) a speech, of which there is no trace whatever either in Felix or in Ord. Vit.; this is the case also with the life in Capgrave (Surius), which is manifestly re-written from Felix.

66 Bale gives an account of Felix and his supposed works (Scriptores [fo. Basil. 1559] cent. I. p. 92), ending:

'Porro non sine mendaciis et erroribus multis, a Vuilfrido abbate ac Cyssa presbytero instigantibus, edoctus prosa et carmine quaedam congessit, atque Elfvualdo suo olim Maecenati (Ehvoldum Polydorus [Vergil fo. Basil. 1570, p. 68, l. 35] habet) orientalium anglorum dedicavit,

Vitam Guthlaci reclusi   Lib. j. Jussionibus tuis obtemperans, lib. [a]
Miracula ejusdem Guthlaci Lib. j. Quodam tempore jucundae recorda. [b]
De translatione ejusdem   Lib. j. Erigite charissimi aures, omnes. [c]
Epitomen vitae Guthlaci   Lib. j. Vitam beati Guthlaci confessoris. [d]
Gesta abbatum Crulandiae Lib. j. [e]

a. This is the actual life by Felix, beginning: 'Jussionibus tuis obtemperans libellum quem de vita .. Gudlaci componi praecepisti...institui' (Birch p. 1);

b. this is printed after Felix' biography in Acta Sanctorum of the Bollandists Apr. ij; it begins 'Quodam tempore jucunda recordationis abbas Ingulfus...';

c. this work is the account of the translation of St Guthlac in 1136 1 Steph.; it is also printed in Acta Sanctorum Apr. ij;

d. this 'epitome' might be Ord. Vit. abridgment (§ 64).

e. this work, whatever it was, can hardly have been written by Felix; it may have been the 'Vitae abbatum Croylandiae' in MS. Cott. Vesp. B. xj. fol. 76 – 78.

67 One of St Guthlac's companions was Cissa, who (according to Felix, Ord. Vit. and Fl. Wig.) succeeded him: Ingulf knows nothing of this, while Felix says nothing of any monastery founded at Croyland by Æthelbald, saying only, that, after Guthlac's death [11 Apr. 714] and first burial, his body was removed a year after, and so in 715, into a certain 'memoriale,' 'quod nunc ab Æthelbaldo rege miris ornamentorum structuris in reverentiam divinae potentiae aedificatum conspicimus; ubi triumphale corpus tanti viri usque in hodierni temporis cursum feliciter pausat' (Birch p. 60).

This Life must have been written before the death of king **68** Alfwold in 749 (Sym. Dun.), and not very long after the summer of 715, still not too soon, as the expression 'usque in hodierni temporis cursum' would then hardly be appropriate. Some years also are necessary to allow for the increase of the power of Æthelbald who became king in 716, corresponding to the words: 'Ex illo...tempore usque in hodiernum diem infulata regni ipsius felicitas per tempora sequentia de die in diem crescebat' (Birch p. 62).

In Ingulf the king is said to have reigned 41 years 'juxta prophetiam sancti patris Guthlaci' (Fulm. p. 5), referring to the indefinite words of Felix (Birch p. 62): 'Non solum autem ut fertur regnum sibi prophetavit, sed et longitudinem dierum suorum et finem vitæ suæ sibi in ordine manifestavit.'

The date 714 as that of St Guthlac's death is given by five of the six chronicles; the sixth, the Abingdon chronicle C, places it in 713, while Ord. Vit. places it 'anno ab Incarnatione Domini DCC°X°V°.'

The book is also to some extent dated by the mention (Birch p. 51) of Cissa a presbyter, St Guthlac's companion, 'qui nunc nostris temporibus sedem sancti Guthlaci viri Dei possidet (v. l. possedit).'

Fl. Wig. incorporates into his notice of the death of St **69** Guthlac s. a. 714 the words 'animam ad gaudia perpetuæ emisit exultationis' from the life of the saint (Birch p. 57). The notice of his entering the monastery at Repton is in like manner derived from Felix: 'Sanctus Guthlacus, **cum-ætatis-suæ-xxiv peregisset annos**, pompis abrenuncians sæcularibus **relictisque suis omnibus monasterium Hrypandun** adiit, ibique **sub-abbatissa-nomine-Alfthrytha, tonsuram** et **clericalem habitum suscepit**.' The abridgment of Ord. Vit. runs thus: '**xx° iv° ætatis-suæ anno** abrenuncians sæculi pompis **Ripadum monasterium** adiit ibique **sub-abbatissa-nomine-Elfdrid tonsuram habitumque clericalem suscepit**.'

Matthew Paris, whose Chronica Majora goes on to 1259, **70** has s. a. 714 (R. S. j. 324 – 8) a long account of St Guthlac, but with no mention of the foundation of Croyland abbey, saying simply: 'in suo oratorio in honorem beati Bartholomæi dedicato, sepulturam accepit; quo in loco omnes, qui cum pio affectu deposcunt, divinæ miserationis indulgentiam consequuntur.' This account is to be found in 'Matth. Westm.' R. S. j. 362 – 5 in identical words.

The remains of St Guthlac were twice translated, once in 1136, an event referred to in the First Anonymous Continuation as the first translation, and again in June 1196 (Fulm. p. 463). The translation of St Guthlac commemorated by the Abbey, 'St Guthlac in August' (Gough, Croyl. App. p. 62) was 30 Aug. (Nicolas, Chron. of Hist. p. 143). The former translation is also mentioned in Joh. Petrib. (s. a. 1136): 'Translatio Sancti Guthlaci ab Alexandro Lincoln. episcopo solemniter celebrata;' it is the translation described in the work mentioned by Bale (§ 66). The later translation is not recorded by Joh. Petrib. The translations of earl Waltheof were in 1090 and in 1219.

71 This latin life of St Guthlac has been printed in the 'Acta Sanctorum' of the Bollandists (fo. Antw. 1675) Apr. ij. 38 – 50, in the 'Acta Sanctorum ordinis S. Benedicti' of Mabillon, and in Gough's Croyland App. No. LXIV. pp. 131 – 153, also in Birch's 'Memorials of St Guthlac of Crowland' (8º Wisbech 1881) from Royal MS. 13 A. xv. in the British Museum.

The Anglo-Saxon Life of St Guthlac is given in: 'The Anglo-Saxon Version of the Life of St Guthlac, Hermit of Crowland, originally written in Latin by Felix (commonly called) of Crowland. Now first printed from a MS. in the Cottonian Library [Vesp. D. xxj]......by Ch. Wycliffe Goodwin M.A. [8º Lond. 1848].

72 Churches dedicated in St Guthlac's name and in his honour are St Guthlac's at Fishtoft Linc., Paunton parva Linc., Market Deeping Linc., Passenham Northants. Near Swaffham Norf. was a hamlet originally called Guthlake's stow from the chapel then dedicated to St Guthlac (Gough). There was also St Guthlac's priory of White Friars near Hereford (Ellis Introd.

j. 431. Dugd. Mon. 1816, iij. 620 ff.). One of the wapentakes of Leicestershire is that of Guthlacston.

'In a niche in the wall of the parish church of Fishtoft' [near Boston] 'is a statue of St Guthlac the patron saint; and there is a tradition connected with this statue, that so long as the whip, the usual insignia of the saint, remained, the parish of Fishtoft should not be infested with rats and mice.' (Thompson, Hist. of Boston 1856, p. 311).

The name of this saint is the name also of an early king of Denmark, who appears in Geoffrey of Monmouth as 'Guichthlacus Dacorum rex,' and in Pierre de Langtoft's Chronicle (R. S. j. 44) as Guthlak. According to Langebek ij. 155 this king Guthlac is the same that invaded Gaul c. 515, and whose name is given by Greg. Turon. iii. iij. as Gothilaeus, and by the northern annalists as Huglekær [Hugleikr] with variations. He appears as Hygelac in Beowulf and is identified with the Chochilagus of the 'Gesta Francorum.'

A namesake of the patron of Croyland was Guthlac abbat of 73 Glastonbury in 824 (Dugd. Mon. [1817] j. 3). The name occurs also among the signatures to Worcester charters (Birch C. S. 75 (691), 76); a book by a certain William, 'de Vita et moribus Philosophorum ad Guthlacum,' formerly in the library of St Paul's cathedral in London, is mentioned by Leland (De Scriptt. p. 216), who adds 'sed an is sit Rameseganus [William of Ramsey] nescio.' Dr Stubbs (Will. Malm. G. R. [R. S.] j. pref. p. cxlij.) would be willing to identify the author with Will. Malmesb.; however among the works of William of Ramsey, Bale enumerates: 'De legendis ethnicorum scriptis Lib. j. Amico suo Guthlaco, Guilhel.' (§ 65. cent. iij. p. 217); this is perhaps the same work; a person named Godwin the son of Guthlac ' in fabulis antiquorum valde praedicatur' according to the 'De gestis Herwardi' (Geffrei Gaimar R. S. j. 372; Fr. Michel ij. 50).

A relic of St Guthlac at Abingdon is mentioned in Chron. Mon. de Abingdon R. S. ij. 158.

A life of St Guthlac, 'liber de vita ac miraculis ejus,' 74 referred to by Ingulf (Fulm. p. 2), in the long passage quoted above, has perhaps given rise to the statement by Fulman: '*Scripsit* [Ingulfus] *etiam librum* De vita et Miraculis S. *Guthlaci,* Croylandensium *Patroni, ut ipse testatur; qui tamen hodie extare non videtur,*' (Fulm. 'Lectori').

75 The 'Codex Exoniensis,' edited from the MS. in the Cathedral Library of Exeter by Benj. Thorpe (8° Lond. 1842), contains a metrical A. S. life of St Guthlac (pp. 107—184). In this poem hardly any proper names occur, not even Croyland, besides the name of the saint; the others are Bartholomew, Adam and Eve, Britain and England; Beccel his companion and Pega his sister are described, but not named.

76 In Joh. Petrib. (MS. Cott. Claud. A. v.) the following notice occurs, which is not referred to in Hardy (D. C.).

'A°. 1237 obiit dominus Henricus de Longo Campo, abbas Croylandiæ, ad cuius petitionem magister Petrus Blesensis, archidiaconus Bathoniensis tunc eloquentissimus, vitam Sancti Guthlaci heroico stylo, et magister Henricus metrico stylo, venustissime dictaverunt.'

77 A MS. of the Cambridge University Library, Dd. xj. 78, contains a metrical latin life of St Guthlac, 'vita beati Guthlaci metrice composita,' of 1666 lines, dedicated to Henry de Longo Campo abbat of Croyland 1190–1236. Mr Birch gives some long extracts from this MS. in his 'Memorials of St Guthlac' p. xxiv ff., and it is quoted by Camden (Britannia 1607, Leic. p. 361).

In it mention is made of the Psalter of St Guthlac, its loss and recovery (§ 61), and of the scourge of St Bartholomew his especial patron saint; these are not spoken of in the Life of St Guthlac by Felix, but figure prominently in Ingulf's account of the destruction of Croyland by the Danes in 870.

78 The dedication is as follows:

Invocacio auctoris ad H. de Longo Campo abbatem Croilandi (sic, see § 354).

  At tu, quem Longus ad celsos Campus honores
  Protulit, abbatum rutilans Henrice lucerna,
  Dum me compellis præsumere, dum mihi stulto
  Imponis sapientis onus, præsumpcio partim
  Est tua, præsumptum partim dignare tueri.

The last section concerning the beginning of the abbey
is here transcribed:

'De munificentia regis Ethelbaldi.
Regis Ethelbaldi devotio perstat, et ipso
Diligit affectu rex, quo dilexerat exul
Guthlacum, stabilemque fidem nec temporis acti
Longa retro series nec adeptio mutat honoris;
Solliciteque cavens ingratus posse videri,
Guthlaci devotus adit penetralia, quorum
Cum nimis arta, nimis antiqua domus, nimis ima,
Et nimis esset egens, rex inclitus ampliat artam,
Innovat antiquam, levat imam, ditat egentem.
Nec solum terram, cuius Croilandia nomen,
Sed circumpositæ telluris dat penes Eurum
Leucas quinque, penes Aquilonem quinque, penesque
Austrum quinque, penes Zephyrum tres, singula cunctis
Consuetudinibus, cunctis exempta tributis;
Quorum Guthlaco successurisque ministris
Inconcussa datur possessio jure perhenni.
"Sic exercet ibi se munificentia regis,
Ecclesiamque gravi vult ædificare paratu.
At quia tam mollis, tam lubrica, tam male constans,
Fundamenta palus non ferret saxea, palos
Præcipit infigi quercino robore cæsos.
Leucarumque novem spatio rate fertur harena,
Inque solum mutatur humus; suffultaque tali
Colla basi multo stat consummata labore."
Indignans regalis apex desistere cœptis
Ornamenta loco quæcumque decentia donans,
Induxerat monachos, quorum non destitit omni
Tempore quo vixit bona multiplicare, querelas
Exaudire, preces attendere, jura tueri.
Hoc monachi celebrant ex illo tempore claustrum,
Quos oculata fides, quos testificata vetustas,
Quos infallibilis docet experientia, quanti
Sit Guthlacus apud Dominum, qui demoniorum
Præcipuus domitor, quos vivus vicerat hospes,
Mortuus exturbat, energumenisque medetur.
Omnia Guthlaco succumbunt monstra, suique
Militis imperio subicit fantasmata X*p*istus,
Rex regum; cum quo sit Patri Spirituique
Sancto, sicut erat in principio, decus et laus
Et virtus et nunc et semper et omne per ævum.'

It will have been noticed, that the poet says nothing of any destruction of the abbey or of its restoration by Turketul.

The seat 'sedes' of the monastery is very differently given in different accounts. According to Ord. Vit. it extended five miles to the E., three to the W., two to the S., and two to the N.; Felix says nothing, as he does not speak of any monastery. This life (§ 77) of St Guthlac (c. 1200) says: five leagues to the N. S. and E. and three to the W.; Capgrave (Surius) says the same; Ingulf says four leagues in length by three in width.

The eight lines in inverted commas are those quoted in Camden's Lincolnshire (§ 77). Another quotation from this poem occurs in his Cambridgeshire.

The poem is ascribed, possibly from Bale (Script. cent. III. pp. 216 – 7), in a modern hand to William a monk of Ramsey abbey, the words 'auctore Gulielmo monacho Ramesiensi' being written on fo. 61.

80 The description of the 'bugges of Crowland' from this MS. is quoted by Camden in his 'Remaines' (4° Lond. 1657) p. 310 with the remark :

'If a painter would portraite divells, let him paint them in his colours, as FELIX the old Monke of *Crowland* depainted' them 'in his verses, and they will seeme right hel-hounds.'

This had already been done by the artist, who drew the scenes of the life of the saint in the Guthlac scroll (§ 82).

81 There are other small works referring to St Guthlac mentioned in Mr Birch's Memorials, mostly poems. The MSS. referring to the saint are enumerated in Th. D. Hardy's Descr. Cat. R. S. j. 404 – 410.

82 Besides these literary monuments of the saint, there exists the Brit. Mus. MS. Harl. Y. 6, a very curious pictorial roll, 9 feet long by 6½ in. wide, containing 17 circular panels and one half one, filled with drawings of the life of the saint, 'in brown or faded black ink, heightened with tints and transparent colours lightly sketched in with a hair pencil,' accompanied by short descriptions of the events depicted. It is probably incomplete beyond the loss of the half of the

first vignette, as that only illustrates his life as a soldier, his earlier life being thus utterly unrepresented. In the 8th we see St Bartholomew rescuing St Guthlac from the power of the local demons with the inscription: 'Sanctus Bartholomæus fert flagrum Guthlaco,' no notice being taken of the Psalterium. The 5th roundel represents the saint building a chapel: 'Guthlacus edificat sibi capellam '; this is not related by Felix, although the building of a hut, 'tugurium' (Birch p. 21), is mentioned, and the saint had also an 'oratorium' (Birch pp. 33, 59) or 'ecclesia' (Birch p. 49). Bishop 'Hedda', who ordains Guthlac in the 11th scene, is stated to be 'episcopus Wintoniensis'; in the life by Felix his see is not given.

The Harley Roll has been engraved several times; the best reproduction is that in autotype in Birch's Memorials.

The last of the roundels represents the thirteen principal benefactors of the monastery making their offerings at the shrine of the saint, their benefactions being inscribed on long labels which they hold. They range from king Æthelbald in 716 to Alan de Croun the donor of the priory of Freston in 1114 (Fulm. p. 119) or rather c. 1150 (§ 406; Dugd .Mon. j. [1657] p. 443), and include one not mentioned by Ingulf, viz. Algar the deacon, who thus speaks of his benefaction: ' Ego Algarus diaconus do tibi [pater Guthlace] terram de Duvedic et ecclesiam cum pertinentiis.'

The scroll cannot be earlier than 1114 even according to the Historia Croylandensis, and as none of the architectural details represented belong to the First Pointed or Early English style of architecture, which came in with the 13th century, it probably belongs to the middle of the 12th century or c. 1160. Not noticing the date of Alan de Croun, whose benefactions belong to the time of abbat Joffrid, if not later (§ 406), Mr Birch thinks, that 'this roll' is 'the work... perhaps of the celebrated Ingulph, the well-known literary abbat of that monastery' (Memorials p. xxxvi.); but Ingulf died in Dec. 1108.

The foundation of the abbey is thus referred to:
' Ego rex Ethelbaldus do tibi sedem abbatie cum per-

tinentiis suis soluta*m* et libera*m* ab om*n*i secu*l*ari exactione', words which differ from those used concerning the same matter by Ingulf (Fulm. p. 2).

84 A life of St Guthlac is mentioned in the First Anonymous Continuation c. 1186 (Fulm. p. 453):

'Abbatia de *Croylandia*, quam incepit beatus *Guthlacus* confessor transactis quadringentis annis et eo amplius, qui et ibidem requiescit, propria Eleemosyna est regum *Angliæ*, de donatione eorum speciali ab antiquissimis temporibus *Anglorum*, postquam eam fundavit *Ethelbaldus* rex, donando Mariscum, in quo sita est, sicut et continetur in Vita ipsius sancti ab olim scripta: longius enim à cætera terra constituta est Abbatia in medio Marisci.'

There is nothing to this effect in Felix' life of the saint, as Mr Riley (Archæol. Journ. 1862, p. 116) seems to think. The foundation as thus dated in 1186 would fall some years before 786, the Ingulfine date being 716.

85 A 'Vita Sancti Guthlaci' was in the library of Peterborough (Gunton, App. p. 174). According to Bale, Peter of Blois is the author of a Life of St Guthlac (cf. § 76),

Vitam Guthlaci confessoris Lib. j. Quia gesta virorum illustrium solet (sic).

86 Felix' life of the saint is to be found in

Acta Sanctorum of the Bollandists (with many additions),
Acta Sanctorum ordinis S. Benedicti ;

a variation of it is given in

Capgrave, Nova legenda Angliæ (4to. Lond. 1516),
Surius, De vitis Sanctorum.

Other accounts will be found in different collections of lives of the saints, such as Hierome Porter (4° Douai 1632) etc.

He is also mentioned in Fox, Book of Martyrs (ed. Townsend, 1843) j. 357.

87 St Guthlac attained a certain degree of renown beyond the limits of Croyland. Bishop Ecgwin's spurious charter of foundation of Evesham abbey (Chron. Evesh. [R. S.] p. 17) is dated '714...post parvum tempus migrationis beati Guthlaci de hoc seculo.'

He is also occasionally found commemorated in the calendars and services of the mediæval church of England.

His death is stated by Fl. Wig. to have happened on

Wedn. after Easter, iij. Id. Apr. 'indictione xij', which can only mean 11 Apr. 714. Felix the monk gives the Wedn. after Easter in the 15th year of his sojourn at Croyland (Birch pp. 53, 54); according to Fl. Wig. he settled there in 699. (His death is put by A.S.Chr. C in 713, but by the rest in 714.)

Accordingly 11 Apr. is the day on which he is commemorated in English service books, a day which was also dedicated to St Leo.

The MS. Psalter 7. F. 1 in the Fitzwilliam Museum, Cambridge, has on 11 Apr. in the Calendar 'Scōrum Leonis et Guthlaci'. That MS. has also on 6 March 'Scārum Kyneburge et Kyn[eswithe] ac Tibbe'. The four local saints are invoked in the Litany.

His translation is given as on 30 Aug. (§ 70). It is mentioned, in Leland Itin. (1744) iv. App. p. 132, as taking place in 1 Steph. 1136, but the day and month are not there given.

1. In bishop Leofric's Missal in the Bodleian Library, **88** Bodl. MS. n° 579, edited by the rev. F. E. Warren B.D. (4° Oxf. 1883), St Guthlac is found:

in the Calendar [c. 980]: ·F·[estum] Sc̄i Guthlaci anachoritae' (p. 26),

in the Litania: 'Sancte Gudlace [ora]' (p. 210),

but no service is given for the day. Leofric was bishop of Exeter 1046 – 1072.

2. In the Red Book of Derby in the Parker Library MS. C.C.C.C. n° 422 [c. 1061], described by Mr Warren, St Guthlac is found:

in the Calendar: 'S. Guthlaci presb.' (p. 272),

but with no especial service, the Proprium de Sanctis being wanting.

3. In the Missal of Robert II. surnamed Champart, abbat **89** of Jumiéges 1037 – 45, bishop of London 1045 – 51, archbishop of Canterbury 1051 – 52 in the Rouen Municipal Library, MS. Y. 6, [c. 1010], described by Mr Warren, St Guthlac is found:

in the Calendar: 'Guthlaci Conf.' in golden letters (p. 280).
in the Litania: (p. 281).
in the Proprium Sanctorum:

III. id. apr. Nat. S. Guthlaci.

[Fo. 1. c.] Adiuua nos, Domine, deprecatione sanctorum tuorum; et praecipue huius beati famuli tui Guthlaci, presbiteri atque anachoritae intercessione, quaesumus, ab omni aduersitate protege, cuius hodie sollempnitatem (sic) diem cum lætitia spiritali ueneramur, ut quorum festa gerimus sentiamus auxilium. Per.

[Secreta].

Respice, Domine, propitius super haec munera, quae pro omnium sanctorum tuorum, et specialiter pro beati Guthlaci presbiteri et anachoritae, cuius hodie ueneranda est festiuitas, commemoratione deferimus, et pro nostris offensionibus immolamus. Per.

Præfatio.

U[ere] D[ignum] æterne Deus. Te quo maxime hodie in hujus beati famuli tui Guthlaci, presbiteri et anachoritae, natalicia uenerari, et in tuorum omnium te glorificare honore sanctorum in sempiternum; quia infirmitati nostræ talium tuorum filium præstitisti suffragia, ut eorum intercessionibus nostri misereri digneris. Per Christum.

Post communio.

Deus, fidelium remunerator animarum, præsta ut beati Guthlaci, presbyteri et anachoritae, cuius uenerandam celebramus sollempnitatem, praecibus indulgentiam consequamur. Per Dominum. (p. 282)

4. In the late 11th century English Missal, MS. Cott. Vitell. A. xviij, described by Mr Warren, we find
in the Calendar: 'Sancti Gudlaci anachorite';
in the Proprium Sanctorum:

III id. Ap. Nat. s. Guthlaci anachoritae.

[fo. 87. a] Deus, qui nos beati Guthlaci confessoris tui annua sollemnitate lætificas, concede propitius, ut sicut ille per ardua solitariae uitae instituta ad tuae uisionis gaudia peruenit, ita ipsius intercessione ad eadem peruenire mereamur. Per.

Secreta.

Da nobis, quaesumus, Domine, semper haec tibi uota gratanter persoluere, quibus sancti confessoris tui Guthlaci depositionem recolimus, et praesta ut in eius laude semper tuam gloriam praedicemus. Per.

Postcommunio.

Protector in te sperantium Deus, familiam tuam propitius respice, et per hæc sancta quæ sumpsimus, interueniente beato Guthlaco confessore tuo, a cunctis eam aduersitatibus (sic) [aduersantibus] potentiæ tuæ brachio defende. Per. (p. 303)

5. In his Memorials of St Guthlac Mr Birch has printed [91] some liturgical matter connected with the saint:
from MS. Harl. n° 1117, fo. 65;
from MS. C.C.C.C. n° 198 fo. 377 b.;
from MS. Arund. (Brit. Mus.) n° 201. fo. 92 b. a hymn in his honour beginning: 'Vera regni perfruens perhennique pace,' the tune of the hymn being there given.

6. St Guthlac is mentioned in some printed service books. [92] In the Prymers he occurs in the calendars:
in the Goodly Prymer in English [1538?];
in the Prymer [1542].

He is found in the Horæ secundum usum Sarum:
4° Antw. 1525;
8° Paris (Regnault) 1535;
and in the Enchiridion ad usum Sarum 8° Paris 1530 (Maskell Mon. III. 207).

The sainted hermit of Croyland is mentioned even in a latin translation of the Prayer book of 1559, 4° apud R. Volfium, Lond. [15..] printed in: Liturgical services set forth in the reign of queen Elizabeth [Parker Society] 8° Cambridge 1847 [pp. 299 – 434] p. 318.

On the other hand he is not mentioned in: [93]
Missale Sarum: 4° Lond. (W. de Worde) 1498.
———————— 8°. Paris (Jehan Petit) 1516
———————— 4°. Paris   1529
———————— ————   ——   1555.
Missale Ebor: 4°. Paris (Regnault) 1533.
Breviarium Sarum: f°. Paris (C. Chevallon) 1531
———————— 4°. Paris (Regnault) 1516
———————— 8°. Paris (Regnault's widow) 1555
———————— 4° Paris (G. Merlin) 1556.

94 Of St Pega nothing seems known beyond what is contained in Felix' life of her brother and in Fl. Wig. She is further mentioned in Ord. Vit. and in Capgrave, but not in Will. Malm. or Matth. Paris.

Accounts of her are to be found (vj Id. Jan. 8 Jan.) in the Acta Sanctorum etc. In the Martyrol. Usuardi monachi ed. J. B. Sollerius (fo Antw. 1714) p. 19 we find

'Item depositio Sanctae Pegae virginis.'

There seems to be no foundation for the statements concerning her, her leaving the scourge of St Bartholomew and her brother's psalter with abbat Kenulf, her journey to Rome after the death of St Guthlac, and her death there, given in the Ingulf (Fulm. p. 5).

In the Martyrologium Benedictinum of N. H. Menard O. S. B. 8° Paris 1629, it is stated 'Romae, Depositio S. Pegae virginis, sororis S. Guthlaci'. But, according to the Biografia universale 8° Ven. 1822 ff. (s. v. Wion, Arnoldo) Menard's work is only a second edition of Wion's Lignum Vitae 4° Ven. 1595 ('è il martirologio d' Arnoldo Wion arricchito di note e d' osservazioni assai ampie'); and there the name of Pega is not found on 8 Jan. The reference to her burial at Rome in Menard is probably derived from Savile's Ingulf printed at London in 1596 and at Frankfurt in 1601.

The cell of St Pega (Fulm. p. 40), and a bell named after her (Fulm. p. 53), are the only other references to her in the Historia Croylandensis.

v. The name of the place, Croyland or Crowland?

95 With respect to the name of the site of the abbey, Mr Freeman has (Norm. Conq. iv. 597) the following observations: 'The true form of the name is *Cruland, Croland, Crowland*. *Croyland* is a form still unknown on the spot, and it is not found in ancient English writers. In Domesday however we have *Croiland* and *Cruiland*. Was this owing to a devout pun *quasi Croix land*?'

There are however several original charters at the Brit. Museum, which do not corroborate Mr Freeman's second statement. Addit. Charter 5863 is a petition to Henry III. 1216 – 72 for leave to elect an abbat of 'Croyland' monastery. Cart. Harl. 44. G. 52 is a final concord before Ralph [Mershe] abbat of 'Croyland' dated 56 Hen. III. 1272. Cart. Harl. 44. II. 7, a similar document with the spelling 'Croyland', is dated Oct. 55 Hen. III. 1271.

The following forms of the name occur:

Crugland = Felix' life of St Guthlac (MS. Cott. Nero E. 1).
Cruglond = Felix (Royal MSS. 13. A. xv., 4. A. xiv).
Cruwland = A. S. life of St Guthlac (Goodwin). Felix (Birch p. 18).
Cruland = Fl. Wig. Ord. Vit.
Inquisit. Comit. Cantabr. (Hamilton).
Liber Eliensis. Gesta Herwardi.
Cart. Mon. de Ramescia [R. S.] j. 188.
A. S. Chr. A. Latin app.
Crulande = A. S. Chr. DE. H. Hunt a. 1075.
Geffrei Gaimar v. 5733.
Crulant = Sym. Dun. a. 1075. R. de Diceto [R. S.] j. 209.
W. de Coventria a. 1075.
Crouland = Hugo Candidus. Felix (MS. Harl. nº. 3097).
Crollande = Geffrei Gaimar.
Croland = Ann. de Wintonia [R. S.] a. 1091. Bale.
Cruiland = Domesday.
Crowland = Fabyan's Chronicle. Hardyng's Chronicle. Fuller.
½ᵈ token 1666: WILLIAM BROWNE IN CROWLAND.
½ᵈ token 1666: WALTER BIRD OF CROWLAND.
Croiland = Domesday.
H. Hunt. a. 726. MS. Cambr. Univʸ. Lib. Dd. xj. 78.
Vita et passio Waldevi comitis.
Guthlac roll ('Vehitur Guthlacus Croilandium').
Gesta Abbatum S. Albani [R. S.] j. 69.
De abbatibus Croilandensis Monasterii (Leland).
Dr Caius.

  Croyland = MSS. Cott. Vesp. B. xj.
       Joh. Petrib. (MS. Cott. Claudius A. v).
       Early charters. Parliamentary writs.
       'Croyland's chronicle'.
       Seal (1512 – 39): 'Sigillum Johannis Welles abbatis de Croylandie'.
       Seal: 'Sigillum commune abbatis et conventus Croylandie'.
       MS. Arund. 178 (Birch).
       $\frac{1}{2}^d$ token 1670: THE POORES HALFPENY OF CROYLAND.
  Croylande = Walter de Coventria a. 1175.
       Cart. Mon. de Rameseia [R. S.] j. 76.
  Croilant = Domesday ('abbas de Croilant').

vj. The text of the 'Historia Croylandensis.'

97 The printed text of the History of Croyland monastery is exhibited in the following editions:

  1. Sir Henry Savile's incomplete text printed in his 'Scriptores post Bedam' (fo. Lond. 1596, reprinted fo. Francof. 1601); this consists of the Ingulf only, and that incomplete, together with the Cambridge fragment of Petrus Blesensis;

  2. W. Fulman's completer text in his 'Rerum Anglicarum Scriptorum veterum Tom. 1' (fo. Oxon. 1684); this consists of the whole Ingulf, Pet. Bles. and the three Anonymous Continuations in their only form;

  3. W. de G. Birch's incomplete text in 'The Chronicle of Croyland by Ingulph' (8°. Wisbech 1883). This, as its title sets forth, consists of the Ingulf only, and that incomplete.

98 There are two translations of Ingulf into English:

  1. H. T. Riley B.A. Clare Coll. Cambr., 'Ingulph's Chronicle of the Abbey of Croyland etc.' 8° Lond. Bohn. 1854;

  2. Rev. Jos. Stevenson M.A. Univ. Coll., Durham, 'The history of Ingulf' in 'Church Historians of England' Vol. II. part ij. 8° Lond. Seeleys 1854.

99 Of Ingulf's history several MSS. are known to have existed; unfortunately they have all disappeared except two, the one an ancient one MS. Cott. Otho B. xiij, and the other, a late one, MS. Arund. 178, both in the British Museum.

The manuscripts of Ingulf may be divided into two classes,

A, the MSS., which do not contain the Laws of William I. or Eadward the Confessor,

B. the MSS., which do contain them.

A. Of MSS., whose text does not include the Laws of king 100 Eadward, we know of the following:
1. MS. Arundel 178 in the British Museum,
2. The MS. used by Savile in 1596.

B. Of MSS., which contain the Laws of Eadward, we have 101 notices of the following:
1. The Croyland 'Autographum' (Selden) or 'Archetypum' (Spelman),
2. The Marsham MS. used by Fulman,
3. The MS. mentioned by Camden in 1603,
4. The Cotton MS. Otho B. xiij in the British Museum,
5. A Cotton MS. mentioned by Fulman ('Lectori'),
6. A MS. apparently in the Cotton Library, used by Selden.

With regard to these several MSS., which are not all different, some further remarks are necessary.

A. 1. MS. Arundel 178 in the British Museum is a very 102 late (Elizabethan) copy of Ingulf. It bears on fo. 2 the inscription in three lines: 'Soc. Reg. Lond. | ex dono Henr. Howard | Norfolcensis'; its class mark was Z. vij. 7. This MS. with the rest of the library of Arundel House was presented to the Royal Society in 1667 by Mr Henry Howard, the second son (b. 1628) of Henry 21st earl of Arundel and the sixth duke of Norfolk, who died in 1684. He also presented part of the Arundel Marbles to the University of Oxford. The historical part of his MSS. was transferred to the British Museum in 1830 (Weld, Hist. of the Royal Soc. 2 vols 8°. Lond. 1848). This MS. has been edited by Mr Birch in 'The Chronicle of Ingulf' mentioned above. It contains only an incomplete text of the Ingulf, extending as far as the Laws of king Eadward; it has, besides, a long paragraph (without any heading) extracted from the Pet. Bles. describing the doings of the Croyland monks at Cambridge in the time of abbat Joffrid, and another paragraph giving an account of that abbat himself, derived from Pet. Bles.

103 A. 2. Towards the end of the 16th century a knowledge of Ingulf had got abroad, and Sir Henry Savile, who first edited it, thus speaks of it: 'Huic [Guilielmo Malmesb.] proximi...... HUNTINDONIENSIS et HOVEDUNUS....quibus INGULPHUM à plurimis antiquitatum nostrarum sitientibus magnopere desideratum adjecimus' His collection called 'Scriptores post Bedam' was printed fo. Lond. 1596 and reprinted fo. Francof. 1601, the leaves in the reprint being paginated, instead of being numbered as in the English edition. Savile gives no information about the MS., which he used, and nothing is known about it. It was very similar to the MS. Arundel 178; they both broke off at the same place, and they both contained (after the imperfect Ingulf) the same two paragraphs about the Croyland monks at Cambridge and about abbat Joffrid. They frequently omit the same words and passages and even long paragraphs, such as Fulm. p. 41, put in Fulman's edition between brackets. But they also frequently differ, Savile's text agreeing with Fulman's text in various readings, as for instance:

Fulm. p. 4.	Sav. 'Ingwaldus'		Arund. 'Ingulphus'
p. 28.	'invadiatus pœnam demeritam'		'absolutus pœnas meritas'
p. 59.	'hoc regis chirographum'		'idem'
p. 68.	'militem corium coctum et'		'militum chorum'
p. 69.	'consummarentur'		'fieret'

and in the insertion of passages omitted by the Arundel MS., as:

Fulm. p. 15. list of witnesses	5 l.	Sav. ins.	Arund. om.
p. 19. list of witnesses	15 l.	ins.	om.
p. 47. list of witnesses	10 l.	ins.	om.
p. 48. paragraph of	4 l.	ins.	om.

The paragraph concerning the Croyland monks at Cambridge is in Savile's edition headed 'Appendix incerti authoris ad Ingulphum'.

There was another person of the same name, Henry Savile of Bank, who was a friend of Camden, and from whose MS. of Asser's life of king Alfred Camden took the interpolation respecting the early history of the University of Oxford; he is by some believed to have been the author of that interpolated passage.

B. 1. This MS. existed at Croyland, when John Selden 104 endeavoured, but in vain, to obtain the use of it for his work (§ 116). Without having seen it he mentions it in his notes to his edition of Eadmer's History (f° Lond. 1623) p. 172, as 'ipsum Historiæ autographum', though on what authority does not appear. Sir Henry Spelman, however, was able later to consult it, and from it he extracted five of the 50 chapters (n°⁵. 1, 17, 18, 20, 36) of the laws of king William, 'leges ipsas ex ipso designavimus Archetypo', which he inserted in his Concilia (2 vols. fo. Lond. 1639 – 64) I. pp. 623 – 5. He speaks of it, from personal inspection, as very ancient 'veterrimum', and as being preserved in the church of Croyland by the churchwardens under three keys 'ab ædituis sub tertia clave'. No one has mentioned it since his time, and in 1684 Fulman had sought for it, or enquired after it, in vain, 'qui tamen hodie non comparet, ut nobis quærentibus relatum est' (Fulm. 'Lectori').

Spelman in his transcript [1639] of the seventeenth law of king Eadward from the Croyland MS., gives the word 'Euestres' for 'Euesqes', and as this mistake could only be made from a MS. of the times of Edward I. 1272 – 1307 or of Edward II. 1307 – 1327, or of c. 1315, there being then very slight difference between the shape of the 'q' and that of the 'tr', Sir Francis Palgrave (Quart. Review 1826, pp. 295 – 6) conjectures, that this was the date of the 'Archetype'. But it is also possible, that this portion of the Croyland MS. was copied at a still later time from a MS. of c. 1315, at a period, when the earlier current writing was already obsolete, and that therefore the mistake was not made by Spelman, but by the scribe of the Croyland MS.

This Croyland MS. contained the Laws of king William

(Fulm. pp. 88 – 91), and hence must have much resembled MS. Cott. Otho B. xiij. and the Marsham MS. But as there are many differences between the five chapters of those laws as given by Spelman and as printed by Fulman, the 'autographum' could not have been the same MS. as Fulman's (Riley, Archæol. Journal 1862, p. 33).

105 B. 2. The MS., from which the rev. William Fulman printed the Ingulf in 'Rerum Anglicarum Scriptorum Veterum' Tom. I. (fo. Oxon. 1684), a collection of which no second volume appeared, belonged to John Marsham, the eldest son of Sir John Marsham bar^t.

106 Sir John Marsham, the father, was born in 1602, and, after being educated at St John's College Oxford, became one of the Six clerks in chancery. He lost his office, when royalty fell, but recovered it after the Restoration; he was knighted, became M.P. for Rochester, and was made a baronet in 1663. He is the author of two works on ancient history and chronology, 'Diatriba Chronologica' (4° Lond. 1649), and 'Chronicus Canon' (fo. Lond. 1672); he is also the writer of the Προπύλαιον to Dugdale's Monasticon. He died 26 May 1685, shortly after the publication of Fulman's collection, and was succeeded by his son, Sir John Marsham the younger, the owner of the above MS.

Sir John Marsham the younger succeeded his father in 1685, and was also a literary man. His son the third Baronet died young; he was succeeded by his uncle Sir Robert Marsham, whose son Sir Robert was in 1716 made Baron Romney; from him the earls of Romney are directly descended.

107 The Marsham MS., which contributed Ingulf and Pet. Bles. to Fulman's work, was complete as to the Ingulf, with the exception of one leaf (Fulm. p. 104), the contents of which were supplied from a Cotton MS. by Thomas Gale the editor of the 'Historiæ Britannicæ et Anglicanæ Scriptores xx.' (2 vols. fo. Oxon. 1691, 1687), and printed at the end of the Pet. Bles. (Fulm. pp. 131 – 2). Fulman does not, unfortunately, record the press-mark of the Cotton MS. He was not himself acquainted with it, when he set up his Ingulf, and has given

no description of it, but it was less complete than the Marsham MS., as it broke off at Fulm. p. 120, whereas the Marsham MS., although also 'in fine mutilus', went on to Fulm. p. 130.

The Marsham MS., which certainly contained the complete **108** Ingulf and the more complete Pet. Bles., may have consisted of only those two parts of the 'Historia Croylandensis', and not, further, of the three Anonymous Continuations. Fulman does not mention, whence he got the text of these three Continuations; and certainly the fact, that in his edition they are separated from the Ingulf and the Pet. Bles. by the Chronica de Mailros and the Annales Monasterii Burtonensis, seems to shew, that, when he made his arrangements for printing from the Marsham MS., he did not know them, and that it was an after thought to print them. They may have come to his knowledge, when he sought for the text of his missing leaf. Smith's Catalogue of the Cotton MSS. was not published till 1696.

The Marsham MS. is now apparently lost. Obadiah Walker, **109** who was Master of University College Oxford in the time of James II., is charged with having appropriated it. He said, that sir John Marsham the younger had given it to him, and that he in return had presented sir John with some copies of Fulman's book. In 1694 Edmund Gibson (b. 1669), afterwards bishop of Lincoln (1715) and of London (1723), writing to Dr Arthur Charlett, Dr Walker's successor, supposed that the MS. was in University College Library,—'there is a curious Ingulphus in your library', he says, 'which, his [sir John Marsham's] family says, Obadiah Walker stole from him' (Gough, Second App. to the Hist. of Croyl. 4º Lond. 1797 pp. 282 – 3), but it is not now to be found in the Bodleian Library, whither the MSS. of University College have been removed. There are papers of W. Fulman at C.C.C. Oxford, but the librarian the rev. C. Plummer says, that there is nothing in them, that throws a light on his edition of Ingulf.

B. 3. This MS. is mentioned, without further information **110** as to ownership or locality, by W. Camden in the Dedication to his 'Anglica, Normannica etc.' (fo. Francof. 1603). He says:

'Henricus Savilus vir exquisitissima eruditione et solidissimo judicio Londini 1596. *Guilielmum Malmesburiensem* qui è nostris proximus ad historiam semi barbaro illo ævo accessit, *Henricum Huntingdonensem, Rogerum Hovedonum*, et qui à nostris plurimum expetiti quia rari *Ethelwerdum* (§ 17) et *Ingulphum*, cuius nunc exemplar inventum est emendatius ac auctius cum Petri Blessensis supplemento [edidit].'

As Camden does not mention the three Anonymous Continuations, this MS. resembles what seems to be the case with the Marsham MS., i.e. that it contained only the Ingulf and the Pet. Bles.

This undescribed MS. Camden probably used in his Britannia of 1607, as he quotes from Pet. Bles. passages, that were not in the MS. Cott. Otho B. xiij, but were in the Marsham MS., so that there is the possibility, that Camden's apparently then recently discovered MS. (B. 3.) was the same as the Marsham MS. (B. 2).

111 B. 4. The Cotton MS. Otho B. xiij. is thus described in 'Catalogus librorum manuscriptorum bibliothecæ Cottonianæ, scriptore Thoma Smitho, ecclesiæ Anglicanæ presbytero' (fo. Oxon. 1696):

'1. Topographica Croylandiæ delineatio.

2. Historia, sive, ut titulus habet, descriptio compilata per D. Ingulphum, abbatem monasterii Croylandiæ, natione Anglicum, quondam monachum Fontavillensem, continuata per Petrum Blesensem et alios, ad tempus R. Henrici VII. Inserta est historia de *Standardo*, ita inscribitur, quasi esset initium operis: sed nihil est, quam narratio de bello inter Davidem, Regem Scotiæ, pro nepote suo Henrico, et R. Stephanum......

3. Chronica de gestis Anglorum post conquestum, ab anno C. 1067 ad annum C. 1307, *h. e.* a coronatione R. Gulielmi I ad mortem R. Edwardi I. Eadem quoad magnam partem habetur apud Matthæum Westmonasteriensem: alia vero in hoc libro fusius enarrantur.'

This account of the MS. is repeated by Casim. Oudin in his 'Commentarius de Scriptoribus Ecclesiæ antiquæ' (fo. Francof. 1722) ij. 869 ff.

112 This MS. suffered most severely in the fire of 1731; it lost its beginning, and its end, and its back, but the separated leaves and fragments that remain, have been very carefully flattened and inlaid in paper, and so rendered available to students. It consists now of part of nº. 1, being a small fragment

of a map; of a few fragments of Ingulf, beginning at Fulm. p. 73, of a leaf containing the last page of Ingulf and the first page of Pet. Bles.; of great portions (from the year 1192) of the First, and (to the year 1470) of the Second Anonymous Continuation (Fulm. pp. 458–554); the remainder of the 'Historia Croylandensis' is entirely gone, together with the whole of N°. 3 of Smith's Catalogue.

From its containing the Second Anonymous Continuation, this MS. of the Hist. Croyl. is certainly not earlier than 1486, whether it contained the Third Anonymous Continuation or not. This MS. is written all through in one hand, and that a somewhat peculiar, but large and very clear hand. As far as one can judge of the MS. in its present condition, the text measured 10 in. by 5 in.

How the MS. Otho B. xiij. got into the Cottonian Library is not known.

The Cottonian Library was created long before 1600 by sir Robert Cotton (b. 1571, d. 1631) B.A. Jes. Coll. Cambr. 1585, and from its collections both John Speed in great part compiled his works published about 1611, and also Lord Bacon obtained materials for his history of Henry VII. published 1621–2, but begun some years before. After having been increased by the son (sir Thomas) and the grandson (sir John) of sir Robert Cotton, it was in 1706 purchased for the nation. In 1712 it was removed to Essex House, Essex Street, Strand, and in 1730 to Ashburnham House in Little Dean's Yard Westminster. Here on 23 Oct. 1731 the calamitous fire broke out, which destroyed wholly or partially over 200 MSS. including the Otho B. xiij. Since 1757 the remains of the Cottonian Library have formed part of the library of the British Museum.

The Cottonian Library was known to John Selden, who from it edited his Eadmer in 1623, but did not then apparently know of the Otho B. xiij, which from its extending to the end of the Ingulf might have contained the laws of king William, which he edited in the notes to that author, though the MS. may have been defective at that place, as it was in several others. Sir William Dugdale also knew the Library, and in his 'Imbanking' published in 1662 he mentions the Life of St Guthlac Nero C. vij. (Birch Memorials of St Guthlac, p. xxij), the Liber Eliensis Titus A. 1, and this very MS. Otho B. xiij. (p. 221 b.).

Speaking of the sale of serfs, Selden (Eadmer p. 208) refers to the Charter of Thorold of 1051, as 'apud Ingulphum in extremo', which is the case in Savile's edition; this again seems to shew, that, although he edited Eadmer from a Cotton MS. in 1623, he did not know the Otho B. xiij.

114 The difference in outward appearance between the Marsham MS. and the Otho B. xiij. was very marked. The text of the missing leaf of the former occupied 63 lines of Fulman's edition, while a leaf of the Otho B. xiij. occupies 70 lines. The Marsham MS. was therefore a smaller book. Also the Pet. Bles. was more incomplete in the Cotton MS. than in the Marsham MS. Still the two MSS. were very similar in their text and in their internal arrangement, having marginal notes, which are given by Fulman from the Marsham MS. The only difference, that has been noticed, is on Fulm. p. 96, where Fulman's margin reads 'Lanfrancus obiit', while the margin of the Cotton MS. reads 'Ob arch lanf'.

The page of this MS. corresponding to Fulm. pp. 93—4 is headed 'lxxv.' The Ingulf and the Pet. Bles. must have been copied into this MS. from one of earlier date, being then followed by the contemporary First Anonymous Continuation.

115 B. 5. This MS., which is mentioned as in the Cotton Library, 'ex codice instructissimae Bibliothecae D. Johannis Cotton', in 1684 (Fulm. 'Lectori'), can only have been Otho B. xiij. (B. 4), which according to Smith's Catalogue (1696) was the only Ingulf in that Library. He had a very high opinion of Ingulf, as in his notes he calls him: 'in hac re testium non tam facile princeps merito dicendus, quam solus forsan cui par sit ut credamus'.

116 B. 6. John Selden brought out in 1623 the 'Historia Novorum' of Eadmer. In the 'Notae et Spicilegium' he prints (pp. 173 – 189) the complete set of the Laws of king Edward the Confessor, that had been granted anew by William I.

These he had in vain sought to procure from the Croyland MS., but actually printed them 'ex codice, ut videtur, Cottoniano' (Fulm. 'Lectori'). Selden mentions, that Savile's Ingulf broke off just before the Laws of the Confessor, and that Savile adds the note: 'Videtur heic leges Edwardi inseruisse, quæ desunt,' and then continues,

'Atqui certò scimus nos cum [Ingulphum] ibi eas inseruisse, quod non solum ex ipso Historiæ autographo, Crowlandiæ in agro Lincolniensi etiamnum servato (§ 104), constat, sed etiam ex recentiori quo usi sumus exemplari ante annos CC. aut circiter exarato....Nam autographo destitutus (quod interea nancisci impensè et volebam et nitebar, sed frustrà) nolui me conjecturarum nugis ultra torquere; sed ubi me prorsus fugiebat (uti sæpe) Normannicæ dictionis significatio, in ipsa versione eam, variato charactere, retexui. Mallem enim me palam inscientiæ reum confiteri, quam, in crassissimis tenebris, oculorum aciem incassum obtendere.'

It would seem, that this MS., which was conjectured to be *about* 200 years old in 1623, or of about the year 1423, cannot have contained the Anonymous Continuation, as the extreme date 1486 would have enabled Selden to fix its age more nearly. It can only have contained the Ingulf and the Pet. Bles., and would be very similar to B. 2. or B. 3., and may have been either the Marsham MS. or the one mentioned by Camden. This MS. had the same mistake in the laws of king Eadward of 'Euestres' for 'Euesqes', as the Croyland Autograph used by Spelman (§ 104) in 1639, and so they may have been derived in both MSS. from the same original.

These laws, besides being given by Ingulf, are also given by the following writers:

1. John Selden in his Eadmer (§ 101),
2. Sir H. Spelman in his Concilia Vol. 1 (1639) pp. 623 - 625,
3. R. Troysden in the second edition of W. Lambard's 'Αρχαιονομία 1644,
4. Dr. David Wilkins in his 'Leges Anglo Saxonum' (fo. Lond. 1721) pp. 219 - 227,
5. Sir Francis Palgrave in 'The rise and progress of the English Commonwealth. Anglo-Saxon period.' Part II. Proofs and Illustrations (4° Lond. 1832),
6. Benj. Thorpe in his 'Ancient Laws and Institutes of England' (fo. Lond. 1840) pp. 201 - 210, the french text from a MS. n°. 228 at Holkham, and the latin text from MS. Harl. 746.

vij. The foundation of Croyland Abbey.

118 The monastery of Croyland is stated by Ingulf and by Ord. Vit. to have been founded by Æthelbald king of Mercia in 716, no day or month being specified; this is further corroborated by the Harley Roll Y. 6 (§ 82), where on the king's scroll we read: 'Ego rex Ethelbald*us* do t*i*bi [pater Guthlace] sedem ab*batic cum* pe*r*tinentiis suis soluta*m* et libe*r*am ab om*n*i secu*l*ari exactione'. The same two writers add, that the first abbat was named Kenulph (Coenwulf), Ingulf stating in addition, that he was a monk of Evesham. Ord. Vit. says, that the king gave the charter of liberties 'sigillo (§ 123, 370) suo signatam', and a charter of king Æthelbald of similar import is given by Ingulf (Fulm. pp. 4 – 7). The foundation is fully described in the Life of St Guthlac by William of Ramsey (§ 77).

There is, however, no mention of the foundation of the monastery by Æthelbald in Beda, A.S.Chr., Fl. Wig., Sym. Dun., the Annales Monastici [R. S.], the Chron. Abbatiæ de Evesham [R. S.], the Chronica Majora of Matth. Paris [R. S.], nor is it mentioned in the Life of St Guthlac by Felix the monk.

119 By some strange accident, Ingulf, in spite of his own words, speaks later (Fulm. p. 80) of a king Æthelred apparently in connexion with the foundation, when giving his version of Domesday:

'Imprimis in Lincolnshire, in Ellowarp, in Croyland Sanctus Guthlacus habuit et habet sylvas mariscosque, quatuor leucas in longitudine et tres leucas in latitudine. Hæc sedes est Abbathiæ tempore regis Ethelredi; estque soluta, et quieta ab omnibus secularibus servitiis.'

This passage is not in Domesday. There were three kings of the name of Æthelred, but 1. Æthelred of Mercia abdicated in 704, twelve years before the foundation. 2. Æthelred of Wessex reigned 866 – 872, while Burgred was king of Mercia, in which kingdom Croyland lay, and 3. Æthelred II. of England reigned 979 – 1016, long after the foundation.

120 From the foundation in 716 to the destruction of the abbey in 870, a period of 154 years, after the account of the deaths of St Guthlac and his sister St Pega, hardly anything referring

to Croyland is given in Ingulf, beyond the charters, some of them very long, of the following Mercian kings: Offa a. 793, Kenulph (Coenwulf) a. 806, Wichtlaf (Wiglaf) a. 833, Bertulph (Beorhtwulf) a. 851, and Beorred (Burgred) a. 868. The names of four abbats only are given for this long period of time; of these one Siward is stated (Fulm. p. 17) to have discharged the pastoral office for 62 years, so that the others must have sat on an average 31 years each. From the restoration in 948 to the year 1075, being 127 years, eight abbats bare sway in Croyland, each on an average for 16 years, or about half the time allotted to the earlier abbats. Abbat Godric elected in 870 is said to have lived on to the year 940.

In the Eulogium Historiarum [R. S.] written by a Malmesbury monk about 1367, the foundation of 'Croland' is ascribed (iij. 21) to king Eadgar; in some other Chronicles (§ 237, 238) it is ascribed to earl Waltheof (§ 228).

viij. The 'Golden Charter' of king Æthelbald.

This is the foundation charter of the Monastery, granted 121 (according to Ingulf) in 716. It was so called from the bright golden crosses, which adorned it at the top and the bottom, and which were inserted also before the names of the signataries. The text is given by Ingulf, but the original is apparently not now extant.

This charter is not the only charter of this monastery so adorned, for in Gough's Croyland App. p. *135, Nº. LXIV, in 'A Noate of such Evidences as belong to the Towne which was delivered to William Wyche', a document 'of the last [the 17th] or preceding [16th] century', are mentioned: 'The great charter with Ethelbaldus his charter' (sic), and 'Six other small charters, the goulden charters (sic)', besides books and maps and other documents.

One of these 'Golden Charters' probably was Eadred's charter of restoration of 948, which, to judge from the transcript of it, which still remains in the Patent Rolls of 1393 and 1399, was ornamented with a series of fanciful crosses placed before the names of the signataries, closely resembling in style those of Æthelbald's charter.

122   These documents had all disappeared from the Church chest before 1783. Fortunately Dr Hickes had the end of the 'Golden Charter' of Æthelbald, consisting of about one fifth of the whole, engraved for his Thesaurus ('Dissertatio Epistolaris' 1703, Tabula D), and from that engraving some idea may be formed of the genuineness (or the contrary) of the 'Golden Charter' of 716.

It was in 1703 in the hands of Dr Thomas Guidet, a physician of Bath; in 1734 it was in the possession of Robert Hunter esq. lord of the manor of Croyland, and was exhibited at a meeting of the Society of Antiquaries by Mr Lethieullier, apparently Smart Lethieullier Trin. Coll. Oxf. M.A. 1723, F.S.A.

123   The 'Golden Charter' of 716 is on many grounds emphatically condemned by Dr Hickes in his 'Dissertatio Epistolaris'. If the original was at all of the same size as the facsimile, it must have been a large document. For the text of the facsimile is $10\frac{1}{2}$ in. wide and about $4\frac{1}{2}$ in. long; as the whole charter occupies 72 lines of Fulman's text and Dr Hickes' facsimile $14\frac{3}{4}$ in., this would make the whole 25 in. long. To this must be further added 2 in. at least each for the upper and lower margins, that contained the very large gilt crosses, so that probably the parchment was 2 ft. 6 in. long and 1 ft. wide. The charter of Eadward the Confessor to Westminster Abbey of 1066 (Brit. Mus. Facs. ij. 18) is 2 ft. 3 in. long by 1 ft. 10 in. wide; it is however a forgery.

In Dr Hickes' engraving, which shews no signs of wear or decay in the charter, no seal is shewn; the words of Ord. Vit. concerning Æthelbald's charter 'et inde cartam sigillo suo signatam...confirmavit', are probably to be understood of the cross ('signum', 'sigillum') made by the king as his signature (Earle, Handbook to the Land charters, p. xxxviij).

The writing is a bad copy of the A. S. style of writing; it has the long e ꝇ, the g ᵹ, the r ꞃ, and the s ſ.

The peculiar crosses before the names of the witnesses

are clearly not the sort, that would be made at the time of signing. Dr Hickes has engraved on Tabula E a charter of William I. for Durham, where the crosses are evidently made as the signatures of the witnesses, being in no very exact order.

The great charter of archbishop Dunstan to Westminster 124 dated 959 (Brit. Mus. Facs. ij. 5) has, besides the two sided seal of the Primate, also golden crosses before the names of the witnesses; but sir Frederick Madden says, that it appeared to him 'extremely doubtful, whether any of the great charters granted to that abbey previous to the reign of Henry I. (including under that term the charters of Edgar, Dunstan, Edward the Confessor, and at least one of William the Conqueror) could be considered genuine or free from suspicion' (Archaeol. Journ. 1862, p. 369).

Ingulf speaks elsewhere (Fulm. pp. 70, 98) of charters 125 similarly adorned. They were 'of extreme beauty, litera publica conscripta et crucibus aureis et venustissimis picturis ac elementis pretiosissimis adornata'; the earlier Mercian charters are spoken of as 'similiter aureis picturis pulcherrima (sic) consignata'. Such documents existed also at St Albans: 'Cumque inspicerentur Regum Anglicorum, Offae scilicet, ac ceterorum, scripta, in quibus, pro sigillis novo modo dependentibus, veteri consuetudine cruces aureae, manu Regum depictae, in principio positae erant, et videbantur quibusdam invidorum nullius esse momenti, quia sigillata non erant,...' (Gesta Abb. S. Alb. [R. S.] j. 151 c. 1160). Charters thus embellished are, however, unhesitatingly condemned by Dr Hickes (Dissert. Epist. p. 82); among these he includes Æthelbald's Foundation charter of 716, although Clemens Reynerus in his 'Apostolatus Benedictinorum in Anglia (fo. Douai 1626), Tractatus j. Sect. i. § 18, had quoted it as an authority.

The foundation charter of 716 is referred to in the sub- 126 sequent royal charters of Kenulph (Coenwulf) 806, of Beorhtwulf 868, and of Eadred 948; but it is not mentioned again except Fulm. p. 85 (c. 1085) and p. 124 (1114), where Joffrid exhibits a copy of the charter of 948 to the convent of Evesham, not having the originals either of it or of the charter of 716 'primae donationis chirographum', (not even Fulm. p. 473 a. 1189, king Æthelbald being there referred to as the founder of the monastery, but only from a life of St Guthlac), till it appears in the Confirmation charter of 1393, which itself is not recited or spoken of in the 'Historia Croylandensis'. It is referred to afterwards, though not immediately afterwards; in 1415 (Fulm. p. 503) in a settlement of the claims of Multon and Weston, and in the same year (Fulm. p. 508) in a similar settlement with Spalding, it is mentioned in the awards of the arbitrators.

The convent does not however seem to have been aware of its existence as late as in 1333 and 1334 in the time of king Edward III. (Gough, Croyl. N°. xxxiv. App. pp. 60, 61), as then the society put the foundation by Æthelbald 500 years before the Conquest, or c. 566; but in 1189 (Fulm. p. 453) it puts it 'transactis quadringentis annis et eo amplius', or previously to the year 786.

ix. Jews in England in A. S. times.

127 Jews are mentioned in Wiglaf's charter of 833. The king confirms to the monastery all possessions, which his predecessors, their nobles, 'vel alii fideles Christiani, sive Judaei, dictis monachis dederunt, vendiderunt, vel invadiaverunt (have pledged, Riley), vel aliquo modo in perpetuam possessionem tradiderunt'. This mention of Jews in England at so early a date is considered suspicious by Mr Riley, although not noticed by sir F. Palgrave (Qu. Rev. 1826); and Mr Freeman remarks (Norm. Conq. v. 818 Note Q): 'I do not remember any distinct mention of Jews in England before the time of William Rufus'; it is however quoted as authentic by Dr S. Goldschmidt, Gesch. der Juden in England im xj. und xij. Jahrh. Berl. 1886 p. 4 (Oxf. Hist. Soc. Collectanea, Series II. A. Neubauer, 'Notes on the Jews in Oxford', 8°. Oxf. 1890). They are not mentioned in the A. S. Chronicle, nor in Fl. Wig.; according to his continuator John, they were charged with crucifying a boy at Norwich in 1137, this being the first mention of them. In Joh. Petrib. (MS. Cott. Claud. A. v.) we find: 'Anno 923 sanguis ex imagine, quam Judaei cruci-

fixerunt Londoniae, effluxit'. The same event is recorded in Matth. Paris [R. S.] j. 446, but the locality is there stated to be 'in Augiam' (Reichenau ?). The account comes from Sigebert, the date vj. Id. Nov. from Marianus Scotus. A later hand has altered 'Augiam' into 'Angliam' in Dr Luard's MS.

'The earliest mention of the Jews in England, which can **128** be relied upon, is that inserted in the Canonical Excerptions published by Ecgbriht archbishop of York in the year 740, chronicled under that year by Johnson in his Ecclesiastical Canons (8°. Oxf. 1850. i. 218). That they were here in the early Norman times seems unquestionable' (Chronica Joh. de Oxenedes [R. S. Sir H. Ellis] Pref. p. xiij).

The canon however as given by Spelman, Concilia (fo. Lond. 1639) p. 275 runs thus: '245. Canon Laodocensis. Ut nullus christianus judaizare praesumat, sed nec conviviis eorum participare.' This Johnson calls 'A Laodicean canon', and adds: 'By this one would suppose there were in this age Jews in the north of England, but I know no other proof of it.'

There is also an ordinance of Eadward the confessor 1041 – 66 entitled 'De Judaeis': 'Sciendum quoque, quod omnes Judaei, ubicumque in regno sunt, sub tutela et defensione regis, Judaei enim et omnia sua regis sunt', which may be found in Spelman, Concil. p. 619 ff; but even this might be too early.

G. B. Depping in his 'Les Juifs dans le moyen-âge' (8° Paris, 1824) pp. 142 ff. has no further references to Jews in A. S. times.

Prynne in his 'Short Demurrer to the Jews' long discon- **129** tinued Remitter into England' (4°. Lond. 1656) knows (p. 4) nothing of any residence of Jews in England 'in any of our British or Saxon kings' reigns.' In his preface he mentions Ingulphus, and quotes 'p. 914' (of the Frankfurt reprint (1601) of Savile) with reference to the Laws of king Eadward, but makes no allusion to Wiglaf's charter of 833.

In Pet. Bles. mention is made of 'fenerantes Judaei' under **130** William Rufus, of 'Judaica perfidia' at Cambridge and 'Judaica pravitas' at Stamford under Henry I.; this quite agrees with Mr Freeman's statement. Among the writings of Peter of

Blois (Migne P. L. Vol. 825) is a treatise 'Contra perfidiam Judaeorum.'

x. The Benefactors of Croyland Abbey during the Mercian period.

131 The following arrangement of the names of the early benefactors of the monastery from 716 to 870, as given by Ingulf, may help to throw some light on the real value of the Mercian charters. The dedications are those given by the Guthlac scroll (c. 1150), the dates are those of the charters recited by Ingulf.

132 Algar, Ælfgar, knight, the son of Northlang (a. 806). 'Ego Algar*us* filius Norlang do tibi [pater Guthlace] Bastune *et* Teford *cum* pertinent*iis*.' His charter is not in Ingulf, but is printed, with the date DCCXXV (for 825 ?) in Gough's Croyland App. n°. XXVII. p. 44.

Algar I., Ælfgar, earl (a. 810). 'Ego Algar*us* comes do t*i*bi terr*am* de Spalding *et* de Pinceb' *et* Quappel' *et* Holeb'.

Algar II., Ælfgar, earl, son of earl Algar I. (a. 868). A charter of this earl is mentioned Fulm. p. 107, but there is no other reference to it; his benefactions are mentioned Fulm. p. 18.

Asketel, king Wiglaf's cook 'cocus' (a. 833).

Edulph, Eadwulf, king Wiglaf's courier 'nuntius' (a. 833).

Fregist, knight, formerly king Kenulf's tutor 'magister' (a. 806). 'Ego Frogist*us* do t*i*bi pater Guthl*a*ce Langetoft *cum* pertinentiis.' His charter is given in Gough's Croyland App. n°. XXVIII. p. 45.

Geolph, 'the son of Malte', 'filius Malti' (a. 806). 'Ego Geolfus do tibi terr*am* de Halintune.'

Grymketel, not further described (a. 868), [bishop of Selsey 1039–47].

Morcard, king Beorred's knight 'miles' (a. 868) [Hunter Magn. Rot. Scacc. 31 H. I. p. 11].

Norman, sheriff 'vicecomes' of Lincoln (a. 833). 'Ego Norma*n*nus vicecomes do tibi terr*am* de Suttune *et* de Sstapeltune (sic).'

Oswy, Oswig, knight (a. 833). 'Ego Oswius do tibi terram de Draitune cum pertinentiis.'
Sigburga, Sigeburh, countess 'comitissa' (a. 833).
Siward, sheriff 'vicecomes' (a. 833), 'vicedominus' (a. 851).
Thorold, sheriff 'vicecomes' of Lincoln (a. 806, § 20). 'Ego Toroldus vicecomes do tibi terram de Buggehale.'
Wulget, Wulfgeat, king Wiglaf's butler 'pincerna' (a. 833).
Wulnoth, Wulfnoth, king Wiglaf's server 'dapifer' (a. 833).
'Ego Wulfno—tus do tibi terram de Adintuñ cum pertinentiis.'
The above names are mentioned in Ingulf; the following is not referred to there:
Algar, Ælfgar, the deacon (a. —). 'Ego Algarus diaconus do tibi terram de Duvedic et ecclesiam cum pertinentiis.'
'Duuedic' was in the possession of St Guthlac at the time of the Domesday Survey, so that Algar the deacon belongs to the Anglo Saxon period. The locality is mentioned also in the Ingulfin charters of Eadred 948 and of Eadgar 966.
Other names pertaining to this period are:
Wibert, Wigbeorht, knight 'miles', seneschal of earl Algar II. [Domesday (Ellis j. 509)];
Leofric, knight, seneschal of earl Algar II.;
Morcard, lord of Brunne or Bourne [Morcard, 'miles' of king Burgred 868 (Fulm. p. 19)];
Osgot, sheriff of Lincoln [moneyer of Æthelred II.; Domesday (Ellis j. 461)], and
Harding, of Rehale, knight [Harding son of Eadnoth the Staller k. 1067 A.S.Chr.; Harding the blacksmith 1051 (Fulm. p. 87); Domesday (Ellis j. 432); 'Hardingus serviens reginae' (Hunter Magn. Rot. Scacc. 31 H. 1. p. 62)].
Here we find some Norse names Asketel (Ascytel) Malte (Langebek [§ 412] cf. Malte Brun, the Danish geographer), and Grymketel (Grimcytel), and also some late names, Norman, Siward and Thorold, besides Fregist (Frithegist), Morcard and Harding.
According to C. H. Pearson the Domesday of Lincolnshire contains a large proportion of Anglo-Danish names (j. 362[1]).
It is also remarkable, how many places with Norse termi-

nations are found in the Ingulfine charter of king Wiglaf dated 833; Langtoft and Aswyketoft, Badby, Holbeck and Pyncebek, many years before the Danes settled in England (Riley). Their first appearance in England was 787 and their first wintering in 851 (A.S.Chr.); and it must have been many years before the places could have acquired Norse names.

xj. The Destruction of Croyland Abbey by the Danes in 870.

135 From its foundation in 716 the monastery of Croyland (as described by Ingulf) went on prosperously for a century and a half. Kings favoured it, nobles enriched it, and the burial place of St Guthlac was surrounded by the tombs of his companions, Ecgberht his secretary 'a secretis et confessor quondam Sancti Guthlaci', Cissa 'sacerdos et anchorita', whom Felix styles Guthlac's successor, Beccelm his servant, Tatwin his guide to Croyland, and of several royal personages, St Ælfthryth, called by Ingulf Etheldrida, Wigmund the son of king Wiglaf and his wife 'quondam regina' Ælfflæd. (Wigmund and Ælfflaed are termed 'rex' and 'regina', equivalent to 'prince' and 'princess', in Chron. Evesham. [R. S.] p. 326.) The action of king Beorhtwulf in taking possession of some of the 'jocalia' of the monastery and ornaments of the church and of the money, which he could find, by a kind of forced loan, is indeed noted with regret; but the greatest blow according to the Hist. Croyl. was given to the monastery by the Danes.

136 The long account given by Ingulf of the destruction of Croyland and Peterborough monasteries in 870 is the most circumstantial narrative in his work. It is unfortunately quite uncorroborated by the A.S.Chr., Asser, Æthelweard, Fl. Wig., his copier Sym. Dun., the Liber Eliensis, and Will. Malm. The history of Ord. Vit. is the oldest document that mentions the destruction of Croyland, and that only in general terms: 'Crulandense monasterium devastatum est, sicut et alia plurima.' Herein it is followed by the Lives of Croyland abbats to be found in MS. Cott. Vesp. B. xj, fo. 70 – 76, which ends with the year 1427. Matth. Paris (c. 1250) just mentions the

destruction of Croyland along with that of Thorney, Ramsey, and Peterborough (Chronica Majora [R. S.] j. 393), this account being copied or repeated by 'Matth. Westm.' [R. S.] j. 433 (s. a. 870):

137 'Et sic nefandi duces, per pagum Eboracensem transitum facientes, ecclesias, civitates, et villas combusserunt,...deinde sursum per flumen Humbri navigantes, consimili ibidem rabie saeviebant; indeque progressi cuncta coenobia in paludibus sita monachorum ac virginum, interfectis habitatoribus, destruxerunt. Horum autem nomina caenobiorum sunt, Crulandia, Thornheia, Ramesia, Hamstede, quod nunc Burgum Sancti Petri dicitur, cum insula Helyensi et coenobio olim famosissimo feminarum, in quo dudum sancta virgo et regina Etheldreda abbatissae officium multis annis laudabiliter adimplevit.'

138 In Leland's Collectanea [1770] i. 221 we find also the following notice, which, however, does not mention Thorney:

'Ex chronicis Ely monaster.
Sexto anno adventus Danorum, hoc est 15. reg: Edmundi [regis Orientalium Anglorum] repetunt Estangliam, flammis destruentes monasteria de Cruland, Burgo Petri, Ramesey, Seham et Ely.'

139 The date given by Ingulf is Aug. or Sept. 870, just before the martyrdom of king Eadmund, which happened on 20 Nov. 870. This seems corroborated by Ord. Vit., who places the destruction of Croyland Monastery at the same time as the destruction of many others, which happened in that year. Mr Freeman (iv. 597) places the destruction of the monastery 'c. 877.'

140 The only account, which seems to agree with Ingulf, is that in the 'Chronicon Johannis Abbatis S. Petri de Burgo.' This chronicle is printed by Sparke in his 'Historiae Anglicanae Scriptores Varii' (f°. Lond. 1723) from MS. Cott. Claud. A. v.; and reprinted (8°. Lond. 1845) by Dr Giles. The MS. itself belongs really to the 14th century, as it ends with the year 1368, but the account of the destruction of the monasteries is written in an Italian (Elizabethan) hand on a blank space, of a column and a half, left in the original MS., and continued on two pairs of leaves of parchment let into the MS. and not belonging to it. This account is nearly identical with that of

Ingulf, but it differs from it by both defect and excess, omitting two long paragraphs referring exclusively to Croyland, and adding towards the end a shorter one referring to some further doings at Peterborough by Toret prior of Ancarig or Thorney with the assistance of brother Turgar.

There are also many minor variations, omissions and additions; according to Ingulf (Sav., Fulm.) the Christian army was after a battle on St Maurice' day reduced by defection from 800 to 200, Joh. Petrib. says from 8000 to 2000.

141 Sparke prints this Elizabethan interpolation without giving one hint of its true character, and hence, possibly, Mr Riley thinks, that it is a real part of MS. Cott. Claud. A. v. and the original of the account in Fulman. He says: 'The basis of the story of the Danish ravages at Croyland A.D. 870...is probably to be found in the account of the destruction of the monastery of Medeshamsted given in the *Chronicle* attributed by Sparke to Abbot John of Peterborough; considerable additions being made, the inventions, in all probability, of the compilers.' The destruction of the Monastery of Croyland is mentioned before that of Medeshamsted. It is also quite plain, that the Elizabethan addition to MS. Claud. A. v. is not original, but copied; in three cases portions of the Ingulfine narrative are represented by 'etc.'; through the omission of several words one sentence is rendered unintelligible; 'frater Turgarus', whom Riley makes a monk of Medeshamsted, is first spoken of by Sparke and Giles in such a way, that he must have been mentioned before, which could only have been in the long paragraph concerning Croyland, which is omitted; though it is also clear, that he belonged to Croyland, since the Croyland monks are termed 'fratres sui commonachi.' The passage, which is added in MS. Claud. A. v. to the Ingulfine narrative, refers to personages mentioned before, but it also is a copy from some other document, as it speaks of 'sanctissima pignora beatarum virginum Kynesburgae etc.'

Still more strangely Dugdale (Monast. Vol. I. 1657, pp. 68 ff.) has transcribed the whole of this Elizabethan insertion in MS. Cott. Claud. A. v. from that MS. with all the '&c.' and without any hint of its being other than contemporary with the rest of the MS.

It may be on account of this narrative, that Freeman (iv. 472 n. 5) speaks of the Peterborough Chronicle as 'nearly as mythical as Ingulf himself.' The remainder of the chronicle is however very meagre. He also remarks: 'Everybody knows the legendary, but highly interesting story [of the destruction of Croyland monastery] in the false Ingulf. It may have some foundation in fact, but if so, it is strange to find no mention of it in Ordcric.' But see § 136. **142**

The history of Peterborough by Hugo Candidus, also printed by Sparke (Vol. II. p. 14), mentions without details the ruin of Peterborough monastery, as well as that of other houses, but without giving even the names of these.

After the departure of the Danes from the ruins of Croyland and of Peterborough, the surviving monks of Croyland, having, according to Ingulf (Fulm. p. 24), done what was possible at their own ruined home and chosen a new abbat in place of the murdered Theodore, went to Peterborough to bury the slaughtered monks of that house; they gathered up their 84 corpses and buried them in a common grave, placing upon it a pyramidal stone 3ft. high, 3ft. long, and 1ft. broad. This Ingulfine account is probably founded on the stone still remaining in the Cathedral, which is however by Mr M. H. Bloxam ascribed to the time of abbat Elsin (d. 1055). as having been erected by him over some of the relics, with which he enriched his church (Archæol. Journ. 1862, pp. 142 – 4). There were burial pyramids at Glastonbury, but of very great size, one being 28ft. high and another 26ft. high (Will. Malm. Gesta regum [R. S.] j. 25). **143**

There is something wrong with the Fulman-Ingulf dating of the events connected with the destruction of Croyland. A battle is mentioned in the month of September, which was fought in Kesteven on the day of St Maurice the Martyr 22 Sept.; this must have been fought not far from Threkingham (near Folkingham about 17 miles N. W. of Croyland), as the Danes buried there the Three Kings of their nation slain in that battle. Three recumbent figures are still shewn **144** there as their monuments (Thompson Hist. of Boston 1856 p. 21). There is a place called Laundenthorp near Grantham, about ten miles from Threkingham; Ingulf however gives Laundon as the earlier name of Threkingham. Another battle was fought on the following day, 23 Sept. In it the christians consisted of the men of Hoyland led by earl Ælfgar II. and his seneschals Wibert [Wigbeorht] and Leofric, with 200 men from Croyland under the command of a soldier-monk named Tolius, 300 from Deping and Baston under Morcard lord of Brunne or Bourne, besides his own retainers, and 500 men under Osgot sheriff of Lincoln, and the men of Stamford under Harding of Rehale [Ryhall, Rutl.]. Earl Ælfgar, 'comes Algarus junior', must have been then of considerable age, as he may be traced back through 868 to 851 and thence back to 810, when he signed a charter of his father, earl Ælfgar the elder, given in Fulm. pp. 85 ff. (Birch 331). In spite of their valour, the christians were defeated. The news reaching Croyland on the following night 'proxima nocte sequente', 24 Sept., some of the monks were sent away by abbat Theodore to Ancarig or Thorney. On the arrival of the Danes, the abbat and the remaining monks were slaughtered; on the third day after their arrival the Danes burnt the monastery, it being then vij. Kal. Sept. (Fulm. Birch) or 26 Aug., and proceeded to Peterborough on the following day. After the slaughter of the monks and the destruction of Peterborough, the Danes 'quarto die' removed towards Huntingdon; the Croyland monks also returned from Ancarig some few days after the murder of abbat Theodore, and having cleared away the ruins, which were still in parts burning, they chose Godric as their abbat; he then with some of his monks went to Peterborough and buried the slain, that day being the feast of St Cecilia, 22 Nov. In the Elizabethan insertion in MS. Cott. Claud. A. v. the above day is called vij. Kal. Oct. (25 Sept.), but there is no mediæval authority for this various reading in the Ingulf; although 25 Sept. is a more possible date, it is perhaps too soon for the arrival at Croyland of the Danes from the battle-field near Threkingham.

The names of the Danish leaders mentioned by Ingulf 145
in 870 and 871 are given in different histories, the A.S.Chr.,
Fl. Wig. etc., but Ingulf seems to have misread his authorities;
he has 'Gogroum' (Fulm. p. 21) for Guthrum, called also
'Gurmund' (Ingulf [Fulm. p. 26], Will. Malm.) and 'Gytro'
(Matth. Paris); this may however be a mistake of the scribe,
as he is afterwards called Godroun; he has also 'Orguil'
possibly for Eowils (Fl. Wig. a. 911), and other minor variations.
'Comes Fungus' and 'Tulba frater Hulbæ comitis' have no
counterpart in the histories, but may be mistaken readings.
According to Matth. Paris j. 399, 'Gutro' did not join the
two leaders Ingwar and Ubba till after the martyrdom of king
Eadmund; the A.S.Chr. does not mention Oskitel and Hamond
till 875.

In J. Major, Historia majoris Britanniæ Paris 1521, we
find (reprint, 4º Edinb. 1740, pp. 87, 88) Hungus and Hubba
mentioned together, as Hinguar and Hubba by Will. Malm.
G. R. j. 98, 264, as murderers of St Edmund king of the East
Angles; Hungus, Fungus and Hinguar seem to be the same
personage. Langebek has (v. 36) an extract from Fulm. pp. 24,
25, and on the words 'Fungo comite' has the note 'Hic
non invenitur apud alios'. In the Index (vol. ix) we find
'Fungus, comes Danicus, in Anglia occidit 871, v. 36'.

The Ingulf tells us nothing of the destruction of Thorney
mentioned by Matth. Paris; but this may be a mistake on the
part of the latter, as the Thorney monastery of later days
was not founded till 972. According to Ingulf there were
at Ancarig a prior (Toret), a subprior (Tisa) and several
'fratres'.

Ingulf gives us a considerable number of names as of 146
monks at Croyland at the time of its destruction in 870.
These we may put together:

Abbat: Theodore.

Prior: Asker. Danish name: (archb. of Lund. d. 1137)
cf. earl Asccr, charter of Burgred a. 868, Æsca, who signs Birch
nº 518 a. 868, Asker (= Asser) bishop of Sherburn (Fulm.
p. 28).

Subprior: Lethwyn (Lethunius Birch).
Monks: Grimketul, æt. 100. Danish name: [moneyer of Cnut at Lincoln; bishop of Selsey 1038 - 45].
Agamund æt. 100. Danish name: [danish chieftain k. 911 A.S.Chr.; moneyer of Harold II.; Liber Eliensis, p. 277; Domesday Linc. XXVIII.].
Paulinus: [Bishop of Rochester Fl. Wig. a. 626].
Herbert, Herebicht: [Ealdorman a. 838].
Elfget, Ælfgeat: [moneyer of Æthelred II].
Savine, Sæwine: [moneyer of Æthelred II.; Domesday (Ellis j. 483)].
Tolius, Toli. Danish name: (Langebek, Index): [Sheriff Earle, p. 343, c. 1060. Tolig (Freeman ij. Ed. III. 573) temp. Eadw. Conf. Domesday. Hunter Magn. Rot. Scacc. 31 H. I. pp. 11, 113].
Egelred, Æthelred: [Late form, occurring Fl. Wig. a. 986 ff. etc.].
Wulric, Wulfric: [The king's house thane d. 897 A.S.Chr.].
Sweinus, Swegen. Danish name: [Hunter Mag. Rot. Scacc. 31 H. I. Index].
Osgot d. 940 (Osgod?): [see § 133; moneyer of Æthelred II.; Osgod Clapa, d. 1054].
Clarenbald, æt. 66 (46 Savile), d. 972 æt. 168 (148 Savile): [Abb. of St Augustine's 1116].
Swartting, æt. 40; d. 973 æt. 142: [moneyer of Æthelred II. at Lincoln; Domesday (Ellis j. 488)].
Brunus, Brun, æt. —; d. 973 æt. —: [moneyer of Æthelred II.; Domesday T.R.E. Ellis j. 387].
Aio, gen. Aionis, æt. —; d. 973 æt. —.
Thurgar æt. 10; d. 974 æt. 115. Danish name: [Thorgeir Torgerus, Langebek Index, pp. 754, 727].
Bricstan (Biscanus Birch) 'quondam cantor': ['Brizstanus' sochemannus homo abbatis Ely'

(Hamilton, Inquis. Com. Cantabr. p. 110), 'Briztan homo Gilleberti de Gant' (Hamilton, p. 99). Briestan of Chatteris 1116, Ord. Vit. iij. 123; II. Hunt. Book ix. R. S. p. xxv]. Godric elected abbat 870 d. 940.

Besides these, two anchorites at Ancarig (Thorney) are mentioned by name:

Prior: Toret, Thoreth: [son of Gunnor, earl of Deira, a. 966; earl of the Middle Angles. Freeman, Index; Domesday Wilts. Ellis i. 331.]

Subprior: Tisa: [moneyer of Eadward the elder 901 – 925.]

Here, as in the list of benefactors of the Mercian period, besides purely A. S. names, which occur also in historical works, and late names, which are found on English coins of the Danish period and in Domesday, we find Danish names Grymeytel, Agamund und Sweyn. With regard to the very strange name Aio, can it have anything to do with the inscription on the boundary stone:

'Aio hanc petram Guthlacus habet sibi metam'?

A charter of Berhtwulf king of Mercia dated 25 Dec. 841 (Kemble 248*, Earle Second. Doc. p. 312) begins: 'Aio et alto domino deo Zabaoth regnanti in aeuum', the first word standing for 'Agio' or 'Hagio'. There is however a very common Norse name Ako, which has many variations (Langebek, Index), as Ago, Agho, Aho, Awo, which 'Aio' may represent.

147

xij. Turketul [Thurcytel] abbat of Croyland, and the Restoration of the Monastery in the year 948.

Unlike the greater part of the English monasteries, that had been desolated by the Danes, Croyland according to Ingulf's statement remained in the possession and occupation of its society (Fulm. p. 84). This is corroborated by Ord. Vit. who (ij. 280) says: 'nec unquam post primam instaurationem, quam idem rex [Edelbaldus] fecit, sedes Crulandiae religiosorum habitatione monachorum usque in hodiernum diem caruit'. And this happened, although the monks were reduced to a very

148

small band and to such extreme poverty, that 'nullus...deinceps pro nimia loci paupertate ad conversionem venire voluit'. Godric, having for 70 (!) years ruled his monks, who in that period of time fell from 28 to 7, died in 940 in the time of king Eadmund the elder. King Æthelstan had proposed to restore the monastery, but was prevented by death at the age of 45 years; this was the case also with his brother and successor Eadmund. The little society lived on, without an abbat, in possession of the old site, in hopes of happier times. At length in the year 948, in the reign of king Eadred, according to Ingulf, relief came in the restoration of the monastery by Turketul.

149 The continuity of the monastery from 716 to the conquest is somewhat doubtful. Dr Stubbs, Epistolæ Cantuarienses R. S. j. p. xviij., states that 'very few of the religious houses which perished during the Danish wars ever rose again from their ashes....It is certain that in 942 there were no real Benedictines in England (Anglia Sacra ij. 91, 194 etc.); Odo, Oswald, and probably Dunstan, sought the knowledge of true discipline at Fleury which had been just reformed under the spirit, if not under the name, of the Clunial revival', and that 'Monasticism...had become (so far as the scanty notices of the chronicles teach us) extinct before the reign of Alfred (Asser; Camden's *Scr.* p. 18)'. Ingulf's statement 'Nec unquam post primam fundationem,...Monasterium Croyland Religiosorum inhabitatione Monachorum caruit, usque in dien? hodiernum' (Fulm. p. 4) is plainly only the same as that of Ord. Vit. above given. How far the statement of Ord. Vit. may be derived from the information of the Croyland monks, we cannot tell; at all events none of the abbats mentioned in Ingulf before the time of Turketul occur in the mortuary roll of the abbess Matilda of 1113. Dr Lingard (A.S.Ch. [1845] ij. 262) says: 'By the death of Alfred the monastic order lost a powerful and zealous protector. During the reigns of his immediate successors, some feeble attempts were made to restore it to its former celebrity; and the origin of several monasteries is referred by their respective historians to this doubtful period.

But their existence is denied by the positive testimony of King Edgar; and unless we accuse that prince of sacrificing the truth to his vanity, we must believe that under the reigns of his predecessors every monastic establishment was abolished[1].'

Turketul has a real existence, if the statements of Ord. Vit., the Guthlac roll, the mortuary roll of Mathilda abbess of Caen of 1113 (§ 478), and the 'Vitæ abbatum' in MS. Cott. Vespas. B. xj. (§ 6) may be taken as history. The date of his death is given by Ingulf (Fulm. Birch) as 'Quinto nonas Julii, id est in translatione Sancti Benedicti'; the former day however is 3 July, the latter 11 July. Besides this Ord. Vit. and the Cotton MS. give the day as 'iiij. Idus Julii' or 12 July, which coincides with neither of Ingulf's statements. Probably 'v. Non. Jul.' is a mistake for 'v Id. Jul.' 11 July, a day which agrees with the festival.

Turketul is said by Ingulf to have died in 975 at the age of 68 years, his birth being thus placed in 907. He was buried at Croyland, where 'the tenants of the scite of the abbey lately dug up his stone coffin among many others' (Stukeley, Palæographia Britannica 1746 ij. 35 quoted in Gough's Croyl. p. 17).

Turketul is stated by Ingulf to have been a nephew of king Eadward the elder 901 – 925, being the eldest son of Æthelweard the king's brother (Fulm. p. 36), who was Ælfred's youngest child (Fl. Wig. s. a. 871) and died in 922. It is a strange circumstance, that, though Ingulf mentions (Fulm. p. 38) that king Æthelstan buried at Malmesbury his two kinsmen, Elwin 'Ælfwine' and Æthelstan, sons of his uncle Æthelweard, who had been slain in 937 by the Danes at Bruneford ('Brunanburh' Fl. Wig.), he does not say, that they were Turketul's

[1] 'Temporibus antecessorum meorum, regum Anglorum, monasteria tam monachorum quam virginum destructa (et) penitus rejecta in tota Anglia erant' (Wilkins Concilia [1737]. i. p. 239), and Wolstan, the contemporary author of the life of St Ethelwold, (963–984) observes, that when that prelate was made bishop of Winchester, the only monks in England were those whom St Dunstan had established at Abingdon and Glastonbury. 'Nam hactenus ea tempestate non habebantur monachi in gente Anglorum, nisi tantum qui in Glestonia morabantur et Abbandonia. (Act. Sanct. Ord. S. Bened. sæc. v. p. 615.)' [Note by Dr Lingard.]

brothers, nor in his account of the battle that Turketul's brothers were also in the fight. Elwin and his brother seem to rest on the authority of Will Malm. (Gesta pontif. R. S. p. 401), but he calls Ælfwine's brother not Æthelstan but Æthelwine. Although Turketul's connexion with the royal family of Wessex is attested by Ord. Vit. and the Cotton MS. Vesp. B. xj., yet his exact place in that pedigree is not given.

Ingulf seems not to have been very clear in his chronology, for he represents Turketul's uncle king Eadward as wishing to promote him to ecclesiastical dignities, among them to the bishopric of Winchester, an office which Turketul declined and persuaded his foster brother 'collactaneus' Frithstan to undertake, who was accordingly consecrated by archbishop Plegmund (890 – 914) in 910 (A.S.Chr.), and this, when Turketul was only three years old. Frithstan resigned his bishopric in 931 and died 10 Sept. 933, but his 'foster brother' lived on to 975.

151   King Eadward finding, that his nephew, though a cleric, had no inclination to take upon him the responsibilities of the episcopal office, declining also the bishopric of Dorchester, made him his chancellor, and by his advice Frithstan and six other priests were appointed to seven vacant sees and were consecrated on one day and at the same place by Archbishop Plegmund. This event is variously dated by different writers, but, according to Ingulf's statements, 914 is the latest possible date, when Turketul was 7 years old, while, if Dr Stubbs' date 909 (Registrum, p. 13) is accepted, the consecration of the seven bishops took place, when Turketul was only 2 years old.

Some of this difficulty would disappear, if in the account of Turketul's death we might for lxviij read lxxxviij, as that would put his birth in 887; he would then be 23 years old, when offered the bishopric of Winchester, and might easily be the king's chancellor, and in 946 might speak of himself as verging on old age. But Ord. Vit. gives no information, and the texts (Fulm. Sav. Birch) agree; and the further difficulty presents itself, that Æthelweard the youngest of the five children of Ælfred, who married in 868, would be born c. 878, and that Turketul his eldest son would be born at the earliest c. 898.

Turketul is described as first cousin to king Eadred, being **152** the son of his uncle Æthelward, as the holder of a very rich prebend 'pinguissima prebenda' in the church of York, and as that king's chancellor also. In the History of Ord. Vit., who got his information at Croyland about 1115, and in the above mentioned Cotton MS., he is spoken of as only a clerk of London, though also 'de regali progenie'.

He is said (Fulm. p. 38) to have presented to St Dunstan **153** (b. 924 Fl. Wig.), who was abbat of Glastonbury, having been appointed in 942 æt. 18, a very beautiful chalice, which was preserved at Glastonbury 'ad hæc Normannorum tempora'; there is, however, no trace of Turketul in the 'Memorials of St Dunstan' R. S.

Dunstan is also mentioned (Fulm. p. 41) as the 'nutricius' pupil or 'foster-child' (Riley) of Turketul, and again (Fulm. p. 38) in the time of king Eadmund the elder 940 – 947 as 'confessionum suarum communicator', 'the receiver of his confessions' (Riley). In the latter case Dunstan as abbat was between 18 and 22 years old.

Ingulf's account (Fulm. p. 37) of Turketul's prowess at the **154** battle of Brunanbuch (§ 290) has been condemned as childish by sir Fr. Palgrave. He headed his men, 'penetransque cuneos hostiles prosternit a dextris et a sinistris….Tandem multo sanguine ad ipsum regem [Constantinum] perveniens, equo dejecit'; the king being afterwards killed by a certain 'centurio' named Singin or Singrin; yet immediately afterwards we read : ' In tam duro certamine sæpius se gloriabatur a Domino conservatum Turketulus, et se fœlicissimum et fortunatum, quod nunquam hominem occiderit, neminem mutilaverit, cum pugnare pro patria, et maxime contra Paganos, licite quisque possit' (§ 251). This account Mr Riley thinks, is apparently an amplification of the narrative of H. Hunt. lib. v. § 19 [R. S.] p. 160; that is a translation of the Brunanburh war song in A.S.Chr. a. 937, but there seems only the one verb 'perforare' common to H. Hunt. and to Ingulf. The name of the 'centurio',

Singin or Syngrin, does not seem to occur elsewhere; this name is not found in Langebek (Index).

155 Having as chancellor gone on a journey to York, he happened to make the acquaintance of the small remnant of the Croyland monks, and was so touched by their courtesy and liberality and by their entreaties, that he first determined to restore their ruined house, and soon afterwards resolved himself to become a monk there. This resolution he carried out, assuming the monastic habit and being appointed abbat by the king, who then immediately began the work of restoration. He was blessed by Ceolwulph bishop of Dorchester, according to Ingulf, one of the seven bishops of 909; but unfortunately Ceolwulf's (or rather Cœnwulf's) successor Winsy signs charters in the years 926 – 934.

156 Ingulf says, that, when Turketul became a monk at Croyland, he transferred to the king the 60 manors that he possessed, reserving only the tenth manor for the service of God, being the six situated nearest to the monastery. This agrees with the statements of Ord. Vit. and the 'Vitæ abbatum'; but in the Guthlac Roll (§ 82) of the 12th century (c. 1160), among the benefactors to the abbey is shewn 'Turketellus' holding his scroll thus inscribed 'Ego abbas Turketellus do ti*bi* [pater Guthlace] sexta*m* parte*m* hereditatis meæ Wenliburch (Wellingborough), Bebi (Beeby Leic.), Cotcham (Cottenham Cambs.) Hokintune (Hockington Cambs.), Elmintune (in Oundle parish Northants), Writhorp (Worthorp in the parish of St Martin, Stamford-Baron),' Turketul's manors being therefore reduced from 60 to 36.

157 Besides bestowing thus his own estates on the monastery, he is represented as recovering many estates, which had in the time of Burgred king of Mercia become after 870 the possession of the royal treasury, and as redeeming for money many that had fallen into private hands; other estates however were totally lost to the monastery (Fulm. p. 25).

158 Turketul is also mentioned as abbat of Croyland by Joh. Petrib. (s. a. 948), but as previously being only a clerk of London, this author not even making him a member of the royal family.

Ingulf in his account of Turketul professes to write, not **159** only from information derived from the monks, but also 'secundum chronicorum fidem' (Fulm. p. 36; Sav.; 'chronicarum' Fulm. marg. Birch), an expression which he might find in Fl. Wig. 'secundum Anglicam chronicam' (a. 672), 'secundum Anglicas chronicas' (a. 734); yet there is no mention of him in the following works: A.S.Chr., Fl. Wig., Sym. Dun., Geffrei Gaimar, Will. Malm., Roger de Hoveden, Matth. Paris, Capgrave, the Histories of Abingdon and Ramsey abbeys [R. S.] 'Matth. Westm.', Holinshed, Grafton, Leland, nor in Twysden's Scriptores Decem (fo. Lond. 1652), although in the Index are the articles 'Crowland', 'Guthlacus', and 'Waltheofus'.

It is remarkable, that a man of the position of Turketul, a **160** near relative of the king, his chancellor, a valiant warrior, 'ac omnium hostium Anglici regni triumphator strenuissimus', a passage in king Eadgar's charter left untranslated by Mr Riley, a pious abbat, who had raised the number of the inmates of his house from five monks to 47 monks and 4 laybrothers, should have escaped the notice of so many writers.

Although Turketul is described as chancellor (§ 170) to the **161** kings of England from c. 910 to 948, being appointed, 'ut quaecunque negotia temporalia vel spiritualia regis judicium expectabant illius consilio et decreto...omnia tractarentur', yet his name nowhere occurs in the lists of witnesses, sometimes very long, attached to the genuine charters of those kings (Earle, p. 166 ff.). Ingulf's mention of the relationship of Turketul to Oskytel the archbishop of York is corroborated by, or derived from, Ord. Vit.; according to the A.S.Chr. B C, archbishop Oscytel was kinsman to Thurcytel abbat of Bedford (§ 166). Nothing seems known of Oscytel's parentage or family.

Thurcytel Turketul is not mentioned again in the Hist. Croyl. after the close of Ingulf's history (Fulm. p. 107), till the year 1415 (Fulm. p. 501).

Hardyng's Chronicle (c. 1460) makes Turketul chancellor of **162** king Æthelbald of Mercia 716 – 755, instead of chancellor of king Eadward 901 – 925 and of his successors:

'Whiche Ethelbalde in Merse oone and fourtye year
Hade reigned hoole and divers abbeys founded,
In Merselande at Crowelaud oon full clere
Of monkes blacke within the fennys grounded,
To which Turketyll his chauncellere indede
Gave sixe maners to theyr foundacion,
And abbot there was made by installacion'

(Hardyng's Chronicle [4° Lond. 1812] p. 185, MS. Harl. 661 fo. 73 b).

163 The restoration of the monastery was completed by the grant of a charter to Croyland, made by king Eadred in 948 (Fulm. pp. 32 ff.). This charter gives the boundaries of the site of the monastery, and recites the estates, that had been the property of the abbey, but that for this purpose Turketul and his monks had resigned into the king's hand. The author of the present form (at least) of this charter, which is not mentioned in Ord. Vit., although it is mentioned in the Ingulfine charters of Eadred, Cnut, Eadward the Confessor, William I. and Henry I., introduces into it law terms, which according to Stubbs (Const. Hist. j. 213³), Kemble (C. D. j. p. xliv.), Earle (Handbook, p. xxiij.) are not found in charters of undoubted genuineness before the time of Eadward the Confessor. They are 'Soch, Sach, Tol and Tem, Infangthef, Weif and Stray'.

164 On the accession of king Eadgar, abbat Turketul procured a similar charter of confirmation in the year 966. This alone seems to have been known to Ord. Vit., who says:

'Hic [Turketulus] magna generositate fuit, et lx maneria de patrimonio parentum suorum possedit, pro quorum animabus sex villas.... Crulandensi ecclesiae dedit, et testamentum inde sigillo...regis Edgari... signatum confirmavit' (ij. 282).

165 The name Turketul, also written Turkitel, Thurketel, in H. Hunt. Turchetel, in the Guthlac scroll Turketellus, is the Danish name Thurcytel, a name of the same kind, as Oscytel bishop of Dorchester and archbishop of York 950 – 971, Grimcytel, Ascytel, Alfcytel, Wulfcytel, Holmcytel, Thurfcytel, Æruycytel (Hickes Dissert. Epist. p. 9ᵃ). It was borne by many historical personages. Thurcytel jarl of Bedford occurs in 915, 921 (A.S.Chr. A B C D); Thurcytel Myranheafod occurs in 1010 (A.S.Chr. B C); Thurcytel son of Nafena was killed 1016 (A.S.Chr. B C); Turchetellus was a monk at Saint-Evroul in 1070 (Ord. Vit.); a coin of Eadward the Confessor bears on the reverse the moneyer's name and the mint THORCETL ON LUND; others (or the same) were moneyers of Æthelred II. 989 – 1016 at Torksey and of Cnut at London; Turchetillus, Turold de Neuf-Marché, was 'nutricius' of the young duke William of Normandy and was murdered in 1035 (Freeman ij. Ed. III. 195; Ord. Vit. iij. 229). It is found also in Hunter 'Magnus Rotulus Scaccarii 31 H. I'.

The name Thurcytel was cut down to Thurkill, as was Ascytel to Askill, Ulfcytel to Ulfkil (Domesday: Ulchel), and Grimcytel to Grinchel (Domesday); the town Thurcaston Leic. is given by Ord. Vit. in a charter of William I. as Turchille-stona, and in the notes as Turchitelstone, and in Domesday is called Torchitelestone. A Thurkill was killed in battle against the Welsh in 1039 at Rhyd-y-Groes (A.S.Chr. C. Fl. Wig.).

There was also a Thurcytel, abbat of Bedford (§ 161), who is mentioned in A.S.Chr. B C (s. a. 971) as having buried there archbishop Oscytel his kinsman, who had died at Thame. Bedford seems to have been in Danish hands in 915 (A.S.Chr. Fl. Wig.), when another Thurcytel 'Turketillus' a Danish chieftain or jarl submitted to king Eadward the elder; this jarl in a few years went to France with his adherents. A further notice of Thurcytel of Bedford is found in the Liber Eliensis (§ 205, ed. D. J. Stewart, p. 145), where it is said that he was expelled from Bedford, 'eo tempore quo expulsus erat de Bedeford', after 971. He is also described (p. 136) as abbat of Ramsey: 'Turkitelus abbas Ramesiae vendidit Æthelwoldo episcopo unam hydam apud Dudingtune...eo pacto, ut per amicitiam liceret sibi frui et possidere terram de Bebuni, quam Oschetelus episcopus moriens dimisit Ædelwoldo episcopo'. When however Ramsey was first founded in 974, Ædnoth was head of the monastery with the title of prior; he became abbat in 993 and died in 1008 (Chron. Abb. Rames. R.S.). The 'Historia ecclesiæ Eliensis' is also in Gale Scriptores Vol. I. p. 463 ff., and his reference in the Index to this Thurcytel is in the same words as the text: 'Turkitelus Abbas Ramesiæ vendit Ædelwoldo Episcopo [unam] Hydam [apud Dudlingtune]'. The 'Historia Ramesiensis' is in the same volume p. 383 ff., but no Turketul seems to have been found by Gale among the abbats.

167 In the charter of king Eadgar to Ely monastery granted in 970, (Liber Eliensis, p. 110 ff.) in the long list of witnesses we find 'Đupcytel Abb.', as also two knights 'milites' of the same name.

In Birch C. S. Nos. 1017 – 20 are undated charters in A.S. of one Thurkytel, being grants of lands at Culeford or Culford Suff. to the monastery of St Edmundsbury, printed from the MS. Univ. Cantabr. Ff. 2. 33. He had two nephews Ulfketel and Thurfketel. A Thurcytel might in like manner have a relation Oscytel, but it is hard to see, how a Danish name of that form could belong to an Anglo Saxon family, whose members bore the names Æthelred, Ælfred, and Eadred, etc.

The name still exists in the debased form Thurkettle.

168 The succession of the abbats of Croyland is continued after Thurcytel by 'two successors of his own kindred' (Freeman) Egelric (Æthelric) I. 975 – 984 and Egelric II. 984 – 992, who sat in somewhat peaceful times, when the monastery prospered. The Danish troubles began in the days of abbat Oscytel 992 – 1005, and continued through the whole time of abbat Godric II. 1005 – 1018, when the exactions of the English rulers and of the Danish plunderers reduced the monastery to a very low estate. In the quieter times of king Cnut and his successors, abbat Brichtmer or Brihtmær 1018 – 1048, being in favour with Cnut and Harold I., was able to restore what had been destroyed; his time of rule extended into the reign of king Eadward the Confessor.

169 In Fulm. pp. 25, 39, we find many nobles mentioned

belonging to the beginning and end of the period of Croyland's desolation 870 – 948:

870. Ethelwulf, Æthelwulf, earl 'comes'.

Langfer knight, pannier 'panetarius' of king Burgred 852 – 874, born c. 840.

Fernod knight, king Burgred's standard bearer 'vexillarius'.

Turgot earl; he signs the Ingulfine charter of king Burgred a. 868 (§ 382).

948. Lewin, Leofwine, earl ('Li quens Lewine', Geffrei Gaimar l. 4917); the name occurs also in Domesday, Linc. (Ellis Introd. j. 444).

Alpher, Ælfhere, earle; he signs the Ingulfine charter of king Eadgar a. 966, as 'dux', caldorman of Mercia; d. 983. A.S.Chr. E. etc. Fl. Wig. a. 975.

Athelwold, Æthelwald, earl; caldorman of the East Angles, first husband of Ælfthryth d. of Ordgar caldorman of Devon. (Fl. Wig. a. 964).

Ailwin, Æthelwine, earl (d. 992 Freeman j. Ed. III. note AΛ. pp. 633 ff.)

Oslac duke 'dux' caldorman; he however obtained this rank only in 966 (A.S.Chr. E) Freeman j. Ed. III. 266 note KK. pp. 659 ff.).

Langfer (see above) d. c. 930, æt. c. 90; his daughters, born c. 870, survived Turketul (d. 975); and so must have been c. 110 years old at their death. This name still exists in the form of Lankfer near Wisbech.

Osbricht duke 'dux'.

xiij. The king's Chancellor in Anglo-Saxon times.

Turketul, the refounder of Croyland monastery, is spoken of **170** by Ingulf as having been by king Eadward the elder appointed his Chancellor: 'Cancellarium suum cum constituit, ut quaecunque negotia temporalia vel spiritualia Regis judicium expectabant, illius consilio et decreto...omnia tractarentur, et tractata irrefragabilem sententiam sortirentur' (Fulm. p. 36), and on the strength of these words Lord Campbell enrolls him among the predecessors of the Lord Chancellors of mediaeval and modern times.

171 Lord Campbell thoroughly accepts the Ingulfine history of 'Lord Chancellor Turketul' and even adds some improvements to the Ingulfine story (8° Lond. 1845 ff. vol. j. pp. 32 ff.). Turketul took 'priest's orders', though preferring civil appointments to ecclesiastical posts; by his advice Æthelstan first took the title of 'king of England'; he refused to mix in the fight at Brunanburh, because he was a clergyman; he was the chief administrator of justice, and even had to 'command the military force both against foreign and domestic foes during the greater part of the reign of Eadred, owing to the lingering and painful disease, with which the king was afflicted', (the illness being mentioned in Byrhtferth's life of St Dunstan: 'per omne tempus imperii sui nimium languens' [Memorials R. S. p. 171], and in Will. Malm. Gesta regum: 'tortiones crebras corporis' [R. S. j. 162]); having become abbat of Croyland he relinquished in the charter granted by Edred the privilege of sanctuary from his 'experience as chancellor' as to its misuse; and he later declared, that he was happier as Abbot of Croyland than as Chancellor of England. For all this Lord Campbell's reference is: 'Ingul. 25 – 52, Ordine 340', the reference to 'Ingul.' being the whole history of Turketul Fulm. pp. 25 – 52, and the 'Ordine' representing the extracts from Orderic printed in Maseres 'Historiæ Anglicanæ...monumenta' (4°. Lond. 1807).

172 According to better authorities, the chancellor first appears in England, by that name, in the reign of Eadward the Confessor, although the name and office had been familiar on the continent since the days of the first Karlings (Kemble, Saxons in England ed. Birch ij. 112 ff.). Rembaldus chancellor of Eadward the Confessor is mentioned in Domesday (Ellis j. 345).

The chancellor may, however, have been an officer at the royal court in yet earlier times, as Matth. Paris (R. S. j. 452) copying Bridferth's 'Vita sancti Dunstani' says, that the king ordered him to be deprived of the office of chancellor, whereas he is elsewhere described simply as priest of king Eadmund or as priest of the royal palace. Leofric, bishop of Crediton 1046 and of Exeter 1050 – 72, is stated by Fl. Wig. (a. 1046) to have been previously 'regis cancellarius', while in A.S.Chr. E F he is called 'the king's priest'. Dr Stubbs also says, that the chancellor was the most dignified, if not the actual head, of the royal chaplains. In a charter of king William Rufus of 1088, printed in Hickes Dissert. Epist. p. 47, 'Rotbertus cancellarius' signs among the 'capellani' of the king. But it would seem, that Ingulf took a more modern view of the office of the A. S. chancellor.

The Liber Eliensis (p. 194) says, that Æthelred II. granted **173** to Ely, that the abbat should, with the abbats of St Augustine's and of Glastonbury, hold the office of chancellor in the king's court, 'in regis curia cancellarii ageret dignitatem', dividing the year between them, 'cum sanctuariis et ceteris ornamentis altaris ministrando'; on this the editor has this note: 'Cancellarii dignitas. There seems no mention of this elsewhere. It seems to imply the royal chaplaincy, rather than the chancery'.

Several priests of the kings of Mercia are mentioned in Ingulf: Tilhere king Offa's priest 793, Sigga king Kenulf's priest 806, Bosa king Wiglaf's priest 833. Turstan king Wiglaf's priest 819 is mentioned in a charter of Fregist the knight in Gough, Croyland, App. N" xxviij.

In Hugo Candidus (Sparke) we find mention of Adulph chancellor of king Eadgar, who became monk first and abbat afterwards of the restored abbey of Medeshamsted.

After the Conquest the mention of the chancellor is frequent. In 1093 Robert Bloet bishop of Lincoln is mentioned by the A.S.Chr. E. as chancellor. The charters of king Stephen mention several chancellors (Ord. Vit. v. 119^3).

Hardy's Catalogue of Lords Chancellors etc. 8° Lond. 1843 begins only with the Conquest.

xiv. Great Britain.

174 In three Ingulfine charters, that of Eadred to Croyland of 948 (Fulm. p. 32), that of Eadgar to Croyland of 966 (Fulm. p. 42), and that of the same king to Peterborough of 970 (Fulm. p. 46), the king styles himself in different formulae sovereign of Great Britain 'Magnae Britanniae'. In the last case Ingulf is supported by Hugo Candidus (Sparke) in his transcript of the charter, where Eadgar calls himself 'regno praesidens Magnae Britanniae'. In A.S.Chr. E s. a. 963, where the same charter is referred to, the king's style is not given.

175 I. The expression 'Great Britain' seems hardly to be used else until the union of the two crowns of England and Scotland on 24 March 160$\frac{2}{3}$. The name for the whole island or for England alone is 'Britannia major', which occurs in Higden, in Matth. Paris etc., when it is necessary to distinguish it from Britany, which is then called 'Britannia minor' or 'Britannia transmarina' (Will. Malm.). In Will. Gemet. c. 1080 (Duchesne, p. 304 B) we find: 'Major Britannia, quam nunc Angliam vocant'. Bale also calls his work (1557–59) 'Illustrium majoris Britanniae Scriptorum summarium'.

In the Proœmium of Walter de Hemingford's chronicle (Gale II. 455; E. H. S. i. 1) we find '...Anglia nostra, quae olim Major Britannia dicebatur, eo quod a Britannis inhabitata erat et possessa, quorum reliquiae modo sunt Wallenses'.

176 But there are a few exceptions:

a. Ptolemy uses the name ἡ μεγάλη Βρεττανία.

b. The Historia Anglorum of Henry of Huntingdon, as printed in the R. S., consists of eight books. To these several MSS. add two other books, 'De summitatibus' and 'De miraculis', numbered in some cases viij and ix, in others ix and x.

The book 'De summitatibus' consists of an epilogue and three epistles:

1. addressed to Henry I. 1100 – 1135, written after 1131.
2. addressed to Warinus, a brief epitome of Geoffry of Monmouth, of 1139.
3. addressed to Walter, 'De contemptu mundi', of 1135.

The book 'De miraculis', which is always styled 'Liber nonus', relates the miracles of 19 saints, mostly those given by Beda, 'cuius auctoritas firmissima est'. In this book is found (R. S. Introd. p. xxviij):

'Hos de multo sanctorum numero brevitati studentes perstrinximus, qui per loca distincta splendorem salutiferum Britanniae Magnae, quasi caeli luminaria decentissime administrant. Multos namque praeterimus, quorum nomina et gesta in ecclesiis ex eorum nomine Deo dicatis luculenter irradiant. Felix Anglia, tantorum patrum tantis insignita splendoribus!'

c. In the 'Livere de reis de Brittanie' [R. S.], which with 'the Livere de reis de Engleterre' runs on to 1326, we find (p. 2) 'Cist Brutus a soun moriant fist sun eyne (aîné) fiz, ki fu apelle Locrinus, roi de Engleterre, et apella la terre Brittanie la Grande, a pres sun nun'.

In Pierre de Langtoft's Chronicle (R. S. Tho. Wright) similar expressions occur: 'La Grande Brettayne' (j. 228, 278), 'Brettayne le (sic) Grande' (j. 94).

d. Hardyng's Chronicle in metre to 1461 (4° Lond. 1812), p. 179, has under the head of

'The lamentacyon of the maker of this boke, and his counsayle to my lorde of Yorke [Richard] for good rule in this realme of England',

'O Gracyous Lorde, O very heyre in ryght
Of Great Britayne enclosed with oone sea,
O very heyre of Logres, that now England hyght,
Of Wales also, of Scotland, which all three
Britayne so hyght of olde antiquitie....'

At p. 182 Cadwalader is called 'King of Great Brytain.'

e. Jehan de Waurin styles his chronicle [R. S.], which extends to 1477, 'Recueil des Chroniques et anchiennes istories de la Grant Bretaigne, à présent nommé Engleterre'; he frequently uses this expression in his work (j. 6, 35, 100, 116 etc.); Britany he calls 'le petite Bretaigne'; he says (j. 5):

'Et lui dura ce nom d'Albion jusques au temps d'un prince appellé Bructus...lequel l'appela Bretaigne la Grant d'oultremer, à la difference de Basse Bretaigne.'

f. In Caxton's Chronicle (4° Lond. 1480) sign. c. 2 we find 'Amorican' (sic) called 'Litell Britaigne', and England 'Moche

Britaigne' and 'Grete Britaigne'. There are later editions of 1498 and 1515.

178 *g.* It was suggested in 1559, that queen Elizabeth should take the title of queen of Great Britain :

'Sur quoy considérant la trop grande affection que la dicte Dame (queen Elizabeth) et les siens ont à l'union des dictez deux royaulmes, ils ont pensé au différent, qui pourrait sourdre sur la préférence des deux coronnes, et que, pour l'éviter, on pourrait supprimer le titre de l'une et de l'aultre pour redonner à toutes deux ensemble le nom ancien de la Grand Bretaigne.' 30 Dec. 1559.

[Alex. Teulet, Relations politiques de la France et de l'Espagne avec l'Écosse au xvj^e. siècle, 8° Paris 1862, j. 384. 'Mémoire baillé à M. de la Mothe'] (Encycl. Brit.).

179 *h.* In Harryson's Description of Britain in Holinshed (fo. Lond. 1577), Vol. I. fo. 43, b. 1, Eadgar is stated to have 'reigned ouer the whole monarchie of Great Britaine'. He says again (fo. 41, b. 2), that Maximian, after subduing Armorica, gave it 'to Conan his cosin, to be afterward inhabited by Britons, by the name of Britayne the lesse : and hereof this realme tooke name of Britayne the greate, which name by consent of forreine writers, it kepeth unto this day'. Of this the former part is taken from Matth. Paris, Chron. Maj. [R. S.] j. 171 – 2 or ·Matth. Westm.' [R. S.] j. 196 – 7, Maximianus being Magnus Maximus emperor 383 – 388 ; Matth. Paris often calls Britany 'Britannia Minor' and England 'Britannia': ' Magna Britannia' seems not to occur.

180 II. Camden (Britannia 1607, p. 101) has nothing definite ; he says:

'Gravius fortasse erit, si posteris......prodam quod nos vidimus, scilicet ut Egbertus hanc citeriorem et suam Britanniæ partem ANGLIAM jussit nominari; ita...... R. Jacobus, totius insulæ Monarchiam......adeptus, ut hæc insula quæ in se una existit......uno etiam esset nomine : nomen, titulum, et stylum Regis MAGNÆ BRITANNIÆ sibi...assumpsit'.

He however (p. 99) mentions the use by king Eadred in 948 of the title of king of Great Britain, but without comment.

181 In king James' ' Proclamation concerning the king's Maiesties stile, of king of Great Britaine' [20 Oct. 1604], he states, that Great Britain is 'the true and ancient name, which God and

Time have imposed upon this Isle, extant, and receiued in histories, in all Mappes and Cartes,…warranted also by Authenticall Charters, exemplification under Seales, and other Records of Great Antiquitie…' (a Booke of Proclamations published since the beginning of his Majesties most happy reign over England [fo. Lond. 1609] p. 82 ff.). The authorities of the Map Department of the British Museum do not know of the use of the name 'Great Britain' before Camden's Britannia of 1607; it does not occur in Ortelius' atlas of 1595.

Spelman (Concilia 1639, p. 428) prints part of Eadred's charter including the king's title, but with no note of doubt.

As the expression 'Magna Britannia' is used in the In- **182** speximus charter of 1393 reciting the two charters of 716 and 948, it would be interesting to discover, whence the author of the charter derived it, and what meaning was attached to the title.

Albion is another name for England found in the Ingulf. **183** It occurs also frequently in Earle (Land charters. Genuine records) in the fantastical titles of Æthelstan: 'Æthelstanus per Omnipatrantis dexteram apice totius Albionis sublimatus', of Eadred: 'Eadred rex divina protegente gratia Albionis summam possidens', of Eadgar: 'Eadgar Dei omnipotentis nutu rex totius Albionis insulæ', and of Eadward the Confessor. The word is used by Beda and by Fl. Wig. (s. a. 926) for the whole island, and also by Ord. Vit. (iij. 216) for England.

xv. The royal title.

In the printed texts of the Ingulf, the kings are sometimes **184** styled after their territories, and not after the inhabitants of those territories.

Thus we find both 'Rex Merciæ, West Saxoniæ, Est-Angliæ, Angliæ, Franciæ', and also 'Rex Merciorum, West Saxonum, Est-Anglorum, Anglorum, Francorum'. Fl. Wig. (d. 1118) seems never to use territorial titles; both styles, however, are found (a. 1126, 1140) in his continuators in Thorpe's edition; Beda also seems always to use the national style.

185 This use by Ingulf of the territorial style can hardly be deemed an additional sign of forgery, since some of the above territorial forms may be due to mistaken expansions of the lost MS. text. But in early days also the use is not constant; thus on coins the style is OFFA REX MERCIORVM, CNVT REX ANGLORVM, but Æthelstan on some coins calls himself ÆDELSTAN REX TOT BRI—T. Will. Malm. generally has 'Rex Merciorum' etc., but in the Gesta regum [R. S.] i. 7 we find Vortigern called 'Rex Britanniæ', where Beda has 'Rex Brettonum'. Hen. Hunt. (c. 1150) uses both forms, but more usually 'Rex Merce', 'Rex Westsexe', 'Rex Estangle', 'Rex Angliæ'. The title 'Rex Cantiæ', though not so frequent as 'Rex Cantuariorum', is yet found in some of the 'genuine records' in Earle's Handbook (pp. 35, 58, 76, 79, 81), while 'Rex Britanniæ' occurs in 736 (p. 30).

186 'Rex Franciæ', which occurs in Ingulf (Fulm. p. 51) has a suspicious look, but it may be found in Dudo of St Quentin c. 1015 (Duchesne), p. 76 D. Willelmus Gemeticensis (c. 1125) also has 'Reges Franciæ' (Duchesne, pp. 304 c, 305 A), 'rex Scotiæ' (p. 297) and 'Rex Northwegiæ' (p. 185).

187 In Ingulf (Fulm. p. 37) we find 'the Emperor' styled rightly 'Imperator Romanorum', but also styled 'Imperator Alemanniæ'. Fl. Wig. calls him 'Imperator de Alemannia' (s. a. 1106), 'Rex Teutonicorum et Imperator Romanorum' (s. a. 1111); H. Hunt. has 'Imperator Alemanniæ'; while other forms are 'þam casere of Sexlande' (A.S.Chr. E. a. 1106), 'Imperator Alemannorum' (Ord. Vit.); and Mathilda the daughter of Henry I. is called 'Imperatrix Alemanniæ' (H. Hunt.). In Stapleton's Magni Rotuli Scaccarii Normanniæ, Vol. I. (8° Lond. 1840) pp. 136, 137 we find mention of certain 'nuntii Imperatoris Alemañ' in the year 1180.

188 The 'prima manus' of A.S.Chr. E. extends to 1122, only a few years after the conclusion of the Ingulf; in it several territorial styles of sovereigns occur:

       s. a. 1085 'Cnut cyng of Denmearcan',
             1087 'Willelm Englælandes cyng',
             1108 'se cyng of France, Philippus'.

This occurs also in D, 'secunda manu' from 1016 to 1079, ending abruptly; there s. a. 1034 we read 'Malcolm cyng an Scotlande'. But in earlier days we have 'Carl Francne cyning' (A s. a. 855, 885) and 'Cosstantin Scotta cyning' (D s. a. 926), while all the English kings are styled as in Fl. Wig.

Ingulf speaks of the Conqueror as 'Gulielmus primus' **189** (Fulm. p. 106). In Fl. Wig. he is 'Willelmus senior' (s. a. 1092), his son being 'Willelmus junior' (s. a. 1100). However the three dukes of Normandy, who bore the name of Richard, are distinguished by Fl. Wig. as 'primus' (s. a. 1002), 'secundus' (s. a. 1013), and 'tertius' (s. a. 1026).

The son of the Conqueror is called 'Wilelmus Rufus' by **190** Pet. Bles. (Fulm. p. 110), as also by Joh. Petrib. (s. a. 1087), and by the Liber Eliensis (pp. 279, 284), but Ord. Vit. likewise gives him that name (j. 186, 187; ij. 105, 189 etc.).

xvj. Coronations in A.S. times.

In his charter of 833 Wiglaf king of Mercia (Fulm. p. 9) **191** speaks of the 'purple chlamys', which he wore at his 'Coronation'. Other kings from Æthelred II. to William I. are mentioned by Ingulf as having been 'crowned'. The word used by Fl. Wig. and his continuator John is 'consecrare', and that used by A.S.Chr. is 'to hallow'. The only use of 'consecrare' in Ingulf is in the charter of Eadgar to Malmesbury of 974; the word 'consecratio' occurs in the charter of Ceolwulf of Mercia (Earle, p. 100) of 822.

On the other hand the word 'coronare' which is found in the Vulgate (2 Tim. ij. 5, Heb. ij. 7, etc.) is used by Joh. de Taxster (Fl. Wig. ed. Thorpe) 1152 - 1265, and other later writers. Ord. Vit. (d. c. 1144), (ij. 164. 374), as also Will. Malm. (c. 1130) Gesta regum (R. S. j. 124, 180, 186, 239), and Hen. Hunt. (R. S. p. 204) have the word 'coronare'. The use of the word by Pet. Bles., whose professed date is c. 1190 (Fulm. p. 111), is not therefore an anachronism.

xvij. **The two charters of 17 July 17 Ric. II. 1393, and of 1 Nov. 1 Hen. IV. 1399.**

192 In the Patent Rolls at the Public Record office are two charters of Inspeximus and Confirmation of 17 July 17 R. II. 1393, and of 1 Nov. Hen. IV. 1399. These are of nearly identical contents; the former recites and confirms the charter of foundation of Æthelbald king of Mercia of 716 and the charter of refoundation of Eadred king of England of 948, while the latter recites and confirms the whole charter of Richard II.

193 The peculiarity of these two charters is the series of crosses prefixed to the names of the witnesses in 716 and 948, which are the same in the two charters of Richard II. and of Henry IV.

194 The 'Golden charter' of Æthelbald of 716 (§ 121), engraved by Dr Hickes, exhibits the same series of crosses, as is found in the charter of 716 as recited in the two charters of 1393 and 1399.

The style of the gilt crosses of the 'Golden charter' of 716 is so different from anything, that is otherwise known in genuine A.S. charters, that on that ground, as well as on others, Dr Hickes condemned the document as a forgery, describing the crosses as 'signa crucis aurea phantastico, si dicam, more facta'.

It is remarkable, that in the Patent Rolls the crosses prefixed to the names of the 13 witnesses of the charter of 948 are of precisely the same style as those of the 19 witnesses of the charter of 716, seven being absolutely identical, so that the lapse of 232 years had apparently brought about no change in the style of writing of the charters. It may however have been, that the documents bearing date 716 and 948, which were transcribed into the Inspeximus charters, were copies of earlier, plainer charters, which (on account of their importance in connexion with the history of the abbey) had been enlarged and illuminated in a supposed archaic style, without regard to the difference of date, by the same hand.

Dr Hickes knew only one 'Golden charter', that of 716, of which he gives an engraving; he was acquainted with Eadred's charter only from Ingulf's text. But among the 'Evidences' belonging to the Town of Croyland (Gough, Croyl. App. p. *135) are mentioned some 'goulden charters', one of which may have been the charter of 948. Dr Hickes does not seem, either, to have been acquainted with the two entries, in the Patent Rolls, of the Inspeximus charters.

Of course the charter of Richard II. proves, that in 1393 the two charters of 716 and of 948, as given by Ingulf, were already in existence.

Perhaps the most curious circumstance connected with the two Inspeximus charters of Richard II. and Henry IV. is, that the 'Historia Croylandensis' makes no mention of them either at their dates or later, though the First Anonymous Continuation is quite perfect from 1388 to 1470, unless they are the undescribed charters of those kings referred to in the award of the arbitrators between Croyland and Spalding in 1415 (Fulm. p. 508).

xviij. The Sempects.

Sempects 'sempectæ' are mentioned in the ordinances of Turketul for the management of the monastery (Fulm. p. 49). They are described as monks, who had reached the 50th year of their monastic life, and who would therefore be at least 60 years old, supposing that like Thurgar (Fulm. p. 22) and Ordericus Vitalis (ij. 300 – 1, v. 135) they had become monks at the early age of ten years. This title, which was of Turketul's choosing (Fulm. p. 49), is only really used of the five monks, who lived through the period between the destruction of the house in 870 and its restoration in 948 (Fulm. p. 107); and Ingulf in his ordinances c. 1091 (Fulm. p. 105), while preserving the three classes of monks established by Turketul, viz. those of less than 24 years, those of less than 40 years, and those of more than 40 years, of monastic life, gives to the latter no especial name.

Thirty-one monks escaped the murderous hands of the

Danes in 870 (§ 146); one of them, Thurgar, was a boy of ten years of age, and another (perhaps) Briestan, 'quondam cantor', who wrote a poem on the ruin of the house. They elected as abbat one of their body named Godric; and he, with a small number of monks, remained, though in great poverty, in possession of the site till his death, 70 years later, in 940, when the monks were reduced to seven, of whom two, Sweyn and Osgot, soon followed their abbat to the grave. Of the five survivors 'Brunus' went away to the monastery of Winchester, and Aio to that of Malmesbury, where they remained till 948, three monks only being thus left at Croyland.

198 In that year, when Turketul began to restore the monastery of Croyland, where he had found the three, Clarenbald, Swartting and Thurgar, he sent for Brun and Aio to come back. His messengers departed from Croyland soon 'mox' after the Eve of the Assumption of the B. V. M. (14 Aug.), and such was their speed, that they returned with the two old monks by the vigil of St Bartholomew's day (23 Aug. or 24 Aug. § 60), though the distance of Malmesbury from Croyland in a direct line is about 110 miles, and that of Winchester about 120 miles.

These five, who are called 'the five sempects' (Fulm. p. 107), thus reunited, assisted Turketul in compiling the history of the monastery before its destruction, which they had witnessed (Fulm. p. 48), and in reviving the ancient observances of the house. Their activity is the more remarkable, that they were of very considerable age;

Clarenbald d. 972 aged 168 (v. l. 148) years,
Swartting d. 973 aged 142 years,
Brun   d. 973 aged —? years,
Aio   d. 973 aged —? years,
Thurgar   d. 974 aged 115 years.

At the restoration in 948, therefore, their ages were between 89 and 144 (124) years; at the destruction of the monastery in 870, their ages were between 10 and 66 (46) years.

Besides the above men of great age, we find in Ingulf mentioned, as over 100 years old, the two monks Grymketul and Agamund, who were slaughtered in 870.

The word 'Sempecta' has been much discussed. Ducange thinks, that the aged monk was so called, because a συμπαίκτης was assigned him, a younger monk who was to minister to him. It is used by Ord. Vit. (iij. 330): 'Hoc animadvertentes, Cenomanni valde lætati sunt, et majorem ei [Hugoni comiti Cenomannorum] metum sempectas incusserunt', Le Prévost suggesting the reading 'per sempectas', 'par les anciens du pays'.

'It is also applied to a class of monks in the order of St Benedict, and an early use of it, though apparently in another sense, is to be met with in the Lausiac history of the Eastern Solitaries, by Palladius a christian bishop' (Riley, Archæol. Journ. 1862, p. 130).

In the Rule of St. Benedict (Nova Biblioth. Patrum, fo. Paris 1639, Vol. I. p. 697) in cap. xxvij. we find: 'Senipectas, id est seniores et sapientes fratres'.

The word συμπαίκτης occurs in the Anthologia Palatina (ed. F. Jacobi, 4 vols. 8vo. Lips. 1831) vol. I. p. 146 (v. 214) as used by Meleager (I cent. B.C.).

The following is Ducange's explanation (Gloss. fo. Par. 1736, vj. 350):

'Nam Quinquagenarios monachos *Sympectas*, appellatos admodum vero simile est, non quod ipsi *Sympectae* essent, sed quod ad ætatis provectioris solatium darentur iis συμπαίκται, seu juniores Monachi, qui eis ministrarent, et cum iis mensæ assiderent, ut ex[s]erte scribit Ingulphus: quomodo ejusmodi seniorum Monachorum συμπαίκτας habet Palladius in Hist. Lausiaca cap. 24. 83. quos *Collusores* vertit vetus Interpres cap. 24, unde liquet ab Ægyptiis et Orientis monachis id vocabuli acceptum.'

The editors then add:

'Probabilissima tametsi videtur vocis *Sempectae* interpretatio, quam ad mentem Ingulfi exponit Vir eruditus: mirum nihilominus est *Sempectas* nuncupatos, non juniores qui eo nomine designandi erant, sed seniores quibus ad solatium ii concedebantur. Ut ut est aliud sonat *Sempecta* in Regula S. Benedicti: eo quippe loci de excommunicatis sermo est, quibus Abbas fratres submittit, qui iis consolationem exhibeant; unde *Sempectas* hic intelligo sodales, socios seu familiares, qui amicum facilius ad meliorem frugem adducere valeant; qui tamen, ut vult S. Benedictus, inter seniores sapientes potissimum eligendi sunt. Vide Menardum in Concordia Regul. et Martenii Commentar. in Regul. S. Bened. pag. 378'.

200   In 'The inventories of Westminster abbey at the Dissolution' published by the rev. Mackenzie E. C. Walcott, B.D. in the Publications of the London and Middlesex Archæol. Soc. iv. 1878, 313 – 364, we find (p. 335) 'xij albes...for the elder men', to which is appended the note: 'Elder monks, here called "Seupectæ", *i.e.* senes sapientes or Synpaiktai mates. See my Interior of a Bened. Monast. drawn up from Ware's Custumal, 1266, now in the British Museum, and printed in the Ecclesiastic [and Theologian], 1866, p. 533'.

There seems to be no corroboration of this alleged use of the word 'Sempecta' at Westminster.

Clem. Reynerus in his Apostolatus Benedictinorum in Anglia (fo. Douai, 1626), though apparently knowing Savile's Ingulf, when mentioning (2d pagin. p. 139) Clarenbaldus, Swartingus and Turgarus who died at very advanced ages in c. 974, does not call them by the name 'Sempectæ' which Ingulf uses, and has no reference to that word.

201   Speaking of the regulations made by Turketul, Dr Hickes has the following observations:

'Præsertim vero in describendis statutis et ordinationibus, quas Turketulum abbatem in monasterio suo Croylandensi observandas dedisse scribit, omnia pro moribus Nortmannicis et temporibus Turketuli, qui mortuus est anno Christi incarnati 975, prorsus aliena tradit' (Thes. præf. p. xxix).

He instances the use of the words 'sempecta' and 'indentura'.

The words 'garcio' and 'armiger' used in the regulations are also suspicious. The former occurs with 'froccus' in 'Gesta abbatum S. Albani', [R.S.] p. 367, c. 1340; and in Oliver, 'Monast. Dioc. Exon.' (præf. p. vj) we find, that in 1526 one John Amadas received grant of a corrody at Tavistock abbey; it consisted of certain food and a furred robe at Christmas yearly, 'of the same kind as that of our esquires', and when at the abbey such accommodation 'as one of our esquires receives', commuted at the Dissolution by the Court of Augmentation for an annuity of £5. But 'Nicolaus scutiger Wandregisili' is mentioned Hunter Mag. Rot. Scacc. 31 H. I. p. 19: he may have been esquire of the abbat of Saint Wandrille, and the esquires 'armigeri' of the abbat of Croyland are mentioned in 1326 and 1338 (Gough, Croyl. App. pp. 60 – 62).

xix. Hereward.

Hereward, the doughty enemy for some time of the Norman **202** invaders of England, 'the mirror of Knighthood in the Saxon period' (Ellis), 'the very Hector of his time' (Croyland's chronicle), has been brought prominently before the English public by Charles Kingsley's novel of 'Hereward the Wake', and his history has been closely investigated by Professor Freeman (Norman Conquest iv. 454 ff. The revolt in the Fen country; note OO, The Legend of Hereward, p. 804 ff.).

His history is given with many variations by the Ingulf, the Gesta Herwardi, the Liber Eliensis, and from them by the usual historians and chroniclers, but not in Hardyng's chronicle.

In the Ingulf and in the 'De gestis Herwardi Saxonis', Hereward is described as the son of Leofric lord of Brunne or Bourn Linc. and of Ædiva [Ingulf] or Eadgifu [Freeman] called Ædina in the Gesta. A genealogical roll of the lords of Brunne and Deeping, of the 15th century (Cottonian charter xiij. 9; Chron. Anglo-Norm. vol. ij. p. xij ff.; Freeman ij. 629) makes his parents Leofric earl of Chester and Godgifu or Godiva his celebrated countess. Hereward would then be the brother of earl Ælfgar and uncle of the two earls Eadwine and Morkere, a connexion accepted by Dugdale (Hist. of Imbanking 1662, p. 186, col. 1), but of which there is elsewhere no hint, and against which are the circumstances, that Leofric died 1057 some years before the conquest, whereas Hereward's father died after it, and that Godgifu was one of the few English ladies, who retained their lands (Pearson, England j. 366 – 8). But, historical personage though Hereward be, nothing, according to Mr Freeman, is known of his parentage.

1. The 'De gestis Herwardi Saxonis', contained in the one **203** mediæval MS. in the library of Peterborough cathedral, consists of 36 chapters. Beginning with its hero's youth, whom it

makes godson 'filiolus' of Gilbert of Ghent 'Gisebritus de Gant', the refounder of Bardeney monastery (Pet. Bles. Fulm. p. 127), it relates his adventures in Cornwall, Ireland and the Netherlands, his marriage there with Turfrida, his return to England and his struggles in the Isle of Ely, his successful engagement with the combined troops of abbat Turold and Ivo Tailbois, his capture of the abbat of Peterborough, who was only released after the payment of a ransom of 30,000 'librae', and who by his attempt at renewing hostilities with Hereward, provoked the latter to the grave step of burning and plundering the monastery, his marriage with the widow of earl Dolfin, and the taking of the veil by Turfrida; and it finishes with his submission to king William, his restoration to his patrimony, and his peaceful end.

This work has been edited from the Peterborough MS. in the R S. edition of Geffrei Gaimar j. 339 – 404; there is also a less correct edition by Francisque Michel in his Chroniques Anglo-Normandes (3 vols, 8° Rouen, 1836 – 40) ii. 1 – 98. It is also to be found in the series of publications of the Caxton Society (8° Lond. 1850) edited by Th. Wright.

Two persons named Dolfin occur in the tract 'De obsessione Dunelmi' in Sym. Dun. R. S. j. 215 ff.: Dolfin the son of Torfin, who lived about 1050 (Skene, Celtic Scotland j. 409), and Dolfin the brother of Waltheof abbat of Croyland 1124 – 38. Ulf the son of Dolfin was one of the insurgent thanes of Northumbria in 1065 (Fl. Wig.). The name is found also in Domesday (Ellis, Introd. j. 405).

Michel gives also (ij. p. xv ff.) a long extract from a MS. of the Royal Library in the Brit. Mus., 18. C. 1, p. 26 ff., containing an 'Account of the taking of Ely' by William I, in which Hereward is once mentioned, but with no recital of his deeds.

A few expressions seem to have been borrowed from this work by the author of the Ingulf.

2. The Liber Eliensis Vol. I. (edited by D. J. Stewart, 8° Lond. 1848) B. ij. §§ 102 – 107, pp. 224 – 239, gives only Hereward's doings in the Isle of Ely 'Elyensis insula', and says nothing of his other adventures, of his wife, or of his death,

nor does it relate any of his doings after his firing the siege works of William spoken of in the Gesta Herwardi § 25.

The writer professes to have culled his account of Hereward 'de plurimis historiis', referring for a fuller description of his doings to a 'Gesta Herewardi' by Brother Richard. There is a good deal of the language in the Liber Eliensis cc. 104 – 106, common also to the Gesta, especially in c. 106.

3. In Geffrei Gaimar's 'L'estorie des Engles' (c. 1140) **205** there is much about Hereward vv. 5457 – 5710 (R. S. j. 231 ff., ij. 173 ff.), but nothing before the uprising in the Fens. It describes him as a 'noble man...one of the best of the country'; it tells of the fortifying of the Isle, of Hereward's firing William's bridge, and of his plundering Peterborough. It seems further to imply (Freeman, Legend of Hereward; Kingsley ch. xxxix.), that Hereward married Alftruda, no mention being made of Turfrida, and it gives at considerable length (vv. 5615 – 5700) an account of his murder by certain Norman knights. It mentions (v. 5609), that he had taken part in an expedition of king William into Maine.

4. John of Peterborough (MS. Cott. Claud. A. v.) relates, **206** how that Hereward returned from foreign parts to England in 1068, and that, finding that king William had bestowed his patrimony upon his Norman followers, he killed those that were thus in possession, and began to wage war with the king; he recounts further s. a. 1069, how Hereward captured Thorold the successor of his uncle Brand (d. 27 Nov. 1069, A.S.Chr. E.) at Peterborough, and put him to ransom at 30,000 marks 'marcae argenti', but says nothing of the pillage of the monastery on 2 June, 1070. Under the year 1071 this chronicler tells of Hereward's resistance to the king in the Isle of Ely, but gives no information respecting his pedigree (beyond the mention of abbat Brand as his uncle), his wife, his submission or the manner of his death. He calls him 'Herewardus le Wake', but gives no reason for this appellation. No hint is given in the First Anonymous Continuation, that the Wakes, who are there frequently mentioned, were descended from Hereward.

207   5. Ingulf has a fairly long account of 'the renowned but shadowy form of Hereward' (Fulm. pp. 67 – 8, 70, 71), which is supplemented by a passage in Pet. Bles. (Fulm. pp. 124 – 5). Of it Mr Freeman (iv. 805) says: 'The story in the false Ingulf (pp. 67, 70) is not wholly to be cast aside, as it may contain some genuine Crowland tradition'; Hallam (Middle Ages, Suppl. Notes, 1848, p. 272) apparently accepts it. Ingulf's account of Hereward begins with his pedigree (§ 202), his youth, and his exile about 1062, mentions briefly his journeys to Northumbria, Cornwall, and Ireland, and his exploits in Flanders; it tells of his marriage with Turfrida (a Turfridus is found in Will. Malm. Gesta Regum [R. S.] i. 147 in Northumbria in the time of king Æthelstan), relating also (without assigning any reason for it) her becoming a nun at Croyland in the time of abbat Wulketul, Wulfkytel or Ulfcytel, and her death and burial there 'vix æstate quarta jam transacta' (Fulm. p. 67); it speaks of the renown, that Hereward acquired abroad and at home, so that ballads about him were sung in the streets in the writer's time, 'cumque...ejus...gesta fortia etiam Angliam ingressa canerentur', and 'prout adhuc in triviis canuntur...' (pp. 67, 68); nothing however seems known of any such ballads.

Returning after the Conquest, he expelled those intruders, who had seized his father's lands, and received knighthood at the hands of his uncle 'patruus' Brand abbat of Peterborough (p. 70). After a lengthy resistance to the forces of king William in the Isle of Ely, he made an attack on Peterborough 'Burgum invasit, abbatem fugavit' in the time of abbat Thorold, the successor of abbat Brand (d. 27 Nov. 1069), and even defeated the joint forces of the abbat and of Ivo Tailbois, took the abbat prisoner, and only set him at liberty on the payment of a heavy ransom (Fulm. p. 71), nothing being said of the taking and plundering of the abbey on 2 June 1070 (A.S.Chr. E). Ingulf adds further, that Hereward was the only one of the leaders in the Isle, who refused to follow the example of submission to the new king set by earl Morkere and others, 'se subdere distulit, ac alias divertit' (p. 71), telling nothing of his later life, except that having avenged his widowed mother, and, having 'cum regia pace' recovered his inheritance, he ended his days in peace, and was buried in the monastery of Croyland by the side of his wife, and that 'nuperrime'. Nothing is said of any second wife.

His daughter, the heiress of Brunne, we are told, married Hugo de Evermue, lord of the vill of Deping (p. 67).

Hugo de Ebremou, Hugues d'Envermeu (in Normandy, near Dieppe), brother of Turold d'Envermeu bishop of Bayeux (d. 1146), is mentioned by Ord. Vit. (iv. 18). Joscelin d'Euremou occurs in Stapleton Magni Rot. Scacc. Duc. Norm. c. 1200 (ij. 429). 'Hugo de Euremou .iij. hidas in dominio et .vij. bovatas in Lincolnescira, et servit pro .ij. militibus' (Liber niger monast. S. Petri de Burgo, in Stapleton's Chron. Petrob. [Camden Soc.], p. 174).

The daughter of Hugo de Evermue married Richard de Rulos. Now Hereward was exiled about 1062, and married Turfrida c. 1064, so that his daughter would be born c. 1065 and married to Hugo de Evermue æt. 18, c. 1083; her daughter, called Godiva in Fr. Michel ij. p. xv, would be born c. 1084 and married to Richard de Rulos æt. 18, c. 1102. But Richard seems to be spoken of by Ingulf (Fulm. pp. 77 – 8) as belonging to a period already somewhat in the past, while the marriage, if a real one, could not have taken place till long after 1092, the last date in Ingulf's history. Richard is spoken of as alive in 1114 (Fulm. p. 246).

Richard de Rulos is described (Fulm. p. 99) as lord of Brunne and Deping in 1091; as he became this only by his marriage with the heiress and only child of Hugo de Evermue, her marriage with him would have taken place before 1091, and then we must suppose, that, being an heiress, she was married when a mere child like Judith the wife of king Æthelwulf of Wessex at the age of twelve years, or the empress Matilda the daughter of Henry I. at the age of eight years (Ann. de Wintonia, s. a. 1110), or even like Mahaut d'Avesnes heiress of the Morea in 1299 at the age of five to Guy II. duke of Athens (Gregorovius, Stadt Athen j. 454). If so, Hugo de Evermue may have died c. 1090, and, if there is any truth in the Cotton charter xiij. 9 (§ 220), Hereward may have been killed by him c. 1088, which might answer to the 'nuperrime' of Ingulf (Fulm. p. 68).

Hugo de Evermue is called de Ewnermothe (Cotton charter xiij. 9). There seems no evidence of any connexion with Hereward of Hugo de Envermeu, or of that of Richard de Rulos, beyond the 'Historia Croylandensis' (Fulm. pp. 77, 78, 95, 99, 118). Richard de Rulos (regius camerarius, Fulm. p. 78) is not mentioned in Ord. Vit., or in Domesday under the tenants in capite (Ellis, Introd. vol. I); however in Hunter's Magnus Rotulus Scaccarii 31 H. I. we find mentioned, p. 110 (Linc.) 'Baldewin*us* fili*us* Gislebe*rti* redd*idit* compot*um* de .ccc.li. et .xxxvj. s. et .iiij. d. p*ro* te*rra* Will*elmi* de Rullos cu*m* filia Ric*ardi* f*ra*tris sui' and p. 143 (Westmorl.) 'Ric*ardus* de Rullos debet .j. *marcam* auri'. Rollos, now Roullours, lies in the S.W. part of the dep. of the Calvados, near Vire (Stapleton Magn. Rot. Scacc. Norm. ij. p. viij). In spite of H. Wharton, Dr Hickes, Sir F. Palgrave, and Mr Freeman, we still find writers quoting the Ingulf as trustworthy history: 'whoever... may have been the author of the chronicle attributed to Ingulf, no doubt has been cast on the story of Richard' [Rulos] 'of Deeping, who made a "garden of delight" out of the "horrible fens of Croyland"' (C. T. Elton, Origins of English History, 2nd Ed. 8vo. Lond. 1890, p. 224).

The paragraph in Pet. Bles. (Fulm. pp. 124, 125) concerning Hereward refers to his connexion with the insurgents in the Isle; it mentions the sorceress 'sacrilega', that Ivo Tailbois brought to act against the English, and Hereward's success in destroying the king's bridge and the tower where the witch was stationed (see the Gesta Herwardi, § 204, where she is called 'pythonissa') by fire; it also relates the capture of abbat Thorold and his ransom of 3000 marks (30000 marks Joh. Petrib.). The plunder of the monastery, elsewhere mentioned, is recorded in the Gesta Herwardi as a separate and subsequent event.

6. The A. S. Chronicle E mentions 'Hereward and his gang' (s. a. 1070, other events in which year are ascribed by D [Worcester] to 1071) made up of outlaws, rebellious tenants of

the abbey, and of Danish allies (Freeman iv. 459); it relates at some length, how those men came to Peterborough and, finding resistance, stormed the enclosure of the monastery and burnt it, having plundered all the treasures of the place.

In the following year (E 1071, D 1072) the final struggle of the English and its termination is recounted. It is stated, that 'all the outlaws went and surrendered to the king: these were bishop Ægelwine and earl Morkere' (earl Eadwine his brother had previously been 'basely slain by his own men'), 'and all who were with them except Hereward only and all who could flee away with him. And he boldly led them out'. The later life of Hereward is not touched upon.

The general plunder by king William of the property deposited for safe custody in the monasteries by wealthy Englishmen took place in the early part of 1070 (A.S.Chr. E; D 1071); all the monasteries were searched, and all deposits of this kind were carried into the royal treasury (Fl. Wig. s. a. 1070). Hereward's plundering of the monastery of Peterborough took place the same year.

7. In Fl. Wig. the only reference to Hereward is s. a. 1071, **211** where the insurrection in the Isle of Ely 'Heli insula' is mentioned, and its apparently speedy suppression, 'et omnes, excepto Herewardo viro strenuissimo, qui per paludes cum paucis evasit, regi se dedebant'. This is repeated in Hoveden [R. S.] i. 125 – 6. The style of 'vir strenuissimus' is given twice to Hereward in the same passage, and 'strenuissimus' is used of him by Ingulf. Pet. Bles. calls him 'sagacissimus baro Herwardus de Brunne'.

This somewhat agrees with the short notice in H. Hunt.: 'Rex vero ducens exercitum terra et mari insulam obsedit, pontem paravit, domum belli artificiose construxit, quae usque hodie perstat; viros praedictos (Morkere, Hereward, and bishop Egelwine) occidit introiens insulam [introiens insulam cepit, or occidit v. l.] praeter Herewardum, qui suos viriliter strenuissimus eduxit' (R. S. p. 205).

8. Hugo Candidus (Sparke, p. 48 ff.) gives an account of **212** the plunder of Peterborough by Hereward and the Danes, in

very nearly the same terms as A.S.Chr. E, but bestowing a somewhat greater prominence on him, and fixing the event more definitely close upon the death of abbat Brand, 'quia audierant [Dani] quod abbas [Brando] esset mortuus, et quod rex dedisset abbatiam cuidam monacho Normanno nomine Turoldo'.

213   9. This last account is repeated in 'Historia vetus Coenobii Petriburgensis, versibus gallicanis' in Sparke's collection, pp. 251 – 4.

214   10. In Domesday Book, besides a mention of some lands in the West, which may have belonged to another Hereward, we read among the 'Clamores de Chetsteven' at the end of the Lincolnshire: 'Terram Asford in Bercham Hundred dicit wapentak non habuisse Herewardum die qua aufugiit', and again 'Terram sancti Guthlaci, quam tenet Ogerus in Repinghale, dicunt fuisse dominicam firmam monachorum, et Ulchel abbatem commendasse eam ad firmam Herewardo, sicut inter eos conveniret unoquoque anno; sed abbas resaisivit eam antequam Herenuardus de patria fugeret, eo quod conventionem non tenuisset (p. 376 b. 377). On p. 364 b. Toli and Hereward appear as former owners on the land of the same Oger le Breton (§ 20). 'This is the amount of our positive knowledge. Hereward held lands in Lincolnshire; part of them was held of the abbey of Crowland, of which abbot Ulfcytel resumed possession, because Hereward did not keep his agreement. At some later time, therefore after 1062' (sic, § 453, see also Freeman iv. 598) 'the year of the appointment of Ulfcytel, Hereward fled from the country, but for what cause we are not told' (Freeman iv. 805 ff.). [According to Ingulf, Wulketul (Wulfcytel, Ulfcytel, Ulchel) was appointed abbat by Eadward the Confessor in 1052.] 'But the date and cause of his flight, whether he had drawn on himself the wrath of Eadward, of Harold, or of William, is utterly uncertain' (Freeman iv. 45 b.). If Hereward had recovered his paternal estate 'cum regia pace' (Fulm. p. 68; Gesta Herwardi) at some not very long time after 1072 (§ 216), traces of this might be expected to be found in the Domesday of 1086.

11. In William of Malmesbury's 'Gesta pontificum' (R. S. p. 420) is the following passage concerning Hereward: 'Idem Turoldus [abbat of Malmesbury], dum tyrannidem in subjectos ageret, ad Burh a rege translatus est, abbatiam opulentam, sed quæ tunc a latrunculis, duce quodam Herewardo, infestaretur, quia inter paludes sita erat', the king placing Thorold there on account of his military abilities.

The fact of Hereward having been a principal actor in the insurrection in the Isle of Ely is undoubted (Freeman iv. 454 ff.); his later life and manner of death is however variously given, if it is given at all. The Liber Eliensis, the chroniclers (A.S.Chr., Fl. Wig., Joh. Petrib.) and Hugo Candidus do not refer to his after life. The 'Gesta Herwardi' says: 'Herwardus igitur...a rege in gratiam receptus cum terris et possessionibus multis postmodum vixit annis, regi Willelmo fideliter serviens, ac devote compatriotis placens et amicis, ac sic demum quievit in pace; cujus animæ propicietur Deus Amen'.

The statement in Geffrei Gaimar (§ 205) as to his murder by Norman knights is slightly supported by the Liber monasterii de Hyda [R. S.] p. 295: 'Post multas denique cædes atque seditiones, multa pacis fœdera cum rege facta et temerarie violata, quadam die cum omnibus sociis ab hostibus circumventus miserabiliter occubuit'.

The account in Ingulf (Fulm. p. 70) is not very intelligible: 'Solus prætactus Hewardus prospero fine remurmurabat'[1].

Ingulf says nothing about the second wife named Alftruda (Gaimar), 'quæ fuerat uxor Dolfini comitis' (Gesta Herwardi), nor do these books say anything concerning his burial.

Another account is given by Dugdale, 'History of Imbanking' (1662), p. 192, 'Ex vet. Rot. MS. penes Georgium Purefey de Wadley in com. Berks arm. anno 1653':

[1] Mr Riley translates the verb 'remurmurare' 'to enjoy (a prosperous end)' and Mr Stevenson 'to resist (with eventual success)', both evidently by mere conjecture. But Ingulf had previously said: 'Hewardus .... cum regia pace paterna obtenta hereditate, in pace dies suos complevit, et in monasterio nostro juxta suam uxorem nuperrime sepulturam elegit (Fulm. p. 68)', which agrees fairly well with the 'Gesta'.

'Yet afterwards he made his peace: And having issue one only daughter, called *Turfrida*, married to *Hugh de Evermue* Lord of DEPING (in LINCOLNSHIRE) with the Forest adjoining; entertaining the said *Hugh* upon a time, at his House in HUNTENDON; it happened that through a quarrel which arose there betwixt them, he was there wretchedly slain, by his said Son in law: and buried at CROULAND'.

220 This is found in Michel, Chron. Anglo-Norm. (ij. pref. p. xij. ff.) from a charter of the Cotton Library xiij. 9: 'Rôle de la Généalogie des seigneurs de Brunne et de Deeping', giving the descent of the family and peerage of Wake from Leofric earl of Chester and Hereward the Wake to Edmund Holland earl of Kent in 1407 (§ 227). This document also mentions his exploits and marriage with Turfrida in Flanders, his return to England, his recovery of his paternal estate, his subsequent long struggle against the power of king William, the marriage of his daughter also called Turfrida to Hugo de Ewuermothe, and his death at the hand of his son-in-law; and it ends: 'Iste Herwardus cum Turfrida sua prima uxore jacet apud Croyland tumulatus', no mention however being made of his second wife.

221 Matthew Paris in his 'Historia Anglorum' or 'Historia Minor' (R. S. j. 15 – 16) in a section, which is mostly original, has a very different termination to the story:

'Herewardus tamen comperiens hostes suos diatim sibi nocivum incrementum suscipere, assumptis secum sociorum suorum praelectis, cuneos inimicorum suorum pertranseundo potenter penetravit, et ceciderunt ab eo dissipati vel caesi a dextris et sinistris, et ad Scociam quantocius avolavit; unde adhuc Scocia, cum terris sibi conterminis, primitivo nobilium Anglorum sanguine purpuratur. Residui vero, qui in insula morabantur, tandem capti vel sponte sese regi praesentaverunt, quodlibet supplicium ad arbitrium ejus subituri. Herewardus vero cum suis complicibus regi, quam diu vixit, dampnose nimis et efficaciter adversabatur'.

Hereward is also mentioned, as taking part in the resistance of the exiles against king William, in an account of the monastery of Ely and its holding out against the king, contained in the Royal MS. (Brit. Mus.) 18. C. 1.

222 In the Chronica Majora (R. S. ij. 7) Matth. Paris says:

'Quod cum adversarii ejus (regis Willelmi) cognovissent, omnes, praeter solum Herewardum, qui socios suos ab insula potenter eduxit, ad manum

venientes, Willelmo sese praesentaverunt, quodlibet supplicium subituri
.... Herewardus vero, quamdiu superfuit, regi Willelmo paravit insidias exquisitas'.

In the Liber de Hyda (R. S. App. Chron. Mon. de Hida **223** from MS. Cott. Domit. A. xiv. p. 295) the following curious account of Hereward is to be found :

'Alius quoque extitit, genere quidam infimus, sed animo et viribus praecipuus, vocabulo Herewardus, qui temptans rebellare, conducta undique valida manu mediterranea Angliae loca, in quorum paludibus delitescebat, die et nocte caede et rapina complebat. Inter cetera autem scelera sua Fredericum germanum Comitis Willelmi de Warennia (Franc. Michel ij. 46), genere et possessionibus insignitum, nocte quadam in domo propria fraudibus circumventum occidit. Pro cuius nece tantae inter ipsum et praedictum Willelmum ortae sunt discordiae, ut nulla satisfactione nulla regia (sic) potuerint quiescere. Fertur denique quia semel cum quoddam castrum virtute vellet irrumpere, nec posset, mortuum se finxerat, feretroque impositum cum fallaci luctu ad ecclesiam ipsius castri incautis habitatoribus deferri sepeliendum jusserat. Mox ut securis illatum animadvertit, feretro totus armatus exsiluit castrumque cum habitatoribus fallaciter subjugavit. Post multas denique caedes atque seditiones, multa pacis foedera cum rege facta et temerarie violata, quadam die cum omnibus sociis ab hostibus circumventus miserabiliter occubuit.'

Dugdale in his 'History of Imbanking' has much about **224** Hereward, pp. 186-192; he quotes, besides Ingulf, 'ex vet. membr. penes Georgium Purefey de Wadley in Com. Berks. arm. an. 1653', 'ex registr. de Peterborough penes Will. Pierpont arm.', 'ex hist. eccl. Elien. in bibl. Bodl.', 'ex hist. Elien. eccl. in bibl. Cotton: [sub effigie Titi] A. 1'.

In the account of Lincolnshire in his Britannia [8°. 1590, p. **225** 423, 4°. 1600, pp. 473-4, fo. 1607, p. 400] Camden thus refers to Hereward :

'Vltra vix ad sex milliaria extenditur Hoylandia nostra, quam vniuersam Guilielmi Primi largitione accepit Yuo Tailbois Andegauensis, cuius insolentiam non ferens Herwardus Anglus vir spei bonae, atque acris animi plenus, filius Leofrici Domini de Brune, siue Burne cum sua, et suorum salus iam ageretur, baltheo militari à Brunno (sic) Petriburgensi Abbate, cuius stomachus in Normannos etiam erumperat, cinctus, bellum in illum mouit, saepius fudit; demum me captiuum abduxit' 'et ita redimi passus est, ut ipse in regis gratiam receptus in eius fide, et clientela diem obierit. Hoc etiam meruit virtus, quae et in hoste laudatur [cf. Fulm. p. 71]'.

It would however appear, that it was abbot Turold, whom Hereward took prisoner, not Ivo Tailbois.

226 In the Cartularium monast. de Ramescia (R. S. j. 44) we find mention of Agnes Hereward and Stephen Hereward, belonging probably to the 13th century. Radulphus Hereward is found c. 1280 in 'Gesta abb. S. Albani' [R. S.] j. 479, John and Adam Hereward c. 1330 in Gesta ij. 265, 266; and Hereward, a tenant of the monastery of Abingdon, c. 1160–1180 is mentioned in 'Chron. monast. de Abingdon' [R. S.] ij. 302.

In Ingulf and in MSS. of Hen. Hunt. the name occurs in three forms: Heward, Herward, Hereward. In Hamilton Inquis. Comit. Cantabr. we find (pp. 53, 75, 76) 'Hæc terra inveniebat .i. averam et unum hewardum', with the variation 'incuuard'.

227 It is not clear, how the name Wake came to be applied to Hereward; it is not so used in the Ingulf, or in the Pet. Bles., or in the Gesta Herwardi, or in the Liber Eliensis; Joh. Petrib. alone calls him 'Herewardus le Wake'.

There was a family of Wac or Wake (§ 220), which belonged to Normandy, having lands in the Cotentin and in Guernsey; it had estates also in Bucks. Of this family three in direct descent were named Baldwin; the last of them, who died in 1206, is mentioned in the Hist. Croyl. They became lords of Depyng. Thomas lord Wake dying without issue, his sister Margaret brought the estates of her family to her husband Edmund of Woodstock earl of Kent, son of Edward I., by whom she was mother of Joan the fair maid of Kent, ancestress of the Hollands. The father of the first Baldwin was Henry Wac, who is represented in Dugdale as marrying Emme the granddaughter of Richard Rulos and daughter of Baldwin Fitz Gilbert[1].

xx. Earl Waltheof, the martyr.

228 Siward, a Dane, was earl of Northumberland in the reign of Edward the Confessor. His daughter Sibylla married Duncan king of Scotland 1033–1039, who was murdered by Macbeth.

---
[1] Stapleton, Rot. Norm. ij; Roll of the Pipe 3 John 1301; Rotuli Normanniæ (Hardy) j. 122—143.

Siward avenged the death of his son-in-law, the young king Duncan, by the defeat in 1054 of the usurper, which was followed in 1056 by his death. Siward died in 1055 (Fl. Wig.), and his son Waltheof, who was 'adhuc parvulus' (H. Hunt., Joh. Brompton), obtained only the earldom of Northampton and Huntingdon, and that at a later period.

Abbat Brihtmer was followed by Wulget [Wulfgeat], pre- 229 viously abbat of Peykirk or Pegeland, who having been deprived, first of the site of his monastery by judicial sentence in favour of the monastery of Peterborough, and then of the other possessions of his house (Fulm. p. 63), was by the favour of the Confessor, in compensation, made abbat of Croyland. In his time Thorold the sheriff of Lincoln, brother of the countess Godgifu (Godiva) gave his manor of Spalding to Croyland by a charter dated 19 May 1051 (Fulm. pp. 86 – 7), but of this the monks were afterwards dispossessed by Ivo Tailbois in favour of the monastery of St Nicholas of Angers.

Among the alienated possessions of Pegeland, the manor of 230 Barnack Northants became the property of earl Siward, and, after his death, that of earl Waltheof. Abbat Wulget was succeeded by abbat Wulketul, and he sat till he was deprived in the reign of king William I., Ingulf of Fontenelle being his successor. Abbat Wulketul being engaged in rebuilding his church, earl Waltheof in 1061 (Fulm. p. 67) gave him for the work the lordship of Barnack, 'villam quae Berneche dicitur' (Ord. Vit.); on account of its stone quarries. This property the monastery lost after Waltheof's death.

Waltheof was not present at the battle of Senlac, but was 231 active against the Normans in the Northern counties and especially at York in 1069, till in 1070 he made his peace with William I. He is set down as one of the witnesses to William's charter to Wells dated [summer] 1068, given among the 'Secondary Documents' by Prof. Earle (Land charters, p. 433).

He soon afterwards married Judith the king's niece (Ellis Introd. j. 440), Adelaide William's whole sister and widow of Ingelram of Ponthieu having married secondly Lambert count of Lens, by whom she had two daughters, Judith the wife of

Waltheof and Adelaide the wife of Otho of Champagne earl of Holderness (Dugd. Bar. i. 60).

232 Waltheof was present at the marriage of Ralph de Wader at Exning Cambridgeshire, where some real or fancied grievances caused the guests to enter into a conspiracy against the king. In this Waltheof was to some slight extent implicated; but acting on the advice of archbishop Lanfranc, he crossed over into Normandy to the king, and disclosed the matter to him. The conspiracy having been crushed, the king kept Waltheof with him; but he was accused by his wife Judith of more than a mere knowledge of the plot, and was, after a year's deliberation, during which he was imprisoned at Winchester, at length beheaded there 31 May 1075 (Fl. Wig.) or 1076 (Freeman). But a fortnight afterwards (Fulm. p. 72), 'processu temporis' (Fl. Wig.), Judith, 'whether to save appearances, or really smitten with remorse by the blow, which had made her a widow' (Freeman), requesting it, the king allowed Waltheof's body to be removed to Croyland monastery, and there abbat Wulketul buried him in the chapterhouse. The date of Waltheof's execution is variously given as 1075 (Fl. Wig.), 1076 (A.S.Chr. E, Freeman), 1077 (A.S.Chr. D), the conspiracy being always placed in the previous year.

233 The monks of Croyland, grateful for his benefaction, gladly gave his remains a final resting place, and requested Ord. Vit. to write his epitaph, which was as follows (Ord. Vit. ij. pp. 289 – 290):

'En tegit iste lapis hominem magnae probitatis!
Danigenae comitis Siwardi filius audax,
Wallevus comes eximius jacet hic tumulatus.
Vixit honorandus, armis animisque timendus;
Et tamen inter opes corruptibiles et honores
Christum dilexit, Christoque placere satogit.
Ecclesiam coluit, clerum reverenter amavit,
Praecipue monachos Crulandenses sibi fidos.
Denique judicibus Normannis ense peremptus,
Luce sub extrema Maji petit artubus arva.
Cuius heri globa Crulandia gaudet aquosa;
Quam, dum vivebat, valde reverenter amabat.
Omnipotens animae requiem det in aetheris arce!'

In Hamilton Inquisitio Comitatus Cantabr. we find mention of several persons connected with Waltheof, as: 'quidam sochemannus de Coṁ Wallef' and 'homo comitis Walleui' (pp. 51 ['Trumpington], 68 [Comberton], 69 [Barton], 86 [Hinxton], 92 [Over], 94 [Stanton], 115 [Westwick]).

Sixteen years after his death, in 1091 under William Rufus, **234** abbat Ingulf (Fuhn. p. 101) translated Waltheof's remains into the church near the altar.

Here there is a difference in words between Ord. Vit. and the Ingulf; in the former it is said, that the monks were prepared to wash the bones in warm water, while according to the latter they expected to find the body 'in cineres resolutum', only the dry bones remaining, and nothing is said of any proposed washing. The martyr's body was found uncorrupted; the head was so reunited to the body, that a red line round the neck was the only mark of what Waltheof had undergone.

On 17 March 1219 abbat Henry de Longchamp placed his remains in a marble tomb, engraved with the effigy of the earl. In the account of this second translation (Michel, Chron. Anglo-Norm. ij. 103), it is said to have taken place 129 years after Waltheof's decollation; but it really happened 129 years after the first translation. This second translation of St Waltheof is not recorded in the 'Historia Croylandensis'.

Mathilda, the eldest daughter of earl Waltheof, married **235** Simon of Senlis ('Silvectanensis') or of Saint-Liz ('de sancto Licio') earl of Northampton and Huntingdon; of their three children, Waltheof was abbat of Melrose 1148 – 1159, Simon was earl of Northampton and Huntingdon, and Henry was 'comes Northimbrorum' (Chron. de Mailros a. 1148, 1159). Adeliza or Alice, Waltheof's second daughter, married Ralph de Toesny, miscalled by Ingulf Tornacensis or of Tournay; his third daughter, who is nameless, married Robert de Tonnebrugge. Matilda the eldest daughter of the martyred earl contracted a second marriage with David who was king of Scotland 1124 – 53, and thereby became the ancestress of the Scottish kings of the direct line to Margaret the Maid of Norway (d. 1291) and also of Robert Bruce and his descendants of the house of Stuart (Freem. iv. 604 ff.).

236 Besides the account of Waltheof given in the ordinary chronicles, there is much information to be found in Francisque Michel, Chroniques Anglo-Normandes ij. pp. xx. ff. 99 ff. We find there:
    1. A short account of the passion and miracles of earl Waltheof by William monk of Croyland, mentioning the second translation of the earl by abbat Henry of Longchamp in 1219, ending with the epitaph of the earl in 13 pairs of rhyming hexameters;
    2. 'Gesta antecessorum comitis Waldevi';
    3. 'Vita et Passio venerabilis viri Gualdevi, comitis Huntendoniae et Norhantoniae';
    4. 'Epitaphium sancti Gualdevi comitis', being an account of him somewhat shorter than that in n° 1 (above) and ending with an abridged form of the epitaph in n° 1, consisting of lines 1 – 2, 9 – 10, 15 – 24 only.
    5. 'De comitissa [Juetta, Waldevi comitis relicta]', mentioning her descendants, and among them William the Lion king of Scotland 1165 – 1214;
    6. 'Miracula Sancti Waldevi gloriosi martyris', which are described as happening in some year between 18 May and 14 Aug.

237   Curiously Radulfus de Diceto thus speaks of Waltheof: 'Ecclesia quae dicitur Croilande a Walteolfo fundata est' [R. S. ij. 211], a statement also found in Leland's Extracts in Collect. [1770] j. 26, where it is noted that in his MS. over the word 'Walteulfo' is written 'Ethelwlpho'; Dr Stubbs the R. S. editor of R. de Diceto does not notice anything of the kind.

238   In the 'Liber de Hyda' [R. S.] p. 295 a similar statement is found, that Waltheof, there called 'Edmesau Waldeth', conspiring against the king, is put to death, 'itaque capite truncatus, corpus ejus ad quandam ecclesiam, quam maritimis locis construxerat, defertur, crebraque ad sepulchrum ejus usque hodie, ut aiunt, fiunt miracula'.

239   The chronicle of Pierre de Langtoft [R. S. j. 430] after describing the conspiracy of the earls at Exning, has the following lines on the death of Waltheof:

        'Le counte de la Marche, Whothe, le chef perdist,
        Le ray William a tort decoler ly fist
        Al mount de Wyncestre, ço parust saunz respyt.
        Sun cors est portez al monster, ou il gist;
        Deus i fist miracle en terre, kaunt homme ly mist;
        William de Malmesbyre le parle en sun escryt.'

In like manner in Orderic's opinion, to this judicial murder was due all the ill success, which befel the Conqueror from that time forward.

The account as given by Hardyng (§ 162) is as follows **240** (pp. 236, 237):

> 'The kynge Wylliam than came full glad agaiue,
> At Wynchestre he helde his parlement,
> Wher he than slewe for wrath and grete disdeyne
> The duke Waldeve, that no harm to him ment,
> But oonly for he counceled and consent
> To erle Edgare to gett his heritage
> Of England hole, and made to hym homage,
> Who duke was than of Northumberlonde
> And erle create was eke of Huntingdoñ,
> By chronicles olde as menne can understonde
> Entitelde hoole als and of Northamptoñ,
> Beheded he was by false ymagynacion;
> Whose hede together grewe to the necke againe,
> Buried at Croweland for sainct the sothe to saine.'

There is a Life of St Waltheof, 'Walthenus', a Cistercian **241** abbat of Melrose in Scotland, 'auctore Joscelino vel Jordano monacho Furnesiensi' in Acta Sanctorum Aug. j. 244–277 (Aug. 3). He was grandson of earl Waltheof, being son of his daughter Mathilda, who married Simon earl of Huntingdon, as above mentioned.

In the 'Liber Vitæ Dunelmiensis Eccl.' (p. 99. c) we find: 'Comes Patricius junior filius Waldevi comitis. Patricius avunculus ejus et Cecilia uxor ejus et Willelmus filius ejus.'

In the Heimskringla (8° Christiania 1868) p. 624 are some **242** verses on Waltheof by Thorkell Skallason quoted in Freeman (iv. 269, 597). I am indebted to Mr Eiríkr Magnússon for the following very close translation of them:

> 'The terror-boding battle-sire (Waltheof)
> Let burn to death in flaming fire
> One hundred of king William's host—
> What dreadful night of human roast!
> Beneath the claws—so people say—
> Of troll-wights' colts (wolves) the warriors lay;
> The wild-woods' dusky-coated steed (the wolf)
> On Frenchmen's corpses stilled his greed.'

and:
> 'For sure did William—he, who steel
> Hath often reddened, and with keel
> From south did cleave the hoary sea,—
> Betray bold Walthiof dastardly:
> At arms my lord was bold and deft,
> No nobler sire was yet bereft
> Of life. In England 'twill be late
> Or e'er such murders shall abate.'

243 The name occurs as late as 1174, when 'Waldevus filius Baldewini de Biere' occurs in Bened. Abbas [R. S. j. 67] as one of them, who were captured with the king of Scotland at Alnwick.

xxj. Ivo Tailbois.

244 Ivo Tailbois is a Frenchman, who figures largely in the Ingulf and the Pet. Bles.; he is also mentioned in Joh. Petrib.

His name was Tailbois or Taille bois, in Domesday Tallebose or Taillgebose. He was a native of Anjou, even according to Ingulf and Joh. Petrib. 'Comes Andegavensis', and was 'lord of the whole of Hoyland of the King's gift', who, according to Ingulf (Fulm. p. 94) gave him to wife Lucia the sister of the two earls Eadwine and Morkere, after their death, together with all their lands, in 1071. Eadwine, indeed, was killed in 1071, but his brother Morkere submitted to king William and remained a prisoner in Normandy till the king's death in 1087, when he was released, but only to be put again in custody as before, by order of William Rufus.

The same mistake as to the deaths of the two earls is to be found in Will. Malm., who in his 'Gesta regum' [R. S. ij. 311], states, that they were slain by their own followers, 'suorum perfidia trucidati'. It is made also by Joh. Petrib., who borrows the words just quoted s. a. 1073, although s. a. 1087 he mentions the release and reimprisonment of Morkere; it is found also in Hardyng (§ 248).

Ivo Tailbois is spoken of as being a bitter enemy to Croyland, seeking to do it harm on all possible occasions (Fulm. p. 71). He is mentioned as taking possession of Durham Castle for king William in 1080, in the tract 'De injusta vexatione Willelmi' (in Sym. Dun. [R. S.] j. 192).

He is not mentioned in Ord. Vit., but is found in Domesday and in Cartul. Rames. [R. S.] j. 233.

Pet. Bles. (Fulm. pp. 124, 125) speaks of him as having **245** induced king William to make use of the power of a certain sorceress 'sacrilega' against Hereward in the Isle of Ely, but with no good result, as the bridge and all other siege works made by the king's army were fired, and his soldiers and the sorceress herself were destroyed, by Hereward.

After joining Robert duke of Normandy, for which he was outlawed from England, Ivo deserted from him, when he found his power declining, and returned to the service of Henry I. king of England. Robert having been taken prisoner by Henry in 1106, Ivo retired to Spalding, where Lucia his wife had been living, and there he died, a few years after, of paralysis (Fulm. p. 125).

Lucia, the 'long lived and often wedded' daughter of earl **246** Ælfgar, but not his 'filia unica' (Fulm. p. 66), was married to Ivo sometime after 1071 (1073 Joh. Petrib.), and he died c. 1110; as her father died in 1059 (Fulm. p. 66, 1062 ? E. A. F.), her brothers earls Eadwine and Morkere were grown men in 1066, and her sister Ealdgith, the wife of Harold II. (whom Ord. Vit. ij. 183 apparently speaks of as the only daughter of earl Ælfgar, mentioning as his children the two earls and 'Aldit'), was previously widow of Gruffydd ap Llywelyn king of North Wales, who was killed in Aug. 1063, she must have been born about 1050, being consequently 60 years old at the death of Ivo; yet Pet. Bles. makes her then marry Roger de Romara after the short widowhood of one month (Fulm. p. 125).

She is even credited with a third husband, Ranulf earl of Chester, in Leofric's genealogy (ad calcem Florentii Wigorn. MS. penes Archiep. Armachanum an. 1649) printed in Dugdale Monast. [1816] iij. 192 [Coventry Monastery] (Ellis Introd. to Domesd. i. 490'), and a son Ranulf 'postea comitem Cestriæ' (Camden, Brit. 1586 p. 307). The wife of Roger de Romara was probably a younger Lucia, the daughter of the elder Lucia.

Roumare is in the dep. of the Seine-Inférieure in the neighbourhood of Rouen.

The entry in Hunter's Magnus Rotulus Scaccarii 31 H. I. [Linc. p. 110] concerning the countess Lucy is as follows:

'Lucia Comitissa Cestr. red*didit* compot*um* de .cclxvj. li. *et* .xiij. *solidis et* .iiij. *den.* pro te*r*ra pat*r*is sui. In thesauro .clxvj. li. *et* .xiij. *solidos et* .iiij. *den.*

Et debet .c. li. Et .D. m*arcas* argenti ne capiat virum infra .v. annos.

Et Eadem Comitissa redd*idit* compot*um* de .xlv. m*arcis* argenti pro eadem conventione ad dand*um* quib*us* rex voluerit. Regin*e* .xx. m*arcas* argenti.

Et debet .xxv. m*arcas* argenti. Et eadem debet .c. m*arcas* argenti ut possit ten*e*re rectum in curia sua inter homines suos.'

247 In Stapleton's Magni Rotuli Scaccarii Normanniæ (2 vols. 8° London [Soc. of Antiq.] 1840 – 44) Vol. ij. pp. cliij, cliv, some further information is to be found respecting the family of the two Lucias. The story of Lucia has been discussed by Mr J. G. Nichols in an article on the earldom of Lincoln in the Topogr. and Genealogist [1846] j. 9 ff. 301 ff., and in one in the Lincoln volume of the Archæol. Institute (8° Lond. 1850) pp. 253 ff., entitled 'On the descent of the earldom of Lincoln', and by Mr Freeman (ij. Ed. III. 682).

According to Mr Nichols 'there is ample evidence of the reality of such a person as the countess Lucy', the wife of Ivo Tailbois; unfortunately he mentions only 'the Croyland Chronicles', and a charter of Ivo dated 1085 (Dugdale (1816) iij. p. 216, no. 5), giving the church of Spalding Linc. to the priory of St Nicholas at Angers. She is also mentioned in Joh. Petrib. s. a. 1073, 1074.

248 The marriage of Lucia with Ivo Tailbois is mentioned in Hardyng's Chronicle (§ 162) p. 236; Hardyng died in 1465.

> 'Edwyn the erle proclamed of Leicester,
> After decesse of Algary his father dere
> And erle Morcare his brother that after
> Dyed bothe twoo, Lucy their suster clere
> Of Leicester then and Lyncolne both in fere
> The countesse was, whome kyng William maried
> To Ivo Tailboys erle of Angeou magnified.'

Here we see the same mistake made of calling Algar earl

of Leicester (Legraceaster, Legereyester, Ligoraceaster), instead of earl of Chester (Legaceaster, Ligeceaster) in accordance with H. Hunt. who calls him 'Consul Cestriæ', and also the further mistake of making Ivo Tailbois earl or count of Anjou.

In Ord. Vit., of Ivo Tailbois and therefore of his marriage there is no mention; but in Joh. Petrib. a few notices of him occur. In 1073 after the death of Eadwine **and** Morkere, their sister Lucia was given by the king in marriage to Ivo with all her lands. In 1074 Ivo Tailbois, 'comes Audegavensis', lord of Spalding and of all Holland, gave the cell of Spalding, which had been endowed by Thorold the 'avunculus' of Lucia, the brother of Godiva wife of Leofric earl of Leicester (so also Fulm. p. 86), to the abbey of St Nicholas of Angers.

He is mentioned frequently in the 'Gesta Herwardi' and in the 'Liber Eliensis', but not as being in any way connected with Croyland.

In Domesday he is found both as tenant in capite in Lincolnshire [xiiij. 'Terra Ivonis Taillgebosc' (photozincogr. pp. xxix – xxxij)] and Norfolk (Ellis j. 490), and as tenant of lands belonging to the abbey of Peterborough and others. C. G. Smith in his Translation of that portion of Domesday Book, which relates to Lincolnshire and Rutlandshire (8°. Lond. 1870), though knowing the charge of spuriousness brought against the Ingulf, has a full account of Ivo derived from the Ingulf and from the Pet. Bles.

Two other persons of the same name are found, 'filia Radulfi Tailgebosch', and 'Willelmus Tailgebosch' (Ellis Introd. j. 490). The former held lands in Hertfordshire, the latter in Lincolnshire.

xxij. Alliteration in the Ingulf.

Ingulf is very fond of stringing together a series of words beginning with the same letter, or of words of somewhat similar sound. Thus we find:

p. 8. meruit sive mortem sive membrorum suorum mutilationem, si ministri mei . . . . ;

p. 15. maneria, mansiones, molendina, mersca et mariscos . . . . ;
p. 28. prudenter præditus et pollens tam profunda peritia . . . . ;
p. 40. cum totius conventus sui consensu communi chirographo sui capituli confirmavit . . . . ;
p. 57. comitis confessore, consulente et crebro commonenti . . . . ;
p. 63. misertus etiam vestri, qui non vestra volentia, sed mortis violentia vestrum patrem (p. 64) nuper perdidistis...scilicet prædictum patrem Wlgatum vobis in prælatum præficiendo . . . . ;
p. 65. multa hominum milia morerentur: misericordia motus...... sapienter consulere suppliciter supplicans . . . . ;

and again:

p. 7. prece pretioque; p. 11. nec more nec amore; p. 22. examinati et exanimati; p. 25. plāgam . . . . plāga; p. 26. durius ac diutius; p. 40. impunitatem vel immunitatem; p. 71. torquens et tribulans, angens et angarians, incarcerans et excrucians; p. 74. emundare et emendare; p. 102. mœstus ac mœrens; p. 103. fidus et fidelis; p. 107. risu et derisu.

This alliteration is found also in Pet. Bles. (§ 480).

xxiij. Discrepant marks of the date of the writer (Ingulf).

252 There are many expressions in the Ingulf, which would seem to point out the time of the composition, but they are either not intelligible or not consistent. Thus:

Fulm. p. 57 the manor of Badby was granted to Evesham c. 1013 'per firmam in grano piperis' for 100 years, at a time however, 'when manors did not exist', when 'a demise for a term of years was unknown in England .. and a reservation of a peppercorn rent a thing equally unheard of' (Riley), 'et ultra terminum firmæ adhuc retinetur', so that Ingulf's history would apparently be written after the year 1113. But

p. 85 we read: 'cum adhuc viginti anni de firma illorum restent, antequam centum anni concessi in eo *Normanno* quondam *Edrici* Comitis Vicecomiti compleantur'. The history therefore was in hand in 1093.

p. 61 Wulfsy the recluse was still 'hucusque' living at Evesham, but as he died 1097 (Fl. Wig.) or 1104 (Joh. Petrib.) Ingulf's history would be written before 1097 or at all events before 1104.

p. 64 Bishop Agelwine of Durham 'permansit in eo usque

ad hæc tempora nostra'. Agelwine was bishop 1056 to 1071 (1072), while Ingulf did not become abbat till 1075 (Fulm.) or 1085 (A.S.Chr. A lat. app.).

p. 68 Turfrida, the wife of Hereward, died 'vix æstate quarta jam transacta', 'hardly four summers since' (Riley). This would make her live to the end of the 11th century c. 1090. Hereward was buried by her side at Croyland 'nuperrime', having ended his days in peace (§ 207).

p. 73 The grandchildren of earl Waltheof are spoken of as 'adhuc impuberes et infantes'. As Waltheof married Judith after Jan. 1070, his eldest daughter would be born in 1071. The eldest grandchild might be born c. 1090, so that the date of writing must be some years after 1093.

p. 73 William I. is spoken of as 'inclytus nunc rex noster Angliæ'; he died in 1087, which would apparently put the date of the composition before 1087. His death however is mentioned at p. 106.

p. 82 King Henry is spoken of as 'qui modo regnat in Francia'. This was Henry I. 1031-1060. This mention of him occurs after the Ingulfine transcript of the Domesday of 1086.

xxiv. Chronological and historical mistakes in the Ingulf.

Many mistakes are to be found 1. in the charters, 2. in the history itself of the abbey, and 3. in the general history, which is incorporated in Ingulf's work. They are all no doubt very great, and have been pointed out by several critical writers.

The chief works and articles, which allude to them are:

Henry Wharton, Historia de episcopis et decanis Londinensibus, nec non Assavensibus 8° Lond. 1695.

Geo. Hickes D.D. Antiquæ literaturæ septentrionalis thesaurus 2 vols. fo. Oxf. 1705. In the second vol. is his 'Dissertatio epistolaris De antiquæ litteraturæ septentrionalis utilitate' fo. Oxf. 1703.

Sir Francis Palgrave, 'On the sources of Anglo-Saxon History' in Quart. Rev. 1826 (xxxiv pp. 248-298) pp. 259 ff.

H. T. Riley B.A. Ingulph's Chronicle of the abbey of Croyland.... translated from the latin. 8° Lond. (Bohn) 1854. Introduction and notes.

H. T. Riley M.A. 'The history and charters of Ingulfus considered,' in Archæol. Journ. 1862 pp. 32 ff. 114 ff.

Sir T. Duffus Hardy, Descriptive Catalogue of materials relating to the history of Great Britain and Ireland [R. S.] (8° Lond. 1862) Vol. II pp. 58 ff.

255 Some of these writers, however, in their anxiety to expose the mistakes, and thereby to disprove the genuineness, of the first two portions of the 'Historia Croylandensis', have not only forgotten the numerous anachronisms and mistakes to be found in undoubted mediæval histories, such as those, which are noted in the Prefaces in the R. S. (cf. Annales Monastici j p. xxxij; ij p. xxvii, xlvii; iij p. xxx; iv p. lj; Barth. de Cotton p. xxxiij), and such as Le Prévost notes in nearly every page of his Ord. Vit., but have also, in addition, made mistakes quite as serious as those which they are dragging to light. Ingulf has quite enough to answer for, without being burdened with the mistakes of his critics.

256 a. Sir F. Palgrave has transferred the 'sacrorum librorum ingens bibliotheca' burnt by the Danes in 870 (Fulm. p. 23) from Peterborough to Croyland; the restoration under Eadred in 948 he puts under Ecgberht (d. 837); this restoration under 'Ecgberht' he dates in 966; the manor of Badby he calls Baddeley; the Formulare Anglicanum of Thomas Madox he attributes to one Maddox; the five chapters of the laws of king William, which Spelman transcribed from the 'autographum' at Croyland, nos. I, XVII, XVIII, XX, XXXVI, he speaks of as 'the first chapters of the Norman laws'.

257 b. Sir Th. D. Hardy, besides the slip of mentioning the Ingulf as being printed first in the 'Decem Scriptores' of Twysden (1652) instead of in the 'Scriptores post Bedam' of Savile (1596), has in his account of Ingulf made two unaccountable blunders. Ingulf states, that the name of Philip was so common among the Franks, that king Henry, 'qui modo regnat in Francia', had given that name to his eldest son. Hardy rushes to the conclusion, that the prince mentioned by Ingulf was Philip Augustus, and shews up the anachronism, as exposing the late date of the work, since Philip Augustus was born 22 Aug. 1166. But herein he is wrong, for

Philip Augustus is Philip II, and Philip I was born in 1053 and reigned 1060–1108, succeeding his father Henry I who reigned 1031–1060, whereas Philip Augustus 1180–1223 was a contemporary of Richard I and John, and his father was Louis VII.

Again he calls the father of Eadgar Ætheling Edmund, his name being Eadward.

c. In his translation of the History of Croyland, the cheapest and most widespread form of the Ingulf, and one which Mr Kingsley seems to have used for his Hereward, Mr Riley, who always calls sir Henry Savile Saville, has on the same page (p. 165) two most remarkable mistakes.

In Domesday it is stated, that at Cottenham Cambridgeshire the monastery possessed, besides other lands, meadow land of eight carucates, some pasture land 'ad pecuniam villae', and from the fens 500 eels. (A rent in eels [Ellis Introd. ¡ pp. 103, 140 ff.] is mentioned in the 'Liber Eliensis' B. ij. ch. 21 : 'Wine liberavit abbati in Grantebrucge liii acras et unum gurgitem valentem mille anguillas'.) The passage stands thus in Domesday and in Fulm. p. 82 respectively.

'Ibi ·1· serv*us*. Prat*um* .viij. car^7. Past*ura* ad pecun^7
'Ibi unus servus, pratum, et octo acræ, pastur. ad pet.
uille.　　　De maresch. q*u*ingent^7 anguill'.　et de
villæ　　　de marisco　　D.　　^{J}Aug.　　et de
præsentat^7 .xij. den^7.　　In totis ualent^7 ual*et* et
　præsent. xij. d. .... val ...
valuit .vj. lib.　　T·R·E·　viij lib'　..............
.... tempore regis Ed. octo libris, modo sex lib.'

Fulman puts in his lower margin : '^{J}Angill'. Out of this Riley makes the following translation : 'There is also one serf, and a meadow, and eight acres of pasture land, granted at the prayer of the vill, in the marshes of the lord Angill, and at present paying twelve pence : in the time of king Edward, it was valued at eight pounds, but now at six'. In a note he draws attention to the probable correctness of this translation ; 'ad pecuniam villæ' (made by Fulm. into 'ad pet. villæ') means 'for the cattle of the village', not (as in Riley) 'at the prayer of the vill'.

259   In Ingulf's explanation of a few difficulties connected with the Domesday record according to his transcription, speaking of the name Philip already referred to above, he says (Fulm. p. 82), that in the Scythian tongue 'leucon' means 'Philippus', and continues:

'Unde Magister in *Isagogis* suis [super] O. M. lib. III. & *niveus leucon*, dicit ibi, hunc *leucon* fuisse *Philippum* Imperatorem, qui *niveus* descriptus est, quia *Christianus*, & baptismo super *nivem* dealbatus'.

The 'Magister' and his 'Isagogæ' have not been traced, but the reference is to Ovid Met. iij. 218, 'Et niveis Leucon et villis Asbolus atris', Leucon and Asbolus being two of Actæon's dogs. And Riley has this note: 'It is probable that by the words, super. O. M. Lib. III., he alludes to the Ormista, or History of Orosius; which is supposed to have received its name from the words "Orosii mundi historia".'

Bale mentions several early commentators on Ovid's Metamorphoses, but all very late compared with abbat Ingulf:

<table>
<tr><td>Alexander Necham</td><td>cent. III,</td><td>no. 86. p. 272.</td><td>c. 1227.</td></tr>
<tr><td>Joannes Gualensis</td><td>cent. IV,</td><td>no. 28. p. 317.</td><td>c. 1250.</td></tr>
<tr><td>Joannes Grammaticus</td><td>— —</td><td>no. 40. p. 325.</td><td>c. 1270.</td></tr>
<tr><td>Nicolaus Triveth</td><td>cent. V,</td><td>no. 23. p. 399.</td><td>d. 1328.</td></tr>
<tr><td>Joannes Ridewell</td><td>— —</td><td>no. 37. p. 408.</td><td>c. 1330.</td></tr>
</table>

Besides this we have the following statement in Joh. Petrib. (MS. Cott. Claud. A. v.):

1366. 'Inv[enta] est primo grossa historia totius sacræ paginæ in fabulis Ovidii Metamorphosis a fratre Waltero de Burgo, quondam monacho de Revesby' (Dugd. Mon. v. 453 ff.).

260   Another most startling statement of the translator is, that St Pega, Guthlac's sister, travelled to the threshold of the apostles, and that 'on entering the city of Rome, after suddenly causing all the bells to ring for the space of one hour, she proclaimed to the citizens the merits of her sanctity', the latin being: 'cumque civitatem Romanam ingrederetur, omnium signorum classicum repentinum personans, per spatium unius horæ, sanctitatis ejus meritum universis civibus indicavit' (Fulm. p. 5).

261   Dr Lappenberg in his 'Einleitung' 'Introduction' (not

'Preface', as Riley gives it) to his 'Geschichte von England' (Vol. I. 8° Hamb. 1834) pointed out the mistake in Ingulf's statement, that the Henry I, king of Germany, who died in 936, sought for the hand of the 'englische Königstochter' (the english princess) for his son Otho after the battle of Brunanburh, which was fought in 937, the marriage having really taken place in 924; but Riley translates the German words 'Athelstan's daughter', whereas his Ingulf told him rightly, that she was Æthelstan's sister.

In his translation of Eadgar's charter to Peterborough of 970 he translates: 'unum monetarium in Stamford .... [concedimus]' 'the sole right of coinage in Stamford', instead of 'one moneyer at Stamford', as the A.S.Chr. E has it.

'Transiens ex hoc mundo ad Patrem de sudoribus Abbathiæ ad sinum Abrahæ' (Fulm. p. 52) is by Mr Riley strangely translated: He 'departed this life, quitting the labours of the abbacy for the bosom of his father Abraham', not seeing the reference to John xiij. 1.

Riley says further (p. 177): 'The "ora" [Fulm. p. 88] was a Danish silver coin probably about ten shillings in value', at a time when pennies weighing c. 20 gr. and of the size of a modern sixpence were the only silver currency. It was a money of account frequently mentioned in Domesday as of the value of twenty pence [Ellis Introd. j. 165].

After the fire of 1091 Ingulf speaking of the restoration of the minster says: 'imponentes novam navim tecto ecclesiæ pro vetusta quæ combusta fuerat' (Fulm. p. 101); this Riley translates: 'we placed a new nave beneath the roof of the church, in place of the old one, which had been burnt'.

He also turns 'Anno...pontificatus Domini Papæ Alexandri xj' into 'In the pontificate of our lord the pope, Alexander XI', although Fulman has in the margin 'Alex. 2. p', and although Alexander VIII is the last pope of that name; again 'in strato stertere aut lateri indulgere' (Fulm. p. 112) is made to mean 'to indulge himself in snoring in bed or lying concealed', while 'ductus sōli cupiditate' is rendered 'induced by cupidity alone'; other mistakes will have to be pointed out. He has also omitted in his translation many passages and single words.

It may be therefore doubtful, whether he is quite justified in finding fault with even Ingulf's blunders.

284   d. Sharon Turner in his 'History of the Anglo-Saxons' 8º Lond. 1852) iij. 47 has an account of the gilt cup, which king Wiglaf gave to the monks of Croyland (Fulm. p. 9). It was chased without with savage vinedressers fighting with dragons, and the king called it his 'crucibŏlum' or cross bowl, because a cross was marked within the cup, 'cum quatuor angulis simili impressione protuberantibus', 'and it had four angels projecting like a similar figure' (Turner).

265   e. Sir Frederick Madden even, in his 'Historia Minor' of Matthew Paris [R. S.] ij. 15, prints in the text, '....si sine herede moriretur', with the note 'moriretur] moreretur ms'.

266   f. A description of the soil of Croyland and the means taken by Æthelbald king of Mercia the founder to improve it, is given by Ingulf (Fulm. p. 4) in a paragraph, which Dr Hickes suggests to be spurious; it is however taken almost verbatim from Ord. Vit. (ij. 280).

267   g. Pits, 'De Angliæ scriptoribus' (4º Paris 1619) p. 193 has the following remarks: 'In eo sanè multum laudandus [Ingulphus], quod gratia, qua pollebat apud principes plurimùm, usus sit non tam ad suum privatum, quàm ad publicum ordinis sui commodum. Unde inter alia à Rege Henrico primo [1100-1135] amplissima privilegia pro suo monasterio partim de novo obtinuit, partim vetera confirmari fecit, ut ipse testatur'. This is however quite wrong, as Henry's charter (Fulm. p. 121) was granted not to Ingulf, but to his successor Joffrid.

Fulman ('Lectori') has the following statement derived from Pits: 'Scripsit [Ingulfus] etiam librum De vita et Miraculis S. Guthlaci, Croylandensium Patroni, ut ipse testatur, qui tamen hodie extare non videtur'. It seems to come from the following statement of Ingulf (§ 65, 74): 'Defuncto igitur et sepulto Dei famulo *Guthlaco*, signa virtutum ac sanitatum...coruscare frequenter cœperunt, ut in libro de vita ac miraculis ejus clarius et luculento stylo (prout de memorandis vestris colligere potui) seriatim panduntur' (Fulm. p. 2; 'de memorandis viris' Savile Birch).

h For J. G. Nichol's statement concerning the name 'Egga' see § 387.

i. Cardinal Bellarmine, who seems to have known Savile's Scriptores, can yet write ;

'De Ingulpho Anglo 1077. Ingulphus Abbas in Anglia vivebat anno Dom. 1050, ut ipse testatur in fine historiae suae: sed supervixit usque ad annum Dom. 1100. Scripsit historiam Monasteriorum Angliae, quae amplissima erant, sed attingit multa, quae ad res gestas Regum Angliae pertinent. Incipit ab anno Dom. 664 et desinit anno Dom. 1067, quo Rex Vvillelmus primus regnare coepit. Extat hic auctor cum aliis, qui de rebus Anglicanis scripserunt' (Bellarminus de Scriptt. eccles. 4° Rom. 1613 p. 177).

---

268 Apart from the statements pertaining to Croyland abbey solely, which receive as a rule no corroboration from other writers, and the wording and names of the witnesses to the charters, Ingulf's chief mistakes, or supposed mistakes, not always due to Ingulf himself, are the following.

269 He makes Æthelbald of Mercia great nephew of king Penda through Alweo 'his brother' (Fulm. p. 2), following herein Will. Malm. Gesta regum [R. S.] j. 79, instead of saying his 'nephew', according to A.S.Chr. and Fl. Wig. (a. 716).

270 The Ingulfine date of the foundation of Croyland Monastery 716 must be wrong, as according to Fl. Wig. St Guthlac died 11 Apr. 714, and Felix writing c. 730 gives no intimation of the existence of any monastic establishment.

271 The mention of Black Monks and of the Rule of St Benedict in Æthelbald's charter of 718 (Fulm. p. 3) is the first of the alleged anachronisms noticed by Hickes: 'In istis vero temporibus regulam S. Benedicti habitumque nigrum, a quo monachi nigri appellabantur, nondum innotuisse ipse Mabillonius concedit De re diplomatica lib. i. p. 30'. He puts the rise of this name in the 11th century.

272 The place, where Æthelbald was killed in 755, is called by Fl. Wig. 'Seceeswalde' or 'Secgeswalde'; in this he is followed by Ingulf (Fulm. p. 5), who names it 'Seggeswold'. In the A.S.Chr. a. 755 and H. Hunt. it is called 'Secandune'; Matth.

Paris calls it 'Sacchenda'. Sym. Dun. gives no place and the year 757.

273 The names of the ancestors of king Offa exhibit that confusion between the P and the A.S. W which is elsewhere found; 'Eawa' and 'Pybba' of the A.S.Chr. and Fl. Wig. are given by Ingulf (Fulm. p. 5) as 'Eoppa' and 'Wibba'.

274 He, with Matth. Paris, in a passage which he transcribes from Fl. Wig. a. 794 (Fulm. p. 6), and with the Chron. Monast. de Abingdon [R. S.] j. 18, calls the son and successor of Offa king of Mercia, Egbert; his name was really Ecgfirth or Egfrith (A.S.Chr. Fl. Wig. l. c. Sym. Dun. Hoveden, Matth. Paris). He was consecrated as king c. 787, and signs some charters as 'rex' or 'rex Merciorum' with the name Ecgfrith, but reigned after his father's death only 141 days. A coin of EGCBERHT REX struck by a moneyer BABBA was formerly ascribed to this king, but is now restored to Ecgberht king of Kent 765 – 791? known by charters of 765, 779...(Kemble C. D. 113, 135, 160). Babba was indeed a moneyer of Offa, but one of the same name also was moneyer of Eadberht Pren king of Kent 796 – 798 (Keary, A. S. coins in the Brit. Mus. 8vo. Lond. 1887).

275 According to Riley the use of the word 'manerium' (Ellis Introd. j. 224 ff.), which occurs in the Ingulfine charters of Wiglaf (a. 833) and of Burgred (a. 868), and also in the charters of Ælfgar the knight (a. 825) and of Fregist the knight (a. 819) given by Gough, Croyl. App. pp. 44, 45, is a token of the late date of the composition of their charters, as being 'a term first introduced with the feudal system'. According to E. de Laveleye, Primitive property (8vo. Lond. 1878) p. 242 : ' In the tenth century—even before the Norman conquest—the mark had been already transformed into the manor, although the term was not yet in use'. The reign of Edward the Confessor is the first, in which they are mentioned; the expression 'tenuit de rege E. pro Manerio' is found frequently in the early part of the Survey (Ellis j. 225). It occurs constantly in the Domesday of 1086, and Ingulf was abbat 1085 – 1108.

276 Concerning the word 'miles' knight see § 377 and concerning the word 'leuca' league see § 21. Both these words are said to have come into use, the former with its special meaning, in Norman times.

The daughter of Offa king of the Mercians, who was affianced 277 'sponsa' to St Æthelberht ('Eielbrihtus' Will. Malm.) king of the East Angles, is named by Ingulf (and by Mabillon Acta Sanct. ord. S. Bened. sæc. iv. pars 1. p. 565) Etheldritha, ('Æthelthryth') (Fulm. p. 7). Her name really was Ælfthryth, Alftrida, as is found also in Capgrave Nova Legenda Angliæ (1516) fo. 137 b. col. 2. l. 14. According to Capgrave (fo. 138 b. col. 1), on the death of Æthelberht Ælfthryth declares: 'Croulandiæ paludes Christo disponente videbo, ibique solitariam vitam emulari incipiam, et conventus hominum evitare discam'; Ingulf speaks of her as having become a recluse in the south side of the church of Croyland in a cell 'contra magnum altare', and says, that king Wiglaf, being pursued by Ecgberht king of Wessex and taking refuge at Croyland, lay hid in Ælfthryth's cell for four months: this is not corroborated by the early historians, and the Acta Sanctorum of the Bollandists (Aug. Vol. i. pp. 173 - 5) have no other authority for the statement than Ingulf.

She is also mentioned in John Brompton, Twysden i. 750 - 52: 'Virgo igitur *Althrida* quæ et secundum quosdam dicitur *Alfrida*, castitatem corporis sui Deo devovens, ad palustres *Croylandiæ* tanquam ad heremum curavit finaliter se transferre, ubi contemplationi penitus et devotioni dedita, talari tunica induta, in omni sanctitate vitæ permansit, eligens magis abjecta esse in domo Domini, quam habitare in tabernaculis peccatorum'; and in Polydore Vergil (c. 1525) we find: 'Ipsa vero [Alfreda] virginitate Deo dicata, ad locum cui nomen est Crolandia se contulit, ibique sanctissime vitam egit. Is locus admodum palustris inter Elym insulam et Nynam flumen, olim circiter annum salutis DCXCV cœpit esse celebris, ob memoriam divi Guthlaci monachi, ubi ille diu habitavit et sepultus est. Quare postea mortales miraculis eodem loco visis adducti, cænobium monachorum ordinis Divi Benedicti ad ipsum Nynam posuerunt, quod vel hodie religione floret' (Anglicæ historiæ lib. xxvij fo. Basil 1557 p. 69); this last account does not shew any acquaintance with Ingulf's history.

278   Ingulf says, that Bertulph, Beorhtwulf king of Mercia 838 – 851 was brother of his predecessor king Wiglaf (Fulm. p. 11), but this seems to be wrong (Fl. Wig. s. a. 838 and Geneal.).

The names of the Mercian kings mentioned by Ingulf are fairly well given by him; even the form 'Beorred' (Fulm. p. 17) represents the pronunciation of the form Burhred given by Fl. Wig., though the coins read BVRGRED.

279   He speaks of a miraculous healing, in 851, of a kind of paralysis, attributed to the merits of St Guthlac on the ground of the peculiar subscriptions of some of the bishops appended to the charter of king Bertulph 'Beorhtwulf' of that date (Fulm. p. 16). This miracle must necessarily fall to the ground with the charter itself (Riley). There is no corroboration of this in any account of St Guthlac.

280   The printed text of Burgred's charter gives 'Snothryngham' as the A.S. name for Nottingham; in the A.S.Chr. however it is Snotengaham or Snotingaham; Fl. Wig. has the latter form. In the historical part of the Ingulf (Fulm. p. 18) it is given as 'Nothingham'; but in the continuation of Fl. Wig. s. a. 1140 it is still called 'Snottingaham', even Matth. Paris has 'Snotingaham'. In Hunter's Mag. Rot. Scacc. 31 H. 1 the county is called 'Notingehamscira'.

281   According to Ingulf (Fulm. p. 17) it was shortly after his return from Rome, that king Æthelwulf gave his celebrated, often recorded charter granting the tithe of his kingdom to the church, dated 'nonas Novembris' 5 Nov. 855. According to Fl. Wig. (Asser) the voyage to Rome was in 855 after the granting of the charter. This is so also stated by Will. Malm. G. R. ij. 114 and by Matth. Paris Chronica Majora j. 383 ff. with the date v Non. Nov. 854, an impossible date, iv Non. (2 Nov.) being the earliest day in the Calendar.

282   Ingulf calls the person, who was with king Ælfred in 872 in the isle of Athelney, his mother 'matrem', possibly by a mistake in expanding the contraction for 'ministrum', which is found in the Liber de Hyda [R. S.] p. 46. Judith the child-wife of king Æthelwulf, born not before the autumn of 843 and married in 855 at the age of not more than 13 years, returned to France upon the death of her stepson-husband Æthelbald in 861, and there married Baldwin count of Flanders. Ælfred's own mother was Osburh the daughter of Oslac the butler of king Æthelwulf (Asser). The story is taken from Higden [R.S.] vj. 342.

The division of England into counties 'comitatus' is claimed **283** by Ingulf for Ælfred (Fulm. p. 28). But 'it is evident from [Asser's] silence, that he was ignorant of any new institution of shires' (Lingard); and in the A.S.Chr. before the time of that king 871–901 mention is found of Defnascir' (a. 851), 'Hamtunscir' (a. 755, 860), 'Wiltunscir' (a. 870), 'Bearrucscir' (a. 860), while the other shires do not occur till later, a great number being mentioned in 1011.

The liber de Hyda, written after 1354 has the following (R.S. p. 42): 'Posthæc .. Alfredus .. suam provinciam divisit in comitatus, et comitatus dividebat in hundredas'. Dr Hickes in commenting on this (Dissert. Epist. p. 62ª) adds: 'Notandum præterea est, quam absurde *Ingulphus Decimas* cum *trithingis* confundit, quod nescio an à quoquam antea observatum est'. In his opuscula R. de Diceto (R.S. ij. 234) has similarly 'Rex Aluredus...decimas quas thiethingas vocant, instituit', derived from Will. Malm. Gesta regum [R.S.] j. 129.

According to Ingulf (Fulm. p. 27) the Mercian kingdom **284** came to an end in the year 875 (c. 878 A.S.Chr.) or c. 230 years from its beginning in the first year of Penda its first king, which would be the year 645 (648). But Penda became king in 626 (A.S.Chr. Fl. Wig. 627) or in 633 (Beda). H. Hunt., who is followed by subsequent historians, speaks of Creoda or Crida his grandfather as the first king of Mercia. John Speed in his 'History of Great Britaine' puts the beginning of that kingdom in 582 and its end in 886, with a duration of 202 years.

The statement, that Ælfred caused a roll to be compiled **285** very similar to the Domesday of 1086, has already been referred to (§ 18).

Among the seven bishops, who were consecrated by arch- **286** bishop Plegmund, Ingulf mentions Ceolwulf as bishop of Dorchester. His name was Coenwulf or Kenulf (Fl. Wig. Will. Malm. Matth. Paris). He is, with the same mistake, a signatary to Eadred's charter of 948, but unfortunately his successor Winsy subscribes already in 926. Stubb's Registrum accepts the name Ceolwulf (pp. 13, 162).

287   Ingulf's account of the doings of king Eadward the elder with respect to Mercia (Fulm. p. 28) is not clear: 'Quippe *Merciam* in manum suam sumens a duce Ethelredo, cui pater cum filia sua eam ante dederat, etiam *Norfolchiam*...bellando subegit....Multum adjuvit eum soror sua Ethelfleda, Ethelredi quondam ducis London. relicta,...' He incorporates in the paragraph, where these words occur, words from Will. Malm. Gesta regum [R. S.] i. 135, who thus writes: 'siquidem......iste primum, mortuo Etheredo, Mercios omnifariam,...suæ ditioni subegerit'. From A.S.Chr. (a. 912, 918), however, it appears, that the king 'took possession of London and Oxford and all the lands, which thereto belonged', but that for eight years, till her death, Æthelflæd 'rightfully held the lordship over the Mercians'. Æthelred and Æthelflæd describe themselves in a charter of 901 [Earle, p. 159; Kemble no. 330, Birch no. 587] as: 'opitulante gratuita Dei gratia monarchiam Merceorum tenentes' (Green, Conq. of Engl. p. 144^2); Fl. Wig. (a. 912) describes Æthelred as 'eximiæ vir probitatis, dux et patricius, dominus et subregulus Merciorum'. Fl. Wig. states also, that, after Æthelred's death in 912, king Eadward took possession of only London (see Fl. Wig. a. 886) and Oxford, leaving Mercia under the rule of his sister; but H. Hunt. says: 'Anno sequente, defuncto Edredo duce Merce, rex Edwardus saisivit Londoniam et Oxinefordiam, omnemque terram Mercensi provinciæ pertinentem (R. S. p. 155). Ingulf seems then to have followed herein Will. Malm. and H. Hunt. H. Hunt. a. 910 ff. makes Æthelflæd, the Lady of the Mercians, the daughter (not the widow) of Æthelred, and her daughter Ælfwyn her sister. His whole account of Æthelred and Æthelflæd is utterly wrong.

288   Mr Riley (Arch. Journ. 1862, p. 48) remarks: '*Theoricum verbum* [Fulm. p. 31], "the word of God"' [rather "the divine text"] 'is a phrase probably not to be found before the time of John of Genoa, whose Glossary was written in the thirteenth century'. But Dudo of St Quentin, whose history of the Normans comes down to 1002, has (Duchesne Hist.

Normann. Script. Antiqui, fo. Paris. 1619) θεορητικῆς (sic p. 101) and ΘΗΩΡΙΚΗC (sic p. 102). The passage runs thus: 'Sed si vi potestatis tuæ professor esse huius Monasterii, et regulæ ΘΗΩΡΙΚΗC viæ, relinquens seculum, incumbere malueris, si me quæsieris, nusquam regionis tuæ invenire me poteris'. ΘΗΩΡΙΚΑ occurs again Duchesne p. 158. The explanation given in the Catholicon is: 'Theoricus, ca, cum. in theoro est.' Ducange explains it, 'contemplativus, qui tantum contemplationi vacat. Joh. de Janua. Gr. θεωρικὸς'. In Ingulf it refers to a variation of the passage Matth. xxvij. 65 'Habetis vos custodiam', and seems to have nothing at all to do with contemplation. Dudo belongs to the first quarter of the 11th century, or c. 1015; he is twice mentioned by Ord. Vit.

The first mention of the Triangular Bridge 'pons triangulus' **289** at Croyland is in Fulm. p. 33 in Eadred's charter of 948; it is again noticed in Eadgar's charter of 966. 'Pons de Croyland' is mentioned before this in the charters of Æthelbald of 716, of Wiglaf of 833, and of Bertulph of 851.

Ingulf states (Fulm. p. 37), that at the battle of Brunanburh **290** (Fl. Wig.; 'Brunford' Ingulf; Will. Malm. G. R. j. 142 (v. l.); Brunandune Æthelweard; Brunesburg, H. Hunt.), won by king Æthelstan in 937, Constantine king of Scots was killed. This again is in accordance with Will. Malm. Gesta regum, the Liber de Hyda, and the Annales de Wintonia; in reality, although the king was present at the battle, it was his son, who was killed (Fl. Wig.); the king escaped to Scotland, resigned in 942, became a monk, and died in 952 (Skene, Celtic Scotland j. 360). Skene puts the site of Brunanburh at Aldborough, but Freeman and Stubbs 'abandon the effort to localize it in despair' (Green).

Respecting the marriages of Æthelstan's four half-sisters **291** Ingulf is wrong almost every way; he represents them as all taking place soon after 937 (Fulm. pp. 37 – 38). In company with Will. Malm. he misnames Hugh the Great, duke of France, 'rex Francorum', whose marriage, not that of his son, with Eadhild took place in 926. He calls Henry I. 'imperator', whereas he was only 'rex', as also his coins declare, while later (Fulm. p. 50) he calls him 'Imperator Almanniæ'. He makes

Æthelstan give his sister Eadgyth to Otho of Germany after the battle of Brunanburh in 937, possibly because Fl. Wig. mentions the marriage in 936 the year of Otho's accession, the marriage having really taken place in 924 (A.S.Chr. B C D) or 930 (Will. Malm. Gesta regum [R. S.] i. p. 149³). In the matter of the marriages taking place nearly at the same time, Ingulf was misled by Will. Malm. Gesta regum [R.S.] i. 149), who, after recounting the victories and glories of Æthelstan, says: 'Propter hæc tota Europa laudes ejus prædicabat,......felices se reges alienigenæ non falso putabant, si vel affinitate vel muneribus ejus amicitias mercarentur', proceeding then to speak of the four marriages.

292 The title of 'Courteous Croyland' ('Croyland curteys') or the expression 'Croyland Curtesy', which is said to have taken rise from the hospitality shewn in 948 to king Eadred's chancellor Turketul by the three monks residing at Croyland, may not have been meant to be the very words used in Turketul's time, but only the Norman translation of them due to Ingulf. Bale (Scriptores fo. Basil. 1557) i. 92, writing 40 years before the first printing of the Ingulf in 1596 and 11 years before its first mention by Dr Caius, says: 'Ab hospitalitate civili urbanitatis cognomen facetum accepit'. Croyland is thus spoken of by Fabyan (d. 1512):

'The holy man Cutlake, about the .xxiiij. yere of his age, renouncyd the pompe and pryde of this worlde, and toke the order of munkys in the abbey of Repyndon, and the .iij. yere after he went to Crowlande, and there lad for the whyle an holy ankers lyfe, and dyd there many myracles, and there fynallye was buryed; in which ile and place of his buryinge stondeth nowe a fayre abbey, the whiche for the great resorte of gestes that thyther drawith, and for the good and frendlye chere, that gestes there reseyve and take, the sayd place hath purchasyd a surname, and is named Crowlande the curteys, the which is a place of good fame; and there lyeth also the holy confessoure, Neotus, some tyme dissyple of Erkynwalde, bysshop of London' (Fabyan's Chronicle [printed 1516] 4° Lond. 1811 p. 128).

293 The present text is quite wrong (§ 149) in the dating of the death of Turketul, apart from the difference between the Ingulf and Ord. Vit.

The death of abbat Egelric I, which happened ten years **294** after that of abbat Turketul in 975, is given in all the texts as DCCCCLXXIV instead of DCCCCLXXXIV by the omission of one X.

Ælfthryth, the mother of Æthelred II, called Elfthrida by **295** Sym. Dun., Alfdritha by Matth. Paris, even Elfrida by Will. Malm., is called Alfleda by Ingulf (Fulm. p. 54), the full form of which would be Ælfflæd.

Ingulf mentions with some detail (Fulm. p. 56) a destruction **296** of Peterborough monastery in the time of Æthelred II, by Swegen king of Denmark and his army, in 1013, an event of which no other notice has been found.

He speaks of 'Analaphus' king of Norway, Olaf Tryggvesson, **297** as a leader of the Norse invaders jointly with Swegen king of Denmark, apparently in the whole time of abbat Godric II. 1005-1018. The two kings were allied in 994, and plundered and destroyed in Southern England and in other parts, but through the instrumentality of Ælfheah (Elphege) bishop of Winchester 984-1005, king Olaf promised never to return to England, and 'sua promissa bene custodivit' (Fl. Wig. a. 994).

The demise of the manor of Badby for 100 years at a **298** peppercorn rent in 1013 has already been spoken of (§ 252).

Ingulf speaks of Eadric Streona, 'perfidus dux Edricus' **299** (Fl. Wig.), the betrayer of his country, of his father-in-law king Æthelred II, and of his brother-in-law king Eadmund Ironside, as being 'laqueo suspensus' (Fulm. p. 57), in accordance with Will. Malm. 'faucibus clisus', Joh. Petrib. 'laqueo suffocatus', and others; but the earlier A.S.Chr. and Fl. Wig. (s. a. 1017) merely notice his being slain, while H. Hunt. speaks of his being beheaded.

Fl. Wig. s. a. 1062 mentions a recluse named Wulsius, who **300** had then lived a solitary life 'plus xl. annis'; this would bring the beginning of his life of seclusion to the year 1022 at the latest. The 'Chron. Abb. de Evesham' [R. S.] p. 322, mentions his being a recluse for 75 years 'in diversis locis', which would bring his death to about 1097. Ingulf says, that he began his life of seclusion at Croyland, which may be covered by the 'in diversis locis', and that he removed to Evesham c. 1035. He is spoken of again by Pet. Bles.

301 Ingulf has the almost universally wrong date 1031 for Cnut's visit to Rome, with A.S.Chr., Fl. Wig., etc., instead of 1027 (Freeman j. Ed. III. 434 note IIII.); he calls Rudolph king of Burgundy Robert (Fulm. p. 60), although Fl. Wig. and Will. Malm. give him his right name. In 'Annales de Wigornia' (Ann. Monast. [R. S.] iv. p. 371) it is stated: 'Anno MXXVI. Hoc anno Canutus rex Romam ivit'. He was present at the coronation of the emperor Conrad II. the Salian Easter 1027.

302 The coronation of Harold I, which is mentioned by Ingulf (Fulman, pp. 61, 62), was apparently considered doubtful by Prof. Freeman (j. Ed. I. p. 541), but is now accepted by him (j. Ed. III. 487 – 8 note RRR. p. 778). The coronation was performed by archbishop Æthelnoth [Joh. Brompton, Scriptores Decem p. 932] at Oxford (Rishanger [R. S.] p. 427. Matth. Paris Chron. Major [R. S.] j. 570) where he had been chosen by the Witan. Both Wiglaf of Mercia (§ 191) and Harold I. are said by Ingulf to have bestowed their coronation robes on Croyland.

303 Ingulf makes Leofric, abbat of Peterborough 1052 – 1066, a contemporary of Wulget abbat of Pegeland 1018 – 48 (Fulm. p. 58), who in 1048 became abbat of Croyland. He speaks (Fulm. p. 62) of the same Wulfgeat abbat of Pegeland being subjected to the claims of Elfin 'Ælfsige' 1006 – 42 (A.S.Chr. E.), Arwin 'Arnwi' 1042 – 52, and Leofric 1052 – 66, abbats of Peterborough, and as having in consequence lost the site and estates of his monastery in the days of king Harthacnut 1039 – 41, whereas the last-mentioned event seems to have happened not long before 1048. Here Ord. Vit. quite differs from Ingulf (§ 229); he says :

'Postquam Brihtmerus Crulandiæ abbas vij⁰ Idus Apriles [7 Apr.] obiit, Vulfgeatus Pegelandæ pater Eduardum regem...petiit, ut greges duorum cænobiorum permitteret adunari, Deique ad laudem sub uno abbate et sub una lege unum conventum effici. Quod ille mox benigniter concessit (ij. 284 – 5).'

304 Ingulf follows Fl. Wig. in assigning 1048 as the year, when

Egelric 'Æthelric' monk of Peterborough succeeded Eadred as bishop of Durham; Sym. Dun. [R. S.] j. 91 seems to say in 1042, but the see was vacant from 1019 for nearly three years before the accession of Eadmund, who sat 23 years (Sym. Dun. j. 84 – 5, 91), and Eadred his successor sat for some (short) time. According to Will. Malm. G. P. [R. S.] p. 271 Egelwin 1056 – 71 preceded Egelric 1042 – 56.

Both Egelric 1042 – 56 and Egelwin 1056 – 71 are repre- **305** sented as obtaining the bishopric of Durham through the influence of earl Godwine, who died 1053 (Fl. Wig.). Sym. Dun. says that Egelwin's promotion was due to the favour of earl Tosti, and seems to imply that that of Egelric was due to the favour of earl Siward (Hist. Dunelm. eccl. [R. S.] j. 91, 92).

Of the road called 'Elricherode' made from Deping to **306** Spalding by bishop Egelric (Fulm. p. 64; Sym. Dun. [R. S.] j. 92), Camden says that in his time it was not to be seen; it is however laid down in Bowen's map of Lincolnshire 1767.

Speaking of the countess Lucia the wife of Ivo Tailbois, Ingulf describes her as the 'unica filia' of Earl Ælfgar; she had however an elder sister Ealdgyth, who was the wife successively of king Gruffydd ap Llywelyn and of Harold the son of earl Godwine.

Abbat Wulget 'Wulfgeat' died according to Ord. Vit. on **307** the Nones of July, Fulman's text (p. 65) says, that he died on the Nones of June (5 June) 1052, being buried on the day of St Medardus (8 June).

The death of queen Ælfgifu-Emma the widow of the two **308** kings Æthelred II. and Cnut occurred ij. Non. Mart. (6 March) 1052 according to A.S.Chr. D. and Fl. Wig., but on ij. Id. Mart. (14 March) 1051, according to A.S.Chr. C. Ingulf puts it in the year 1052 (p. 66).

The second outlawry of earl Ælfgar in 1058 (Fulm. p. 66) **309** is considered an error and as 'an accidental repetition, under a wrong year, of Ælfgar's former outlawry three years before' (Freeman), but both outlawries are mentioned by A.S.Chr. D., Fl. Wig. etc.

310   Ingulf erroneously speaks of 'Radinus' the great earl of Hereford as the husband of Goda the sister of king Eadward (Fulm. p. 67). 'Radinus' is Radulphus or Ralph of Mantes, Ralph the timid, who was the son of Goda by her first husband Walter of Mantes. But Fl. Wig. a. 1060 is wrong about Gytha the wife of earl Godwine, making her the sister, instead of the aunt, of king Suanus Svend Estrithson.

311   There is some difficulty about the story of Harold's expedition against the Welsh in 1063 (Fulm. p. 68). Finding the heavy armour of the English a hindrance to their pursuit of the lighter armed Welsh, he, according to Fulman's text, commanded 'militem corium coctum et omnem levem armaturam assuescere', while, according to Savile's text, he commanded 'militum chorum omnem levem armaturam assuescere'. This 'cuir bouilli' has been unfavourably commented on, and no early historian notices it; but in a passage in John of Salisbury (d. 1182) Policraticus iv. 18 'praedurum corium' as a cuirass is mentioned, and the words 'levitatem' and 'levem armaturam' are used, which occur here. A quotation from Statius, which is found in it (§ 427), is also elsewhere used by Ingulf (Fulm. p. 37). The whole passage is as follows:

312   'Anglorum recens narrat historia, quod cum Britones, irruptione facta, Angliam depopularentur, à piissimo rege Eduardo ad eos expugnandos missus est dux Haraldus, vir quidem armis strenuus, et laudabilium operum fulgens insignibus, et qui tam suam, quam suorum posset apud posteros gloriam dilatare, nisi meritorum titulos, nequitiam patris imitans, perfide praesumpto regno decoloraret. Cum ergo gentis cognosceret *levitatem*, quasi pari certamine militiam eligens expeditam, cum eis consuit congrediendum, *levem* exercens *armaturam*, perornatus incedens, fasciis pectus et praeduro tectus corio, missilibus corum levia objectans ancilia, et in eos contorquens nunc spicula, nunc mucronem exercens, sic fugientium vestigiis inhaerebat, ut premeretur '*Pede pes et cuspide cuspis*', et *umbo umbone repelleretur*. Nivium itaque collem ingressus, vastavit omnia, et expeditione in biennium prorogata, reges cepit, et capita eorum regi, qui eum miserat, praesentavit' (Joh. Sarisb. Policraticus [De nugis curialium] Lib vj. Cap. vj. ed. Giles iiij. 16 [8º Oxf. 1848]).

There is nothing about all this in Fl. Wig., Sym. Dun., Matth. Paris, or 'Matth. Westm.'; however in Giraldus Cambrensis it is stated: 'Et sicut longe plenius Haraldus ultimus:

qui pedes ipse, cumque pedestri turba, et levibus armis, victuque patriæ conformi, tam valide totam Walliam et circumivit et transpenetravit, ut in eadem fere mingentem ad parietem non reliquerit' ([R. S.] vj. Descriptio Kambriæ 217).

In the 'Gesta Herwardi' (Geffrei Gaimar [R. S.] j. 361) the expression occurs 'cum tunicis ex corio valde coctis', while Franc. Michel (Chron. Anglo-Norm.) prints '...valde cortis'.

Fulman (p. 68) prints the names of the brothers of 'Griffinus' (so also Fl. Wig.) the Welsh king, as Blethgent and Ruthius. In Fl. Wig. the latter name is 'Rithwalanus', and in A.S.Chr. D (not E) 'Rigwatla'. Griffin (Gruffydd ap Llywelyn) was murdered by his people, according to Fl. Wig., Joh. Petrib. and Matth. Paris, on 5 Aug. 1064, according to A.S.Chr. DE in 1063 (5 Aug. D, Freeman), but according to Ingulf in 1065. **313**

Ingulf represents king Eadward as sending Robert of Jumiéges archbishop of Canterbury (1051-52) to duke William in the same year 1065 to assure to him the succession to the throne of England; Robert however had been expelled from England in Sept. 1052 and died not long after, perhaps on 26 May 1056. This statement seems derived from Ord. Vit. who says: **314**

'Edwardus nimirum propinquo suo Willermo duci Normannorum primo per Rodbertum Cantuariorum summum pontificem, postea per eundem Heraldum integram Anglici regni mandaverat concessionem, ipsumque concedentibus Anglis fecerat totius juris sui hæredem.'

In Will. Gemet. (Duchesne p. 285 B) it is thus put:

'Edwardus Anglorum Rex, disponente Deo, successione prolis carens, olim miserat Willelmo duci Rodbertum Cantuariorum Archipræsulem, ex regno à Deo sibi attributo illum statuens hæredem. Deinde Heraldum cunctorum suæ dominationis Comitem divitiis et honore ac potentia maximum, Duci destinavit, ut ei de Corona sua fidelitatem faceret, ac Christiano more sacramentis firmaret.'

In William of Poitiers, 'Gesta Guillelmi...regis Anglorum' (Duchesne p. 181 D) we find also: 'Optimatum igitur suorum assensu per Rodbertum Cantuariensem Archipræsulem, huius delegationis mediatorem, obsides potentissimæ parentelæ Godvini Comitis filium ac nepotem ei [Guillelmo] direxit [rex Edwardus]'.

315 In speaking of William duke of Normandy, Ingulf always styles him 'Comes', 'Comes Normannorum', but this is in accordance with the practice of Fl. Wig. (Sym. Dun.) and of Ord. Vit. (ij. 35, 39). A.S.Chr. D terms William 'eorl' of Normandy.

316 Another expression for 'earl' is found in Ingulf, viz. 'consul' (Fulm. pp. 75, 76, 102). This word is used by Æthelweard, 'undecim consules, quos illi Eorlas solent nominare' (s. a. 871), and later, in Domesday (Ellis j. 47), by Hen. Hunt., Matth. Paris, etc. Leofric, who is called by Ingulf (Fulm. p. 66) 'comes Leycestriæ', is named by H. Hunt. 'consul Cestriæ'. This latter writer frequently uses the word (cf. a. 1075).

In king Ælfred's translation of Boethius de Consol. Philos. edited by J. S. Cardale (8° Lond. 1829) pp. 2 – 3 we find 'Then was there a certain Consul, that we call Heretoha, who was named Boethius'. In Hamilton, Inquis. Comit. Cantab. 'Consul Alanus' occurs pp. 78, 82. Æthelweard speaks of Hengest as 'Consul et dux de Germania...gentis Anglorum'.

317 Ingulf speaks of the earls Eadwine and Morkere as being both killed treacherously by their men in 1071 (Fulm. p. 70); but only Eadwine it was, who was then killed; Morkere was alive in 1087 (Fl. Wig.), having submitted to William 1. in 1071. Will. Malm. makes the same mistake; he states them to have been 'suorum perfidia trucidati', Ingulf's words being 'ambo a suis per insidias trucidati'.

318 Simon, who married Matilda the eldest daughter of earl Walthcof, is called by Ingulf 'Silvanectensis', of Senlis, and so also by Ord. Vit. (iij. 402). But by others he is called Simon de Seynliz, de sancto Licio (Joh. Brompton s. a. 1075 Twysden i. 974).

319 Another mistake is calling Ralph Radulphus de Toerny, the husband of Alice the second daughter of earl Walthcof, 'Rodulphus Tornacensis' or of Tournay. This was the reading of Fulman's MS., as he himself notes. Both the names 'Rodulphus' and 'Radulphus' occur frequently in Ord. Vit.

320 The council of Windsor of 1072, which made a decree (Fulm. p. 93) relative to the precedence of Canterbury over

York, is stated by Ingulf to be the one, which determined, that the bishops' sees should be removed from small places to the large cities in their dioceses. Dr Stubbs however gives 1075 as the date of the council of London, which operated this change.

According to the Ingulf, Wulketul Wulfcytel abbat of **321** Croyland was deposed by 'the Normans' at a council held at London in 1075, 'cito post sancti martyris [Waldevi] sepulturam', and replaced by Ingulf, who was installed on the feast of the Conversion of St Paul, 25 Jan. '1076'. There was indeed a council held at London in 1075 (Will. Malm. G. P. j. 42), but according to the Latin App. to A.S.Chr. A, and to Gervase of Canterbury (R. S. ij. 367) Wulfcytel was deposed at Gloucester in the 16th year of Lanfranc's primacy (1070 – 1089) at Christmas 1085. He is besides mentioned as abbat in 1080 (Hamilton, Inquis. Com. Cantabr. see § 451).

The statement, that Ingulf, who was born c. 1030, 'in the **322** earliest authentic passage that can be adduced to this point' (Hallam, Middle Ages, 1846, ij. 480), studied Aristotle at the university of Oxford 'studium Oxoniense' (cf. 'studium Aurelianense' Fulm. p. 114) about the year 1048 early in Eadward the Confessor's reign, 'cumque in Aristotele arripiendo supra multos coaetaneos meos profecissem, etiam Rhetoricam Tullii primam et secundam talo tenus (Ovid. M. iiij. 343) inducbam', has given rise to expressions of suspicion, by Gibbon among others, both on account of the subjects of study and on account of the place, the works of Aristotle being (as stated) then unknown, and Oxford being then in ruins. Gibbon's words (Miscell. works 4to. Lond. 1815, iiij. 534) are: 'Ingulphus boasts of his proficiency in Aristotle and Tully's Rhetoric, yet in 1048 Aristotle was unknown; Oxford lay in ruins, had neither cathedral nor monastery, to which the studies were confined. The Divinity Lectures of Robert Pulein in the abbey of Oseney (1129 – 35) I consider as the punctum saliens of the University'. We find however in Ord. Vit. (ij. 210 – 11) writing c. 1130 with reference to archbishop Lanfranc, who was Ingulf's senior, having been born in 1005: 'Admirandum cognoscerent ingenium sibi, studiumque Lanfranci Herodianus in grammatica, Aristoteles in dialectica, Tullius in rhetorica, Augustinus et Hieronymus, aliique legis et gratiae expositores in sacra pagina.' In the library of the monastery of Fécamp (c. 1150) was found 'Topica Aristotelis in corio impresso' (Ord. Vit. v. App. p. xvi.). 'In the Gesta Comitum Andegavensium, Fulk, count of Anjou, who lived about 920, is said to have been skilled Aristotelicis et Ciceronianis ratiocinationibus' (Hallam, Middle Ages, 1846, ij. 480 note). Dr Lingard shews further, that although Oxford was burnt in 1010, yet very shortly afterwards it was a place of importance (A.S.Chr. Fl. Wig. s. a. 1013), indeed of such importance, that meetings of the Witan were held there in 1015 and in 1036 (A.S.Chr. Fl. Wig.). In king Eadward's times it must have been a town of considerable size, consisting of more than 900 houses (Ellis, Introd. j. 193). Dr Lingard also says, that Aristotle was known in some form much earlier than is generally thought, as Alcuin (c. 735, 19 May 804) states, that it was studied at York (De pontif. Ebor. v. 1550), and himself wrote on several treatises of the philosopher (Lingard s. a. 1070). His references are: Canis[ii Thesaurus fo. Amstel. 1725 Vol.] ij. part j. p. 482 (sic); Alc[uini] Opera [fo. St Emmeran 1777] j. 47, ij. 350 [Ep. xxxv De dialectica].

323   The reference to Aristotle is in a metrical description of the library at York, collected by Ecgberht the seventh archbishop (Will. Malm. Gesta Pontif. [R. S.] p. 246), and destroyed in the great fire of 1137 (Gale, Scriptores, j. (1691) 730, l. 1536 ff.):

> 'Illic invenies veterum vestigia Patrum,
> Quidquid habet pro se Latio Romanus in orbe,
> Graecia vel quidquid transmisit clara Latinis:...
> Quidquid et Althelmus docuit, quid Beda magister,
> Quae Victorinus scripsere, Boetius; atque
> Historici veteres, Pompeius, Plinius, ipse
> Acer Aristoteles, Rhetor quoque Tullius ingens....'

Hallam (Middle Ages, 1846, ij. 480 note) supposes, that 'the works of Aristotle intended by Ingulfus were translations of parts of his logic by Boethius and Victorin'. A. Jourdain, Recherches critiques sur l'âge...des traductions latines d'Aristote (new ed. 8° Paris 1843) does not allude to Ingulf. Towards the year 935 Reinhard 'scholasticus' of the monastery of St Burchard at Würzburg composed a commentary on the Categories of Aristotle (Heeren, Gesch. des Studiums d. class. Lit.).

In his account of himself Ingulf speaks of his pilgrimage to **324** Jerusalem before the Conquest, going with some archbishops of the Empire, 'plurimos Archiepiscopos Imperii', of whom the archbishop of Mentz was one, in a company of 7000 persons (§ 436). He says, that at Constantinople he saw the emperor Alexius, 'Alexim imperatorem ejus adorantes'. The earliest emperor of the name of Alexius, however, was Alexius I. Comnenus, who was born 1048 and reigned 1081 – 1118; he is always called Ἀλέξιος on his coins, in Anna Comnena's history, in Matth. Paris, etc., but in H. Hunt. is written : 'Alexi igitur apud Constantinopolim imperante...' (R. S. p. 219) and the same name Alexis is found in Hoveden. This passage of Ingulf is quoted by Baronius Ann. Eccl. Vol. xi. (fo. Antv. 1642) p. 353 in n° XXXIV, where he speaks of the pilgrimage of the German bishops. In the margin he has the following note on the word 'Alexim'—'*Ducam:* pro Duca imperitus librarius *Alexim* posuit, putans non convenire simul Ducam et Imperatorem, nesciens Ducam esse cognomentum Imp. illius. Sed Alexius longe post haec tempora vixit.' The emperor Alexius is called Alexis also by Benedict of Peterborough (R. S. ij. 201). The emperor Constantine XIII. ὁ Δούκας reigned 1059 – 67. Although Ingulf knew the title 'Basileus' (Fulm. pp. 47 – 48), which is continually used as the greek equivalent of emperor, and is also used of Eadgar by Fl. Wig. a. 975, he yet calls the Constantinopolitan ruler 'Imperator'. He however speaks of the great church at Constantinople as the 'Agia Sophia'. (A few other greek words occur ; in Eadgar's charter to Malmesbury (Fulm. p. 48), archbishop Dunstan makes the sign 'hagiae crucis'; he has (Fulm. p. 83) the words 'hierochronographi', 'protodoctorem', and 'neo-apostolus'.)

At Jerusalem Ingulf saw the patriarch Sophronius, who is **325** last mentioned in 1059, but not as dying in that year as

Mr Riley says (Archaeol. Journal 1862, p. 43), while his successor died in 1094 (L'art de vérif. les dates j. 265, 267). Sophronius is mentioned in Will. Malm. Gesta Regum [R. S.] ij. 425, where also 'Achym soldanus' (Fulm. p. 74) is spoken of. He might find 'Agia Sophia' and 'Imperator ejus [Constantinopolis]' in Will. Malm. Gesta regum [R. S.] ij. 412.

326 Ingulf does not give the date of his pilgrimage; it was however between 1051 (Fl. Wig.), when duke 'comes' William visited England, and the Conquest in 1066; and on his return the writer became a monk at Fontenelle, where 'non paucis interlabentibus annis' (Fulm. p. 74) he became prior (as is also stated by Ord. Vit.) apparently (§ 457) not long before the invasion of England. This pilgrimage cannot therefore have taken place in 1065, when some German bishops made a pilgrimage to Jerusalem. Joh. Petrib. puts their pilgrimage in 1064, and mentions the archbishop of Mentz, three bishops and a company of 7000 persons, of whom only about 2000 returned to their homes. According to the complete Fl. Wig. (fo. Francof. 1600), which includes the chronicle of Marianus Scotus, the three bishops were those of Utrecht, Bamberg, and Regensburg.

327 'Achym soldanus' mentioned by Ingulf on this occasion c. 1064 as having 'formerly' 'dudum' destroyed the churches of Jerusalem is Al-hákem beamrillah Mansúr, the Fatimite sultan of Egypt 996–1023; the destruction was in 1010. Riley translates 'dudum' 'lately'.

328 Ingulf states, that duke William, in acknowledgment of the assistance in men and money given him in 1066 by the monastery of Fontenelle or Saint-Wandrille, gave to it by charter the whole of the vineyard 'Cari loci' (Fulm. p. 74). According to Gough (Croyl. 1783, p. 27 note), a place called Carville is found in De Witt's Map of Normandy close to Saint-Wandrille, on the right bank of the Seine, near Yvetot and Caudebec. This donation is not mentioned in the account of Fontenelle in 'Gallia Christiana' ed. P. Piolin, vol. xj, pp. 155–185, 984 [Rouen] fo. Paris 1874.

329 On being appointed abbat of Croyland, Ingulf was installed on 25 Jan. 1075 – 6. Here he found (Fulm. p. 176) 123 monks from other monasteries, who had made Croyland their place of refuge, and among them six monks from St Mary's without York. On this statement bishop Tanner has the following observations: 'I cannot account for the monks of St Mary's without York, mentioned by Ingulf, p. 76, under the year 1076, it nowhere else appearing that there were then any religious of that denomination in that city.' Four other similar statements have been commented on by Tanner. Ten monks had come from St Mary Stow Linc. This church was founded for secular priests probably by Eadnoth bishop of Dorchester c. 1040, and augmented by earl Leofric. Will. Malm. says of bishop Remigius 1067 – 92, 'Coenobium monachorum apud Sanctam Mariam de Stou ex novo fecit,' which Tanner understands to mean, 'After the Conquest the Religious here were changed into Benedictine monks...', 'For monks were placed here before A.D. 1076, as is plain from Ingulf, p. 76.' From Thetford fifteen monks were at Croyland in 1076, and Tanner remarks, 'Monks here were in some place of this town, if not at St Mary's, before the year 1076, when Ingulf...tells us, that of the monks, whom he then found at Croyland, fifteen were at Thetford.' Fourteen monks belonged to Christchurch Norwich; on this Tanner says: 'Among the monks, which Ingulf found in his church of Croyland A.D. 1076, there were fourteen from Christchurch in Norwich, of which Religious house nothing else hath yet occurr'd'. The see of Thetford was transferred to Norwich in 1094, and in 1096 bishop Herbert de Losinga founded the Benedictine priory of the Holy Trinity. With respect to St Andrew's Northampton, from which two monks had come, Tanner says: 'On the North part of this town was, as early as A.D. 1076 the priory of St Andrew', a statement resting solely on Ingulf's authority. This priory was augmented in 1084 by Simon de Senlis, the husband of Matilda, daughter of earl Waltheof.

In Fulman's text (pp. 63, 77, 88) and in Savile's the royal 'justitiarii' are spoken of in 1048, 1075 and 1092, and Riley comments on this early use of the word as an anachronism, 'such a thing' being 'unheard of until about a century later, at the earliest'. In the last two cases in Fulman we find in the lower margin the correct word 'justitiis', which seems from Selden's Eadmer (p. 172) to have been the reading of the MS., 'Justitiis in Ms'. The alteration may then be due to the editors, although the later word is found in the Elizabethan MS. Arundel 178.

331 Soon after his appointment in '1075', abbat Ingulf visits his 'old friends' Lanfranc the archbishop and Odo bishop of Bayeux at London (Fulm. p. 78). Odo was imprisoned in Normandy, at Rouen, by his half-brother William in 1082 (A.S.Chr. E, Fl. Wig., Freeman iv. 684, 711). This visit is therefore incompatible with the apparently certain date of Ingulf's appointment in 1085, and Ingulf's statement renders any conjectural correction of date at the least very difficult.

332 Ingulf (Fulm. p. 79) represents Malcolm III. king of Scotland as doing homage to William I. at Abernethy, at the very time 'tunc', when, to thwart the expected invasion of Cnut V. king of Denmark, the king of England laid waste a great part of Northumberland. But the latter event was in 1085, although Ingulf (Fulm. p. 79) speaks of it as happening a few years before 1085, and the invasion of Scotland and the homage of Malcolm was in 1072 (Fl. Wig.).

333 He mentions Henry I. of France, as: 'qui modo regnat in Francia', whereas the king died in 1060, before the Conquest, and 30 or 40 years before Ingulf wrote his history.

334 He states, that Philip was a name that was very common 'frequentissimum' in France (Fulm. p. 82), but Ducange remarks, that it is scarcely to be found before the time of Henry I. 1031 – 60. It does not seem to occur among the names of the moneyers of the Merovingian period; there Johannes is common, but even Petrus and Paulus only just occur.

335 The double names 'Harald Gower', 'Roller Quater' belonging to dependents of the convent in 1091 (Fulm. p. 104), and also those found in the charter of Thorold of Bukenhale [Bucknall, Linc.] (Fulm. p. 87) of 1051 (§ 391): 'Gunter Liniet', 'Turstan Dubbe' and 'Besi Tuk', have been condemned by

Riley as 'the creatures of an inventive imagination, and no more'; 'the common people...at this time had no double names, such being a usage of Norman introduction' (Archaeol. Journ. 1862, pp. 38, 45). But in Earle's Land charters (p. 257 ff.) is a long series of manumissions of persons bearing double names, not only of trades, as: 'Alger se webba', 'Randolf se cordewan', and of places, as: 'Waltere se Flemig', but also descriptive nicknames, such as: 'Wulfrice Wig', 'Semer Swetleðer', 'Osbern Havoc' etc. These Prof. Earle ascribes to the 11th century. Double names occur earlier among the Danes and Northumbrians, e.g. 'Osferth Hlytte' (A.S.Chr. a. 911), 'Siward Barn' (A.S.Chr. 1072), and nicknames are common at all times and in all countries, and already in c. 775 (A.S.Chr.) we find Offa abbat of Medeshamsted further called Beonna (Hickes, Dissert. Epist. pp. 24 ff.).

Among the moneyers of Cnut we find many double names: Æstan Loc, Edsige Ware, Godric Swot, Godwine Cas, Lefstan Swene, etc.

In the Index to Langebek we find 'Rollerus, Rollo, Rolf, frater Erici Diserti', 'regnum Norvegiæ Gotharo occiso accipit', with the reference j. 86, 88.

Ingulf (Fulm. p. 94) puts the death of queen Matilda in **336** 1085, wrongly for 1083 (Fl. Wig.). He places it in the same year as the death of abbat Wulfcytel, which he gives as in 1085, and two years before the death of king William I., 9 Sept. 1087.

He describes the general homage of 1086, which took place **337** at Salisbury (A.S.Chr., Fl. Wig.) as taking place at London (Fulm. p. 79).

It is not clear, what Ingulf means by the words: 'Verun- **338** tamen in proximo spero tantam præsumptionem cum Regis benevolentia plenius in statum pristinum emendandam, quem per ccc. et fere xxx. annos antea pacifice possederamus' (Fulm. p. 83). This brings us back to a period later than the year 756. King Æthelbald the founder died having reigned 41 years (Fulm. p. 5) from 716 (Fl. Wig.), in 755 (Fl. Wig.), or in 757 (Sym. Dun.). The foundation itself, however, was (Fulm. pp. 2 - 4) in 716. He has also forgotten the events of 870.

339 The 'vicarius' of Wedlongbure, Wendlingborough or Wellingborough is mentioned in 1091 (Fulm. p. 105), 'whereas, in reality, vicars of churches were unknown here till about a century after that date' (Riley).

340 One of the most serious mistakes is making king 'William receive his death wound at Le Mans' [rather in Maine Cenomannia] 'instead of at Mantes' [on the Seine, between Paris and Rouen] (Freeman iv. 600[1]). Ingulf says: 'Post cuius [reginae Mathildis (H. Hunt.)] obitum anno secundo, scilicet Anno Domini M.LXXXVII. cum Dominus meus inclytus rex Willelmus fortissimum contraxisset exercitum, super Franciam equitans Cinomanniam fere ferro flammaque delevit, huius expeditionis nimio studio ac sudore morbum incurrens .....' (Fulm. p. 94). Ord. Vit., after mentioning the death of queen Matilda Nov. 1083 (iij. 192 ff.; cf. Freeman iv. 655 ff.), narrates William's incursion into Maine against Hubert lord of Beaumont, and the two years war or siege of Sainte-Suzanne near Laval (iij. 192 ff.; cf. Freeman iv. 656 ff.); there had been an earlier war in Maine in 1073, but this one was in 1083 – 85. Ordericus then goes on to speak of the invasion of Cnut V. of Denmark (iij. 201 ff.; cf. Freeman iv. 686 ff.), and, after touching upon some other topics, chiefly the translation of the relics of St Nicholas of Myra in Lycia (iij. 205 ff.), comes to William's operations against Mantes (Madantum Ord. Vit., Medanta Will. Gemet., Mathantum Fl.Wig. Lib.Elien., Mathuntum Joh. Petrib., Maantum Matth. Paris, Maante H. Hunt.) and his death, when he speaks of him as dying, not of any 'wound', but through an illness contracted 'ex nimio aestu et labore' (iij. 225 ff.). This is in agreement with Ingulf's statement, though the almost total wasting of Maine 'ferro flammaque' may be a reminiscence imported from the earlier war in Maine into the account of the later war. Ingulf's mistake is leaving out all mention of the expedition against Mantes. He may have been misled by the language of Will. Gemetic. given below, who mentions 'Medanta' immediately after 'Cinomannia' without stating the exact locality. Ord. Vit. and Fl. Wig. a. 1073 call the town 'Cenomannis', the country Maine 'Cenomannia'. But if it be considered, that the words 'hujus expeditionis' altogether warrant Mr Freeman's charge of 'singular carelessness' brought against the writer, then, however mistaken the author of the Ingulf may have been, he yet sins in good company, as a similar, if not worse, mistake is made by Matth. Paris (Historia Minor [R. S.] j. 18) in substituting 'Normannia' for 'Cenomannia' (Freeman iv. 558 [1]).

The A.S.Chr. E and Fl. Wig. know nothing of any 'death wound'; the former says: 'He fell sick and was severely afflicted', and the latter: 'durus viscerum dolor illum apprehendit'; neither of them knows anything of the French king's joke and of William's retort; these seem to come through Matth. Paris from Will. Malm. G. R. [R. S.] lib. iij. § 281.

The account given by Will. Gemeticensis, De ducibus Normannis (Camden, 'Anglica, Normannica etc.' fo. Francof. 1603, Duchesne p. 291), p. 670 is not clear:

'Cum ergo idem Rex victoriosus post plurima bella post multiplices expeditiones tam in Normannia quam in Anglia, et in minore Britannia, seu etiam in Cinomannia prospero exitu consummatas, oppidum quoddam Medanta nomine proprium Philippi Regis Francorum, qui tunc temporis partes Rodberti Ducis bellum patri inferentis juvabat.......Cum igitur Wilhelmus Rex oppidum Medanta assiliens flammis ultricibus tradidisset, pondere armorum, et labore clamoris, quo suos exhortabatur, ut fertur, a ruina intestinorum ejus liquefacta, infirmari non modice coepit, et licet aliquandiu postea vixerit, non tamen solita valetudine usus est. Dispositis tandem rebus suis, et regno Angliae concesso Wilhelmo filio suo, vitam praesentem finivit in Normannia apud Rotomagnum iv. Idus Septembris (10 Sept.)'.

The form 'Cinomannia' occurs in Fl. Wig. a. 1073 and Will. Gemet. (Camden), but on Merovingian and Baronial coins it is always 'Cenomanis'.

H. Hunt. also says: 'Quibus de causis [his cruelty at Mantes] Deus irritatus, regem cum inde veniret (v. l. rediret), infirmitati, postea morti, concessit' (R. S. p. 209).

xxv. Exaggerations in the Ingulf.

342 The writer is much given to magnify the sums of money given to the monastery, or belonging to it.

343 King Æthelbald of Mercia 716 – 755 gave to his new foundation not only the island of Croyland four leagues (leucae) by three leagues in extent and the marshes of Goggisland and Alderland, forming a very large domain, but also £300 'legalis monetæ' and £100 a year for ten years 'ad ædificationem monasterii ejusdem' (Fulm. p. 3).

344 After the destruction of Croyland by the Danes in 870, their vassal-king of Mercia Ceolwulf imposed a tax of £1000 'mille librarum' on the already impoverished monastery, which so nearly reduced the society to ruin, that no fresh candidates presented themselves for admission, and that abbat Godric I. dispersed most of his monks among the friends of the monastery, he himself and a few only of the community remaining at Croyland in extreme poverty (Fulm. p. 27).

345 According to Fl. Wig. a. 694 £3750 ('libræ') was the mulct paid by the men of Kent to Ina king of Wessex for having burnt Mul the brother of his predecessor Ceadwalla; the ransom of bishop Cymelgeac (Fl. Wig. a. 915) was 40 'libræ argenti'. The expression 'libra argenti' occurs in a charter of Eadric king of the Cantware of June 686 and in one of Æthelstan of the year 933 to the bishopric of Crediton in Earle Genuine Records pp. 10, 170. The word 'libra' is frequently used by Fl. Wig.

346 The gifts of money, made to the three old Croyland monks by Turketul the chancellor, were very large for the time; for he gave them first 100 shillings 'solidi', then a little later 20 'libræ argenti', at a time when he was able to recover the former monastic estates of Spalding, Whaplode and Sutterton for 40 'mancæ auri' (Fulm. p. 39) or 'marcæ auri' (Savile p. 870; Ellis Introd. i. 164), Drayton for ten, and Staundon and Badby for other ten.

Mancuses of gold are mentioned in Earle a. 822 'anulus aureus habens .lxx.u. mancusas' (p. 101), a. 988 '112 mancesan goldes' (p. 212), 'Kalicem aureum pensans .xxx. mancusos' (p. 160). The word 'manca' used by Ingulf (Fulm. p. 39) is found in Camden's Brit. 1607 (p. 121) from a latin form of one of the laws of William I., being no. 22 of Fulm. and Selden, and no. 20 of Palgrave (Rise and progress, Part II.). The mancus seems to have been one eighth of a pound, and so $\frac{1}{8}$ of a lb. of sterlings, or also equal to 30d. A mark of silver was worth 13s. 4d. (Stapleton, Magni Rotuli Scacc. Norm. ij. p. xvij); a mark of gold was equal to 10 marks of silver (C. H. Pearson, Hist. of England j. 585³; Twysden, Scriptores x. 1652. Glossarium).

In Eadred's charter to Croyland of 948 a fine of £100 is imposed upon every person, who should in any way injure the monastery or hinder the monks from enjoying peaceful possession of the king's grant (Fulm. p 35).

In 975 the treasure 'thesaurus' of the monastery amounted to nearly £10000 ('libræ'), which must be considered enormous, as the whole of the Danegeld paid in 991 amounted to only the same sum, and in 1018 the impost of London was no more than £10500. The yearly contribution of Croyland in 1005 is stated by Ingulf to have been 400 marks or £266. 13. 4 (Fulm. p. 56), and the whole amount paid by the convent in the days of abbats Oscytel and Godric II. to Æthelred II. and his officers, and to the Danes, to have amounted to £2966. 13. 4, equivalent to perhaps £60000 or £70000 of modern money. The multiplier here used is 20, which is also used for the latter half of the 12th century by Mr C. H. Pearson in his History of England (j. pp. 384, 585, 641).

At the Dissolution 4 Dec. 1539 the gross value of the monastic estates was £1217. 5. 11 per ann., and the clear annual value £1083. 15. 10; the total amount of the pensions was £322. 13. 4, of which the abbat John Welles got £133. 6. 8; the remainder £189. 6. 8 being divided among the 26 monks, who received from £5 to £13. 6. 8 per ann. These numbers must be multiplied by at least 12 to get the present value of the annuities. Dugdale Bar. j. 247 makes the 'augment sixfold' from 1450 to 1675.

At his death, in 975, Turketul left 47 monks and 4 lay

brothers at Croyland; in 1076 there were 62 monks and 4 lay brothers (Fulm. pp. 51, 76); in 1324, on the resignation of abbat Simon of Luffenham, there were found there only a prior and 40 monks, besides 15 corrodiers and 36 servants. There had been evidently at Croyland as elsewhere a very great decrease in the number of the inmates, when the end came.

350 The presents made to Croyland by different kings (Fulm. pp. 8, 9, 11 [Wiglaf], pp. 58, 61 [Cnut], p. 62 [Harold I.]) are perhaps hardly of so great value as to be considered exaggeration. Wiglaf speaks (Fulm. p. 8) of giving to the high altar of the monastery 'calicem aureum, et tabulam capellæ propriæ laminis aureis deauratam', a large gift for the time. The presents and relics sent to king Æthelstan by foreign princes (Fulm. p. 38) are also referred to by Will. Malm. and other writers. In addition, Ingulf mentions the thumb of St Bartholomew given by the duke of Beneventum, whither the body of the apostle had been brought in 809 (Fl. Wig. [fo. Francof. 1801]), to the 'emperor' Henry I. 919 – 936 and by him to Turketul while chancellor. Princes 'principes' continued to rule at Benevento from early times to the year 1077; the prince in 809 was Grimoald IV. 806 – 827; the one, who presented the relic to Henry I., was perhaps Landulf I. 910 – 943. The account in the Ingulf may be derived from the statement in Eadmer Hist. Nov. (R. S. p. 108), that queen Elfgifu-Emma presented to Canterbury an arm of that apostle, which an archbishop of Beneventum had brought to England to sell (Freeman j. ed. III. 442).

351 Ingulf also mentions (Fulm. p. 98) a 'Nadir' a kind of orrery or planetarium, presented to Turketul by the 'king' (duke) of France, of beautiful and costly make, formed of different metals according to the several planets. 'This...was, I make no doubt, of Arabian or Greek manufacture' (Hallam, Middle ages [1841], ij. 353 note). Richard de Wallingford abbat of St Albans 1326 – 35, who was a celebrated mathematician (Fuller, Worthies, Berks), constructed 'præcipuum instrumentum astronomiæ' somewhat on the same principle, which he called by the fanciful name 'Albion—quasi totum per unum'—as though shewing all by one (Gesta Abb. Mon. S. Alb. [R. S.] ii.

207); Leland in his Commentarii de Scriptoribus Britanniæ (§ 470), p. 404 mentions this orrery 'de quo Joannes Stubius mathematicus multa refert'.

There is some tendency to exaggeration in other respects in Ingulf.

Turketul is spoken of in Eadgar's charter of 966 (Fulm. p. **352** 42), in words omitted in Riley's translation p. 85, as 'omnium hostium Anglici regni triumphator strenuissimus', although only one military exploit of his is recorded in Ingulf, viz. at the battle of Brunanburh. The endeavour to give him a heroic character is evident in the description given of his youth.

The ages of the 'sempects' of Turketul's time, and of some **353** monks before the destruction of Croyland in 870, as well as the 70 years rule of abbat Godric I. 870 – 940, are beyond all reasonable belief.

The extent of the fire of 1091, of which strangely the exact **354** date is not given, though it was in Ingulf's time, seems to be exaggerated. The Ann. de Wintonia [R. S.] s. a. 1091 says: 'Ecclesia Crolandi (sic, see § 78) combusta est', and Ord. Vit.: 'Nam pars ecclesiæ cum officinis et vestibus et libris multisque aliis rebus necessariis repentino igne combusta est', words repeated in the 'Vitæ abbatum' MS. Cott. Vesp. B. xi, and condensed in Leland's extracts 'Sub hoc abbate pars ecclesiæ cum officinis combusta'.

In this fire all the muniments of the monastery 'omnia monimenta nostra' (Fulm. p. 98) were destroyed, duplicate copies only remaining. The Mercian charters 'privilegia regum Merciorum', with all their crosses and illuminations, perished; what the other documents 'chirographa nostra pulcherrima', similar in style to the charters of the Mercian kings, were, is not stated. At all events the charter of sheriff Thorold 1051 (Fulm. p. 86), that of earl Algar of 810 (Fulm. p. 95) and that of another earl Algar escaped and were produced in court the year after the fire (Fulm. p. 107). Ingulf however, fearing robbery or fire, so carefully stowed the remaining charters away (Fulm. 107), that in 1114 (Fulm. p. 124) his successor was unable to find them when wanted. The 'charta restaurationis' of

Eadred was apparently in existence after the fire, although the 'chartæ originales', probably the Mercian charters, had perished. There is no statement in the Hist. Croyl., as at present existing, when these charters were recovered; if any such there ever was, it must have been contained in the great lacuna in that history from 1254 to 1388; the charter of Æthelbald however reappears in the Hist. Croyl. in 1415 (Fulm. p. 501) together with those of Eadred and Eadgar.

xxvj. Meteorological observations.

355   The writer, imitating the A.S.Chr. and other historical works of early date, mentions at times the state of the weather.

He says (Fulm. p. 39), that about the year 948 there was so great a drought throughout all England, 'quod triennio non plueret super terram, et siccitas Eliæ a plurimis diceretur'. This is not confirmed by the A.S.Chr., that seems to take no notice of droughts, though it does of heavy rains (s. a. 1098, 1116, 1117), high winds, severe winters, extraordinary lightnings, etc.

There were also great famines in England in 793, 976, 1005, 1044, 1070, 1082, which are recorded in A.S.Chr. The passage, concerning the three years' drought in the Ingulf, may be however out of place, as it occurs in the middle of the account of Turketul's doings at Croyland, before he became abbat there.

We read also of a dreadful famine in king Æthelred's time, followed first by a dysentery afflicting both beasts and men, and then by a pestilence (Fulm. p. 55). In 986 the A.S.Chr. records the appearance for the first time in England of 'the great murrain among the cattle', and in 987 Fl. Wig. that of a fever, which attacked men, and of a dysentery, which destroyed the cattle.

Ingulf mentions an earthquake (felt at Worcester, Derby, and elsewhere, Fl. Wig.) followed by a pestilence as happening in 1048; he gives the day as 1 March wrongly for 1 May. This latter day being a Sunday (Fl. Wig.) fixes the year as given by Ingulf and A.S.Chr. C; A.S.Chr. D gives the year as 1049, which must be wrong. Fl. Wig. mentions also the pestilence.

A famine in the year 1051 is mentioned Fulm. p. 65, but this is not corroborated by A.S.Chr., Fl. Wig. or Matth. Paris. To the pity aroused in king Eadward's heart towards his people by this famine Ingulf ascribes the abolition of the Danegeld which took place in 1052 (Fl. Wig.), in 1051 (A.S.Chr. D).

We are told (Fulm. p. 56) of continued wet weather, that in 1013 rendered the islands of the Fen district inaccessible, and so made them a place of refuge for the population of the neighbourhood from the ravages of the Danes.

In 1075 (Fulm. p. 77) mention is made of a storm: 'tale pluviae diluvium coelum defundebat, quod utique fluentibus aquis dies Noctica credebatur'.

xxvij. History of the Ingulf since the 15th century.

There seems to be no means of finding out, who first **356** brought the Ingulf to light, and when and where the MS. was found. But it must have been early in the second half of the 16th century, as Bale did not, apparently, know Ingulf in 1557, when the second edition of his Scriptores was printed, while in 1568 Dr John Caius speaks freely of him in the first edition of his De Antiquitate Academiae Cantabrigiensis.

As soon as the Ingulf was introduced to the world, it took high rank among the early chronicles of England. Savile, who printed it in his Scriptores post Bedam in 1596, speaks of it as being 'à plurimis antiquitatum nostrarum sitientibus desideratum' (Dedication), and for 100 years it was constantly quoted by historians both at home and abroad as an authentic work of the reign of William Rufus.

It is in consequence referred to without suspicion **357**
by Dr Caius in his De Antiquitate Cantabr. Acad. (1568),
by archbishop Parker in his De Antiquitate Britannicae Ec-
    clesiae (1572),

by its first editor sir Henry Savile (1596),
by William Camden in his Britannia and in his Anglica, Normannica etc.
by Bryan Twyne in his Antiquitatis Acad. Oxon. Apologia (1608),
by John Speed in his Theatre and History (1611),
by John Selden (§ 116) in the Historiæ Novorum of Eadmer (1623),
by sir Henry Spelman in his Concilia (1639),
by sir Geo. Buck in his History of Richard III. (1647),
by Tho. Fuller in his History of the University of Cambridge (1655),
by sir William Dugdale in his several works,
by William Fulman, the editor of 1684,
by James Tyrrell in his General History of England (1700),
by bishop Edward Stillingfleet in his Origines Britannicæ (1710),
by bishop William Nicolson in his British Historical Library (1714),
by David Wilkins in his Leges Anglo-Saxonicæ (1721),
by Hearne in his Ductor Historicus (1724) j. 166,
by bishop Tanner in his Notitia Monastica (1744),
by Thomas Carte in his History of England (1747),
by David Hume in his History of England (1762),
by Tho. Warton in his History of English Poetry (1778),
by baron F. Maseres in his Historiæ Anglicanæ...monumenta (4° Lond. 1807),
by sir Walter Scott in his Ivanhoe 'Dedicatory Epistle' (1817),
by H. Hallam in his Europe during the Middle Ages (1818),
by Dr Lingard in his History of England, and in his Anglo-Saxon Church (1819),
by sir H. Ellis in his General Introduction to Domesday (1833),
by lord Campbell in his Lives of the Lord Chancellors,
by C. H. Pearson in his History of England (1867),

by C. K. Adams of Michigan University in his Manual of
Historical Literature (1882) pp. 504, 506,
by C. T. Elton in his Origins of English History (1890).

On the continent it was quoted as freely as in England: **358**
by Baronius in his Annales Ecclesiastici (1588 – 1607),
by cardinal Bellarmine in his De Scriptoribus eccl. Liber
(1595),
by Clemens Reynerus in his Apostolatus Benedictinorum
(1626),
by Bulaeus in his Historia Universit. Parisiensis (1665),
by Ducange, in his Glossarium (1680),
by J. Mabillon in his Annales Ordinis S. Bened. (1704) and in
the Acta Sanctorum Ord. S. Benedicti,
by Bouquet-Brial in the Rerum Gallicarum et Francicarum
Scriptores (1715 –),
by Langebek in his Scriptores rerum Danicarum (1772),
by Lappenberg, in his Geschichte von England (1834),
by Thierry in his Histoire de la Conquête de l'Angleterre
(1839),
by Huber in his Geschichte der engl. Universitäten (1835),
by F. Gregorovius in his Geschichte der Stadt Athen (8" Stuttg.
1889), j. 173.

At the end of the 17th century, however, Ingulf's good **359**
reputation began to be obscured. Henry Wharton (b. 1664, d.
1695) in his posthumous Historia de episcopis et decanis
Londinensibus necnon...Assavensibus (8° Lond. 1695) first
attacked the Mercian charters of 716, 833, 851 and 868,
drawing attention to the anachronisms, which he had been able
to detect in the list of witnesses appended to them.

In a letter to Robert Harley earl of Oxford (MS. Harl.
7526) dated 6 July 1703, Humphry Wanley, the antiquary,
who was librarian of the Harleian library, mentions, that 'some
learned men' entertained doubts as to the authorship of
Ingulf's history and suspected 'vehemently' some of the
charters, especially the foundation charter of 716, adding that
this 'was, or seems to have been, taken from one now in being,

and not much older, if anything at all, than Henry the Second's time' (1154–89).

360 Among such doubters Dr Geo. Hickes (b. 1642, d. 1715), for whom Wanley worked, was chief. In the preface to his Thesaurus linguarum septentrionalium (§ 254) and in his Dissertatio epistolaris printed with it, he points out the existence of words in the charters not in use at the time, but introduced many years later by the Normans.

361 This has been further worked out by Mr Riley in his article 'The history and charters of Ingulfus considered' in the Archæol. Journal 1862 pp. 33–49, 114–135, where he extends the investigation from the language of the charters to the language of the history itself, touching also on the mistakes, anachronisms and exaggerations to be traced in the historical portions of the work, not always however with sufficient care.

362 Sir Francis Palgrave's words (Qu. Rev. 1826, p. 294) are very decided: "Do we then *bonâ fide* consider the history of Ingulphus as being little better than an 'historical novel'? We must decidedly give an affirmative answer to the question. We believe it to be a mere monkish invention; and the object of the compilation may perhaps be guessed. It was intended to support St Guthlac's title to the lands and possessions of which the deeds were lost, and to give a sterling value to the base metal of the 'golden charter'".

Dr Freeman, while bestowing much attention on Ingulf (iv. 597 ff), considers him as mythical.

According to Ellis (Introd. j. 40), charters were exhibited to the commissioners for the Domesday Survey, as they are mentioned in several places, and he adds: 'A large portion of the forged Saxon Charters which at this day exist are to be referred to the period of the Domesday Survey. They were fabricated by the Monks in anxiety to make the titles to their property good when the Norman Commissioners came amongst them'.

Neither the Ingulf, however, nor the charters contained in it can be of so early a date, as the latter half or the end of the eleventh century.

There are writers, who make a distinction between the historical portions of the Ingulf, and the charters found in it, rejecting the latter wholly, while disposed to accept, more or less, the former. Dr Hickes, while rejecting the charters, seems to have been inclined to accept the historical part, of the Ingulf, at least he refers to statements made in it without, apparently, mark of doubt (Dissert. Epist. pp. 29 n, 36 etc.). E. Edwards also in his Memoirs of Libraries (8° Lond. 1859) i. 114 – 6 takes this view of the comparative value of the two parts.

363

xxviij. The Ingulfine Charters.

In Ingulf's history we find enshrined many charters purporting to have been granted by monarchs and nobles of Mercia, and of England both before and after the Conquest.

364

The few similar documents in the Pet. Bles. (Fulm. pp. 108 – 129), and two from Gough's Hist. of Croyland may conveniently be included.

A. First period of the monastery 716 – 870,
  I. Charters of kings of Mercia:

1.	Æthelbald	dated 716	Fulm.	p.	3 ff
2.	Offa	„ 793	„	„	5 ff
3.	Kenulph, on coins: Coenwlf	„ 806	„	„	6 ff
4.	Wichtlaf, on coins: Wiglaf	„ 833	„	„	8 ff
5.	Bertulph, on coins: Berhtwulf	„ 851	„	„	12 ff
6.	Beorred, on coins: Burgred	„ 868	„	„	18 ff;

  II. Charters of nobles:

7.	Earl Algar or Ælfgar the elder	„ 810	„	„ 95 ff
8.	Fregist the knight	„ 819	Gough App. p. 45	
9.	Algar the knight, the son of Northlang	„ 825	„	„ 44;

B. Second period of the monastery 870 – 1066.
  I. Charters of kings of England:
    10. Edred, on coins: Eadred   dated 948   Fulm.   p. 32 ff
    11. Edgar, on coins: Eadgar   „ 966   „   „ 42 ff
    12. Edgar, charter to Peterborough „ 970   „   „ 46 ff
    13. Edgar, charter to Malmesbury   „ 974   „   „ 47 f
    14. Cnut   „ 1032   „   „ 58 ff
    15. Eadward the Confessor   „ [1048]   „   „ 64;
  II. Charter of a noble:
    16. Thorold of Bukenhale [Bucknall Linc.] „ 1051 „   „ 86 ff;
C. Third period of the monastery 1066 – 1135.
  I. Charters of kings of England:
    17. William I   dated [1086] Fulm.   p. 85 ff
    18. Henry I   „ 1114   ,   „ 121
    19. Henry I, charter to Spalding   „ [1114]   „   „ 124;
  II. Charter of a noble:
    20. Alan de Creoun   „ 1114   „   „ 126;
D. Besides these charters, the following documents are found in the Ingulf:
    21. The statute of Æthelbald of Mercia 719 or 749   Fulm.   p. 5
    22. The charter of Æthelwulf of Wessex 855   „   „ 17
    23. The ecclesiastical censure of 966   „   „ 44 ff
    24. The decree of 1072 concerning the precedence of the See of Canterbury „ „ 92.

365 Nearly all these charters have been condemned as forgeries, on account both of the anachronisms in the witnesses, and of expressions of later date found in them. Prof. John Earle's Handbook to the Land charters and other Saxonic documents (8° Oxf. 1888) may be taken as a sufficient guide as to what may cause an A. S. charter to be at once rejected or not, apart from other circumstances, which may decide for or against the charter. His work is divided into: Part I. Primary documents, I. Genuine records dated [pp. 1 – 248], II. Genuine records undated [pp. 249 – 277]; and Part II. Secondary documents [pp. 278 – 452].

In no case are the boundaries given in the Ingulfine charters, as so constantly in Earle and Birch (Cartularium Saxonicum 8° Lond. 1883 ff), in the A. S. language, and towards the end of the charters.

It is strange, that the writer of the Ingulf should not have had before him any charters of the kind, of which the cartularies and chronicles of the monasteries, such as Abingdon, Ramsey, etc. are full; very many royal charters of A.S. date, granting different portions of land, are there to be found, but they are very unlike the Ingulfine charters.

These charters, Mercian and English alike, are all, with the exception of king Eadred's, called 'chirographum'. This word does not seem to occur in Earle as equivalent to 'charter'; the word there is 'cartula', which is found in the charters of Hlothari king of Kent a. 676 (Earle p. 8) and of many succeeding kings down to Æthelred II. a. 987 (Earle p. 209); the word 'schedula' is also sometimes used.

The word 'chirographum' often occurs in Stapleton's Magni Rotuli Scaccarii Normanniæ in 1198 in the context: 'sicut cyrographum inter eos testatur' (ii. 346, 381, 410, 420 etc.), so that the word seems to mean 'indenture', 'agreement', words not applicable to royal charters. It occurs, indeed, though only rarely in the Primary Documents, viz. in the deed (MS. Cott. August. II. 61) of 12 Oct. 803 of Æthelheard archbishop of Canterbury (Earle p. 70 ff; Birch no. 310), which abolished the archbishopric of Lichfield, where we read: 'Hic sunt nomina sanctorum episcoporum et abbatum qui præscriptum cyrographi cartulam In synodo qui factus est æt Clofeshoum.

anno aduentus Domini .DCCC.III Cum signo sanctæ crucis xp̄i firmauerunt', and in a charter of king Eadgar a. 960 (Earle p. 195, Birch no. 1055). It occurs also in a Secondary Document of Æthelred II. of the year 996 (Earle p. 404), reendowing the monastery of St Albans, where is found: 'Scriptum et renouatum est huius libertatis chirographum...+Ego Æthelredus Anglorum basileus hanc renouationis et libertatis cartam scribere jussi'; in this document the charter itself is variously described by the witnesses as 'hæc scedula', 'hæc diffinitio', and (by bishop Ælfheah of Winchester) as 'hoc chirographum'. The word 'chirographum' is found also in 11th century charters of Worcester diocese among the Brit. Mus. facsimiles, part iv, the word being written between two identical copies of the charter, and the knife or scissors that parted the twin deeds passing through it, e.g. in charters of Wulfstan archbishop of York and bishop of Worcester 1003 - 23 (no. 13; Earle p. 234), of Ælfweard abbat of Evesham 1017 - 23 (no. 15; Earle p. 235), of Byrhtch bishop of Worcester 1033 - 38 (no. 19; Earle p. 238), of Lyfing bishop of Worcester 1038 (no 22; Earle p. 239).

367 The word 'cartula' is found in Ingulf (Fuhn. p. 17) in Æthelwulf's donation of 855, but in no Croyland charter.

The charter of Eadred of 948 (Fuhn. p. 32) styles itself a 'carta', a word, which is otherwise frequently used by Ingulf in his narrative (Fuhn. pp. 2, 6, 8, 12 etc.), 'chirographum' also being there used (Fuhn. pp. 16, 17, 25 etc.), as is also the word 'confirmatio' (Fuhn. pp. 18, 58, 85). The Normans, according to Ingulf (Fuhn. p. 70), 'chirographa chartas vocabant', but the word was perhaps of earlier date (Hickes, Dissert. Epist. p. 63).

xxix. The witnesses to the Ingulfine charters.

368 The witnesses to the charters as set forth in the Ingulf are both lay and clerical.

Of lay witnesses we find personages of the following classes:
    king,
    queen,
    other royal personages,

ealdorman, duke, dux,
earl, comes,
countess, comitissa,
thane, thegn, minister,
sheriff, vicecomes, vicedominus;
of ecclesiastical witnesses:
archbishop of Canterbury,
archbishop of York,
bishop,
abbat,
abbess,
priest.

In addition to these, besides titles belonging to nobles and thanes, as 'princeps' (Earle p. 52), 'patricius', 'pincerna', 'pedesecus', 'præfectus', we find further in Earle as designations of ecclesiastics: archdeacon, subdeacon, priest ('presbyter'), deacon, and presbyter abbat.

The signatures of a charter are not autographs. The name **369** of the signatary is the work of the scribe, and even the cross 'signum', the making of which should be the essence of the signature, and 'which presumably may have been at the outset traced by the hand of each of the signataries', seems also to have been made beforehand by the scribe, while at the time of the execution of the charter the 'signer went over it with a dry pen, or laid a finger upon it', in spite of such expressions as: '...signum sanctæ crucis subscripsi', and 'libenti animo propria manu crucem infixi'. There are some charters, which have also in addition a small cross marked besides above the name of the witness (Earle pp. 174, 176, 191), while many charters in the Brit. Mus. series of facsimiles have no crosses at all prefixed to the names.

The diminutive of 'signum' 'sigillum', which in later times **370** received a different meaning, is found in Ordericus Vitalis' description of Æthelbald's charter of 716, 'inde cartam sigillo suo signatum confirmavit', although the word itself does not occur in the Ingulfine text. Actual seals do not appear attached to genuine charters till the time of Edward the

Confessor. The seal of wax 'cereum signum' is only once mentioned in Pet. Bles. (Fulm. p. 126) about the year 1114. In a charter of Æthelstan of 939 (Earle p. 173 ff) is found '✠ Ego Æthelstanus rex totius Britanniæ præfatam donationem cum sigillo sanctæ ✠ crucis confirmavi'.

371 The signataries are sometimes very numerous. A charter of king Æthelstan of 931 (Earle p. 166 ff; Kemble C. D. no. 353, Birch no. 677) is signed by the king, the two archbishops, two 'subreguli', seventeen bishops, fifteen 'duces', five abbats, and 59 'ministri' or thegns, in all 102 signataries. Another charter of Æthelstan of 934 (Earle p. 171, Kemble no. 364) has a very long list of 90 witnesses. These are far longer lists than any found in the Ingulf.

372 Of these different classes of witnesses it is necessary to say something:

The only queen, who signs in Ingulf, is Editha (Eadgyth) the wife of Eadward the Confessor. But in Birch and in Earle we find several other queens, of Mercia, of Wessex, and of England, signing sometimes with their husbands or sons:

 Cynethyth, the wife of Offa;
 *Ælfthryth, the wife of Coenwlf (Kenulph);
 *Cynethryth, the wife of Wiglaf;
 Saethryth, the wife of Berhtwulf;
 *Æthelswith, the wife of Burgred;
 Judith, the second wife of Æthelbald of Wessex;
 *Eadgifu, the widow of Edward the elder, and mother of the kings Eadmund and Eadred; she signs with her sons;
 Ælfgifu-Emma, 'the lady', the widow of Æthelred II. and Cnut (d. 1052); she signs with Eadward the Confessor her son.

It is curious, that none of these queens sign the charters of their husbands and sons contained in Ingulf, although those marked with * signed charters of later dates.

 Eadgyth signs with her husband Eadward the Confessor and his mother Ælfgifu-Emma Kemble no. 779 (1045), but also with the king alone Kemble nos. 776, 778 (1045), 1335 (1046).

The A.S. title 'caldorman' does not occur in the Ingulf, **373** where all the charters are in latin. The equivalent is chiefly 'dux', less frequently 'comes' (Fl. Wig.), even 'princeps' or 'consul' (H. Hunt.). A comparative list of titles is given in Kemble, Saxons (1876) iij. 127 ff. Heabricht, who is styled 'comes' in no. 2 and in Fl. Wig. (a. 805), is styled 'caldorman' in A.S.Chr. (a. 805).

The title 'comes' occurs in Ingulf together with 'dux' in **374** nos. 5 and 6, and even with 'dux' and 'minister' in no. 10; but in Earle we find the titles 'dux' and 'minister' used almost exclusively. In an A. S. charter of Ælfwerd abbat of Evesham c. 1020 (Earle p. 235), two 'eorls' (Hacun and Eglaf) and an 'caldorman' (Leofwine) are mentioned by name. But in Felix' Life of St Guthlac, as also in the abridgment by Ord. Vit., among his visitors are mentioned 'comites' (no 'duces'), which in the A. S. version is represented by 'caldormen'; in a charter of Æthelbald of Mercia of 736 (Earle p. 29) we find: '✠ ego Onoc comes subscripsi', as well as: '✠ ego Æthilric subregulus atq. comes gloriosissimi principis Æthilbaldi...subscripsi'; Pilheard was 'comis' of Coenwulf, king of Mercia, c. 800, Heardberht was 'comes' in 805—811, Aldhun in 811, Swithnoth in 814, Leofric in 1045 (B. Mus. facsimiles). In Asser [Fl. Wig. s. a. 860] the word 'comes' occurs as the equivalent of 'caldorman', and in A.S.Chr. D E (s. a. 851) of 'dux' (Kemble, Saxons 1876 ij. 125 ff).

In a charter of Æthelbald of Mercia of 742 (Earle pp. lxxv¹, 36-40) 'a list of persons removable from office' is given as 'comes, presbyter, diaconus, clericus, monachus'.

'Still more important is it to keep the Saxon *comes* distinct from the *Comes* of the Normans, which stands for the Latin equivalent of the titular *Earl*. The so-called "Asser" has the *Comes* and it is ominous' (Earle p. lxv¹). On Asser and his life of Ælfred, see Dr Lingard, Anglo-Saxon church j. 420 ff.

A countess 'comitissa' Sigburga (Sigeburh) occurs as a **375** benefactor in no. 4 (a. 833); and Godiva (Godgifu) the wife of caldorman or earl Leofric, who signs no. 16 (a. 1051), styles herself 'comitissa', by which title also she is described in Fl. Wig. a. 1055. The title seems not to occur in Earle's Genuine

Records, and Freeman remarks: 'I may notice, that Godgifu, Ælfgifu, and other wives of earls, are in Domesday and in other Latin writings freely called "comitissa". But I have not found any English equivalent for that title. "Lady" belongs to the king's wife only; an Earl's wife seems to be simply called the Earl's wife and nothing else' (ij. ed. III. p. 683).

376 Sheriffs 'vicedomini' are mentioned in nos. 5 and 10; and sheriffs occur as benefactors in nos. 3, 4, 5 and 6, but the sheriff is called 'vicecomes' in nos. 3 and 4, and 'vicedominus' in nos. 5 and 6. In Eadred's charter no. 10 are found among the signataries 'Byngulph vicedominus' and 'Alfer vicecomes'. Three of the Ingulfine benefactors of 833 (no. 4) are Thorold, Norman, and Siward, all sheriffs ('vicecomes'). These names are all of later date; there is a historical Thorold in Domesday, who is however omitted in the Ingulfine transcript (§ 20), a historical Norman a brother of earl Leofric (A.S.Chr. Fl. Wig. a. 1017), and a historical Siward the earl of Northumberland and father of earl Waltheof. A Thorold was moneyer of Æthelred II. at Lincoln. The sheriffs Thorold and Norman, who were large benefactors, occur in the Guthlac scroll presenting their benefactions to St Guthlac; the gift of Siward was of smaller extent, and his gift is not there referred to. The benefaction of the Thorold of 806 was at Bukenhale [Bucknall], that of the Thorold of Bukenhale of 1051 was at Spalding; the Thorold of Domesday gave to St Guthlac lands at Bukenhale.

377 Knights 'milites' are frequently mentioned in the Ingulfine charters as early as no. 3 (806); and nos. 8 and 9 are records of benefactions by two men of this rank in 819 and 825 respectively. Several knights are mentioned in Earle, 'Secondary Documents' pp. 336 ff dated 855; and in Liber Eliensis, Vol I. pp. 113, 156 we find 'miles' printed, but this might be caused by a misreading of the 'm̅' or 'm̅i' for minister, though in Earle's Genuine Records 'miles' and 'minister' occur together a. 1038 (p. 239), and 'mit' occurs c. 1010 (p. 235). It occurs very frequently in Domesday (Ellis j. 58).

378 The archbishop of York signs after the archbishop of Canterbury very constantly in Earle from the time of king

Æthelstan 925-940. In Ingulf also this is found, but we find, besides, Enbald archbishop of York signing with the archbishop of Canterbury in the charter of Wiglaf of Mercia of 833 (no. 4) as 'archiepiscopus Eboracensis', and the 'archbishops of England' signing Æthelwulf's donation of 855 (no. 22).

On three occasions Ingulf (as printed in Fulm. pp. 45, 64, 66) calls the northern primate 'archiepiscopus Eboracæ'. This might be thought to be a mistake, as elsewhere York is called 'Eboracum'; but in Æthelweard and in the original part of Sym. Dun. 'civitas Eboraca' is common; in Fl. Wig. (not in Sym. Dun.) a. 919 we find: 'Ægelfleda Merciorum domina...Leogereceastram pacifice acquisivit...cui...Dani qui Eboracæ præsidebant,... firmaverunt se ipsius voluntati...consensuros', and in the Latin appendix to A.S.Chr. A again: 'Septimo anno...mandavit...ut Eboracam irent', while in Sym. Dun. [R.S.] ij. App. III. p. 392 we find: 'Habet [Anglia] sedes metropolitanas duas, Cantuariam et Eboracam'. On the York coins of the English kings from Edward I. to Edward VI., 1272-1553, we always find CIVITAS EBORACI. In MS. Arundel 178 the word reads 'Ebor.', 'Eboracensis', 'Eboracæ'. In William of Newburgh [R. S.] 'Eboraca' is very frequent.

In Earle's 'Genuine records' of early date the notices of the **379** sees of the episcopal signataries are scarcely ever added to their names, while in the Ingulf they are uniformly so given. This practice begins with Æthelstan 925-940, though a few earlier examples occur, as 'Mercensis ecclesiæ episcopus' a. 749 (Earle p. 44), 'Archiepiscopus Dorobernensis ecclesiæ', and 'Liccelfeldensis ecclesiæ episcopus' a. 803 (Earle p. 73). Schlumberger, Sigillographie byzantine, gives the seal of bishop John of Athens in the 7th century with the inscription ΘΕΟΤΟΚΕ ΒΟΗΘΕΙ ΙΩΑΝΝΗ ΕΠΙΣΚΟΠΩ ΑΘΗΝΩΝ. In a charter of king Eadgar to Abingdon of 961 (Earle, p. 197) the bishops designate themselves in fantastical ways never found in Ingulfine charters, 'præsul', 'pontifex', 'antistes', 'plebis Dei famulus', 'legis Dei catascopus'.

The names of the abbeys are perhaps never appended to **380** the names of the abbats. The Cotton MS. Aug. II. 38, king

Æthelred's charter to Abingdon of 993, which has names of the monasteries appended to the names of the abbats, is marked by Kemble and Thorpe as 'spurious or of doubtful authority'. The only signature of a possible abbat of Croyland found in charters is that of abbat Brihtmær 1018 – 48, who appears as a signatary to a charter of Cnut of 1031 (Brit. Mus. Facsim. IV. 18), and to two in Kemble C. D. no. 741 (1024) and no. 743 (1026). 'Býrhtmær abbod' is one of the witnesses of a charter of Æthelred II. in 1012, and of the will of Æthelstan Ætheling son of Æthelred II. in 1015 (Earle p. 227), but this must be the earlier (1008 – 1021 MS. Harl. 1008 – 1032 Kennet, Wharton) abbat of Newminster of that name (Dugd. Mon. ij. 427 ff.).

381 In the Ingulfine charters four abbesses are found among the witnesses of charters:

Ceolburga Ceolburh, of Berkeley (d. 805 A.S.Chr. Fl. Wig.) signs no. 2 a. 793;

Merwenna Mærwyn, of Romsey (appointed 967 Fl. Wig.) signs nos. 11 and 23, charters of the year 966;

Herleva Herelufu, of Shaftesbury, and

Wulwinna Wulfwyn, of Wareham, who both died in 982 (Fl. Wig. A.S.Chr. C not E), sign no. 23 of the year 966.

Abbesses are also spoken of as signing no. 22, Æthelbald's donation of 855 (Fulm. p. 17) 'abbatum et abbatissarum, ducum, comitum, procerumque totius terræ, aliorumque fidelium infinite multitudo'. In Birch C. S. several forms of this document are given from different sources, nos. 468 – 9 – 70 – 1 – 2 – 83 – 484 – 5, but in none of them except in 484, which is the Ingulfine no. 22, is any mention of the signature of an abbess to be found.

In Earle the only charter, which has any signature of an abbess, is one of Ceolwulf of Mercia of the year 811 (p. 86 ff., Birch no. 335), where we find:

'+ Cuuocnburg abba sub.
+ Seleburg abb subscripsit'.

In a charter of Æthered and Æthelflæd king Ælfred's daughter, the rulers of Mercia 'monarchiam Merceorum tenentes' of the year 901 to Wenlock abbey (Earle p. 159 ff.,

Kemble no. 330, Birch no. 587), when the abbess Mildburg is mentioned, some undescribed ladies, Wigburg, Cineburg, Æthelswith, Wulfgyth, are found among the signataries.

An archdeacon is spoken of in no. 23 of 966, and this has **382** been commented on by Mr Riley as a mark of spuriousness, archdeacons having been introduced into England only after the Conquest by archbishop Lanfranc. But archdeacons, whatever their functions may have been, are mentioned in Earle's 'Genuine Records'. In charters of Æthelheard archbishop of Canterbury of the years 803 (p. 72 ff.), 805 (p. 78 f.) we find 'Uulfred archidiaconus' (or 'arc diā'). In a charter of 831 (Earle p. 102 ff.) four archdeacons are mentioned.

'+ ego Sigefreth ar̃dc̃ *consensi*
+ ego Ealhstan ar̃dc̃ *consensi*
+ ego Biarnnoth ar̃dc̃ *consensi*
+ ego Wynhelm arc̃d *consensi*'.

In a charter of Æthelberht of Wessex of the year 863 (Earle p. 133 ff.) three archdeacons sign, Biarnheah, Osulf and Sigefreth, and in one of his successor Æthelred I. of the year 867 (p. 137 ff.) also three, Sigefred, Bearnoth and Herefreth; these are followed by signatures of subdeacons. Again in a charter of Suithulf bishop of Rochester of the year 889 (p. 152 f.) the signature of 'Ciolmund archidiaconus' occurs. Other cases are found.

In Goussainville's edition of Peter of Blois (fo. Paris 1667) we find p. 767 ('notæ') references to the office of archdeacons from the sixth century downwards, in Spain and France.

In the Ingulfine charter of Eadgar to Peterborough of 970, **383** a long string of 14 names without designations is found. A parallel case may be seen in Earle p. 113 in a charter of 836, where 12 such persons follow the bishops and 'duces'.

In general, the genuine charters begin with a Preamble **384** prefaced by an Invocation, or with an Invocation itself constituting the Preamble.

Ingulf's Mercian charters 716 – 868 all begin with the king's name and style without any Preamble or Invocation at all; but although some of Earle's 'Genuine Records' of corresponding dates (pp. 15 ff.) have also either only a short Invocation as Preamble, which might easily be omitted by the writer, or else no Preamble at all, there is this difference that they begin: 'Ego N...rex...', whereas Ingulf's Mercian charters all begin with the greeting: 'N...rex Merciorum...salutem...', a form which apparently is not found in any genuine charters of that period, but begins with William I.

Eadred's charter of 948, no. 10, has however a short Preamble: 'Pax in summae Trinitatis nomine, Patris, Filii, et Spiritus Sancti, Amen', while Eadgar's charter of 966, no. 11, has a longer one of the very common type 'Imperante Domino nostro Jesu Christo etc.'

Ingulf's later charters have, like his Mercian ones, no Preamble at all.

385 Not many of these charters are 'Land charters'. Besides the foundation charter of 716, only nos. 7, 8, 9, 16 are grants of lands, the other royal charters being merely confirmations of earlier grants. None such seem to be found in Earle; in the 14th and 15th centuries they were very common.

It is curious, that Ingulf did not find and recite Turketul's deed of gift of the six manors in 948, although he has preserved one such document of 810 (no. 7).

xxx. The anachronisms found in the Ingulfine charters.

386 The anachronisms in the signatures of the bishops first pointed out by Henry Wharton (§ 254, 359), drew the attention of antiquaries to the possible spuriousness first of the Ingulfine charters, then of the Ingulfine history as a whole. Dr Stubbs' 'Registrum sacrum anglicanum' (4°. Oxf. 1858) enables us to investigate this point thoroughly and easily.

It is somewhat remarkable, that the writer should have made so many mistakes about the bishops, when he is so frequently right about the other signataries, where they can be traced. On the supposition of forgery, the question arises, Whence did the forger procure names, that so often fit in so well? The archbishops of Canterbury are always rightly placed, except in nos. 4? and 8.

All these charters are in Kemble C. D. marked with a star as spurious or doubtful. Hallam's note (Middle Ages 1846 ij. 88 note) is 'I do not pretend to assert the authority of these charters, which at all events are nearly as old as the Conquest. Hickes calls most of them in question. Dissert. Epist. p. 66 ; but some later antiquaries seem to have been more favourable. Archæologia, vol. xviii. [1817] p. 49 [Douce, Remarks on the original seal belonging to the abbey of Wilton]. Nouveau Traité de Diplomatique, t. i. p. 348.'

1. Charter of Æthelbald king of Mercia, ...716. **387**
[Kemble no. 66*, Birch no. 135.]

Of the four bishops who sign two are wrong: 1. Wynfrid [Wilfred] bishop of the Mercians [Worcester] 718 - c. 744; and 2. Aldwin bishop of Lichfield 721 - 737. The day of the death of Ecgwin, Wilfred's predecessor, is given exactly by Fl. Wig. as iij Kal. Jan. feria v, Thursday 30 Dec. 717, (the Dominical Letter of 717 being C, the 30 Dec. 717 was really a Thursday), so that Wilfred's promotion fell practically into the following year, 718, although he was elected in the lifetime of Ecgwin, 'illo [Egwino] adhuc superstite' (Fl. Wig.).

Two abbats sign, Æthelred of Bardeney, formerly king of Mercia (d. 716 Fl. Wig.), and Egbald of Medeshamsted [Egwald, Riley, by mistake]. The latter is mentioned in A.S.Chr. E s. a. 686.

The laymen are: 1. Egga earl of Lincoln, known only as such from this place (Dugd. Bar. j. 6. a.), but possibly derived from the comes Egga of the Guthlac Scroll, out of whom St Guthlac drove an evil spirit; Ecgga is also mentioned in Felix' life of St Guthlac (Birch p. 42), but there he is 'præfati exulis Æthilbaldi comes quidam cognomine Ecgga'; in the A. S. translation the 'comes' is the 'gefere'; 2. Leuric earl of Leicester or rather of Chester 'Legaceaster', Leicester being Legraceaster, also known (Dugd. Bar. j. 6. b.) only from this place; Leuric is a form of Leofric, which occurs in Domesday Linc. (photozincograph p. LXXI. a.), in Geffrei Gaimar (Leofric earl of Mercia), and in Hugo Candidus (Sparke), p. 42 ; and 3. Saxulph, Seaxwulf, the son of earl Saxulph. Ingulf a priest signs last.

In his account of 'the Descent of the Earldom of Lincoln' (§ 247) Mr J. G. Nichols says: 'The...name Egga is not merely apocryphal, but purely fictitious. It occurs only among the witnesses to the spurious foundation charter of Croyland abbey, a document fabricated by the monks of a subsequent age'. But besides occurring in Felix' life and the Guthlac Scroll, the name Egga is found also in A.S.Chr. D as that of a 'high reeve' slain in 778.

The abbat of Croyland is Kenulph or Coenwulf, the namesake of king Kenulf of Mercia 796 – 819, of an abbat slain 905 (Fl. Wig.), of a bishop of Winchester d. 1006 (A.S.Chr.) etc.

This is the first charter condemned by H. Wharton; it was however in existence in 1393 (§ 192). Dr Hickes (Dissert. Epist. p. 66) says of this charter: 'Chartam...hanc ementiri necesse habuit coenobium *Croilandense*, qua terras suas sine charta datas, aut quarum chartas perdiderant, servarent à *Nortmannis*, qui nullam fere justam possidendi praedia causam, praeter chartas, Monasteriis indulgebant'. (But see § 126.)

2. Charter of Offa king of Mercia, ...793.
   [Kemble no. 163*, Birch no. 268.]

Here we find all the three bishops wrong: 1. Ægbald [Ecgbald] bishop of Winchester c. 772 – c. 782, Kinbert subscribing 785 – 801; 2. Aldred [Ealdred] bishop of Dorchester c. 839 – 840 (Fl. Wig. Cat.), Unwona subscribing 785 – 799; and 3. Aldulf bishop of Lichfield c. 802 – 815, Higbert subscribing 779 – 801 as archbishop of Lichfield.

Of the other witnesses, Ceolburga abbess of Berkeley and earl Heabriht are mentioned together in Fl. Wig. as dying in 805. Besides these, Beonna abbat of Medeshamsted (A.S.Chr. E s. a. 777 'in the days of king Offa'), and Tilhere priest and scribe are witnesses to the charter. Tilhere bishop of Worcester (the Hwiccii) died in 781 (Fl. Wig.).

The abbat mentioned in this charter is named Patricius. The name does not occur (except as St Patrick) in the indices to the A.S.Chr., M. H. B., or the Scriptores Decem. It was borne however by several abbats of the 12th and 13th centuries, as of Alnwick 1152 – 67, of Melros 1206 – 7, of Calconia 1258 –

60 (Chron. de Mailros, Fulm. Index); Patricius de Evreux earl of Salisbury was killed in 1167 (Dugd. Bar. j. 174. b.). The name Patricius occurs frequently in the additions to the 'Liber Vitæ Eccl. Dunelm.' (Surtees Soc.).

Queen Cynethryth does not subscribe this charter of 793; the latest date however at which her signature is found in Birch is 790.

3. Charter of Kenulph (Coenwulf) king of Mercia,......806. **389**

[Kemble no. 192*, Birch no. 325.]

Again the bishops are both wrong : 1. Kinebert bishop of Winchester c. 783 – c. 801, Eahlmund being consecrated 802; 2. Wunwona bishop of Leicester c. 783 – c. 800, Werenbert being consecrated 802 and subscribing 803 – 814.

Coolred abbat of Medeshamsted is mentioned in A.S.Chr. E a. 852; Cuthred king of Kent 'rex Cantuariorum' died 805 (A.S.Chr. see § 10); Coolwulf 'frater domini regis Kenulphi' succeeded him in 819; he signs a charter as 'rex Cantiæ' with Coenwulf of Mercia in 805 ? (Earle, Genuine records p. 75). The other witnesses are : Algar (Ælfgar) the thane 'minister', and Sigga the priest 'presbyter' and scribe. Ælfgar the thane may be intended to suggest earl Ælfgar; Sigga, the same as Sigfrid, Sigefrith, was the name of a bishop of Selsey 733 – c. 750 (Sym. Dun. a. 733; Fl. Wig. Cat.); the name occurs also in A.S.Chr. a. 789, 793, and in the 'Liber Vitæ Eccl. Dunelm.' (Surtees Soc.) p. 18. c.

The abbat of Croyland mentioned in this charter is Siward, described as brother of Celred (Coolred) abbat of Medeshamsted. The name is late and Danish; it was borne by an archbishop of Canterbury 1044 – 48, by a bishop of Rochester 1058 – 75, also by the father of earl Waltheof (d. 1055).

Queen Ælfthryth, of whom Kenulph speaks as 'regina mea' (Fulm. p. 6), subscribes several charters of her husband from 799 to 817, but here in 806 her name is not found.

4. Charter of Wichtlaf (Wiglaf) king of Mercia, **390**
London, 26 May 833.

[Kemble no. 233*, Birch no. 409.]

Of the ten bishops who subscribe two only are right, the

remaining eight being wrong: 1. Eanbald I. archbishop of York sat 780 - 796, Eanbald II. was consecrated in 796, and although the date of his death does not seem to be recorded, yet on the death of his successor Wulfsy, Wigmund sat 837 - c. 854; 2. Osmund bishop of London 802 - c. 809, Ceolbert subscribing 824 - 839; 3. Helmstan of Winchester 838 - c. 850; 4. Herewin of Lichfield c. 815 - 817, his successor Æthelwald being consecrated 818; 5. Cedda of Hereford was succeeded by Aldberht in 777; 6. Adelstan of Sherburn, apparently another name or a mistake for Ealhstan (Fl. Wig. a. 823) or Heahstan (Stubbs) 824 - 867; 7. Herfred [Herefrith] of Worcester, not known to Fl. Wig. Cat., Eadberht being bishop 822 - 848; in Will. Malm. G. P. (R. S. p. 278) Hereferth is a mistake for Wereferth signing 873 - 915; 8. Godwine of Rochester 995 - ..., who also occurs in no. 5 of 851 and in no. 23 of 966! Archbishop Ceolnoth, who was consecrated 24 Aug. 833 (Stubbs), is represented as signing this charter on 26 May previous; in Fl. Wig. however the consecration is put in 830.

The abbats Hedda of Medeshamsted (killed 870 Ingulf, Joh. Petrib.), Ambert Eanberht of Repton 'abbas Ripadii', and Kynewin of Bardeney are also witnesses; but Dugdale (vj. 429) has no prior of Repton before 1200 (indeed in 697 it was in the hands of an abbess Ælfthryth [Felix, St Guthlac]), nor any other notice of Kynewin than that of this charter (j. 623).

Wiglaf's overlord Ecgberht king of Wessex and his son Æthelwulf also sign.

Of the caldormen, who sign, Wulhard 'Wulfheard' and Athelm 'Æthelhelm' were killed in 837, and Herenbriht in 838 (A.S.Chr. Fl. Wig.). Other witnesses are: Swithun priest of king Ecgberht, and Bosa scribe of king Wiglaf. Bishop Swithhun of Winchester was consecrated in 852, and died 2 July 862; and Bosa was bishop of York (Fl. Wig.) 678 - 705.

The abbat of Croyland is again Siward.

Cynethryth (not to be confounded with the queen of king Offa, or with the sister of St Kenelm), the wife of king Wiglaf, who subscribes two of the few charters of that king, a. 831, 836, does not subscribe here in 833. Fulman in his Index prints: 'Celfreda, ux. Witlafi R.', but Celfreda is a mistake for Alfleda (Ælflæd, Æthelfleda Will. Malm.), and she was wife of Wigmund, king Wiglaf's son. In like manner Fulman (p. 30) prints Cilward for Eilward (Fulm. marg.) or Æthelward; in the Ann. de Waverleia [R. S.] a. 1072 we find Cilricus for Eilric or Æthelric bishop of Durham.

This is the second charter condemned by Henry Wharton.

5. Charter of Bertulph (Berhtwulf) king of Mercia, **391** Kingsbury, 27 March 851.

[Kemble no. 265*, Birch no. 461.]

This charter bears the signatures of six bishops, of whom four are wrong: 1. Swithulph of London (Fl. Wig. Cat.), his predecessor Deorwulf signing 860 – 862; 2. Orkenwald of Lichfield, not known to Fl. Wig. Cat., Tunberht subscribing 844 – 857; in Fl. Wig. Cat. the name Oithelwaldus is found, which is a form of Æthelwald, who was bishop 818 – c. 828; this may have been read Orkenwaldus; it was actually read Herkenwald by Will. Malm. G. P. [R. S. p. 308]; 3. Rethun Hrethun of Leicester 816 – 840, Ceolred subscribing 840 – 869; 4. Godwin of Rochester 995 – ... (see no. 4).

The case of bishop Swithulph of London is somewhat peculiar. In Fl. Wig. a. 897 is recorded the death of 'Suithulfus Hrofensis ecclesiæ præsul'; he does not however occur in the list of the bishops of Rochester in Fl. Wig. Cat., where no names are given between 844 and c. 933, seven bishops being altogether omitted. Fl. Wig. may have entered Swithulf among the London bishops by mistake, and the writer of the Ingulf may thereby have been misled into giving him a place as such among the signataries to this charter. He is found signing a grant of land as bishop of Rochester in 889 (Earle p. 152). There seems no trace of any Swithulf of London.

Three abbats subscribe: Wulfard 'Wulfheard' of Evesham (Chron. Abb. de Evesh. [R. S.] p. 77), Living Lyfing of Winchelcombe, not elsewhere mentioned (Dugd.), and Hedda of Medeshamsted (see no. 3).

The ealdormen (duces) Emulph 'Eanwulf', and Osric are mentioned in 845, the latter also in 860; two more ealdormen (comites) Elhere 'Ealhhere Ealchere' of Kent, and Huda of Surrey occur in A.S.Chr. A E a. 853; Oslac the butler 'pincerna' (Fl. Wig.) and father-in-law of king Æthelwulf died 855 (A.S.Chr.). Earl Serlo (Fulm. p. 15) is an impossibility at so early a date, Serlo being a Norman name that occurs very frequently after the Conquest, when an abbat of Gloucester (d. 1104), a bishop of Séez a. 1120, a canon of Bayeux c. 1100, a dean of Salisbury, and very many other persons of that name occur; it is also very often found in Stapleton's Magni Rotuli Scaccarii Normanniæ, c. 1200. In this charter, however, it may be a mistake for a Saxon name, as 'Scule corl' occurs in charters of c. 930 given in Birch and Earle (Genuine records pp. 172, 183), and Savile prints the name as Serto.

The abbat is still Siward.

Queen Sæthryth, who signs with king Berhtwulf from 840 to 849, may have died in that year, as she does not appear among the witnesses to the king's later charters of 851 (besides this one of Croyland) and of 852.

This is the third charter condemned by Wharton (p. 25); it is also condemned by Dr Hickes, Thes. Præf. p. xxviii.

392   6. Charter of Beorred Burhred Burgred king of Mercia, Snothryngaham, Snotingaham, Nottingham.

1 Aug. 868.

[Kemble no. 297*, Birch no. 521.]

Here, among the five bishops, some unknown ones are found: 1. Elstan of London may be right, as his predecessor Deorwulf subscribed 860 – 862, and he himself died a. 898 or 900; 2. Edmund of Sherburn possibly stands for Heahmund 868 – 871; 3. Alewin of Winchester ('Winton') is not known, Alfred sat 862 – c. 875, and Fulman has in the margin 'Wigornensis', but the bishop of that time is Aelhun 848 – 872; 4. Kyneberht of Lichfield is a mistake made also by Will. Malm. G. P. (R. S. 312) and Matth. Paris s. a. 872 for Kyneferth (Fl. Wig. a. 871 Fl. Wig. Cat.) subscribing 836 – 841; 5. Ethelbert of Hereford is unknown, Deorlaf subscribing 866 – 884.

Three abbats sign: Tivinus of St Albans, and Wulfsy of Evesham, whose names are not to be found in the series of abbats of their respective houses, and Hedda of Medeshamsted, already mentioned in nos. 3 and 4. In a charter of Eanberht of the Hwiccas of 757 (Kemble no. 102*; Earle 'Secondary Documents' p. 307) one of the signatures is: '+ signum manus Tiluuini abbatis'; his monastery is not known.

The charter is signed by Æthelred I. king of Wessex 866–871 and by his brother Ælfred, who were both present at the siege of Nottingham with king Burgred their brother-in-law (Fl. Wig.), and also by Eadmund the martyr-king of the East Angles.

Two 'duces' sign, one being Adelred possibly meant for the 'comes Gainorum' Æthelred Mucel, whose daughter Ealhswith Ælfred (b. 849) married c. 868, the other Osbert, a namesake of the king of Northumbria of 848–867 and of Osbert de Longchamp; 'Osbearht' not further described, signs a charter of king Æthelberht of the year 863 (Earle p. 133 ff.).

The charter has the names of 12 'comites'. Earl Adelwulph 'Æthelwulf' caldorman of Berkshire was killed 871 (Fl. Wig.). Earl Diga is a very curious instance of knowledge, or of chance favouring the writer of this charter, as DIGA is a moneyer of this very king Burgred (Brit. Mus. Cat. of A. S. coins j. 46, 53); 'Dycga presbiter' of the diocese of Hereford signs a decree of archbishop Æthelheard of 12 Oct. 803 (Earle p. 72 ff., Kemble no. 1024). As to earl Burkard, 'Burgheard episcopus' witnesses a charter of king Burgred a. 869 (Kemble no. 299, Birch no. 524), and Burgheard, not further described, subscribes Birch nos. 533 and 534 dated 872 of Werfyrth Werefrith bishop of Worcester. It occurs also in the early part of the Liber Vitae Ecclesiae Dunelm. 'The name Burhhard, though a possible name', says Freeman (ij. ed. III. 680), 'and one borne by several men T. R. E. can hardly be called a common English name'. Other names of earls, which have not been traced are: Wulkelm; Turgot mentioned again Fulm. p. 25 (§ 169) and in Domesday; Alcmund 'Ealhmund'; Lefwine 'Leofwine'; Ascer; Thurstan; Reynard 'Regenheard'; and Tilbrand. Turgot prior of Durham was archbishop of St Andrew's 1109–1115 (Sym. Dun. R. S. j. 111); Wulkelm may be a mistake for Wulfhelm; Ascer may be meant for the same name as Æsca, who signs Birch 518 a. 868 (from the Textus Roffensis), while Ingulf speaks of a contemporary prior of Croyland named Asker (§ 146); Thurstan was abbat of Glastonbury c. 1080, and another was moneyer in the days of Æthelred II. and Cnut.

The abbat of Croyland mentioned is Theodore, the successor of Siward. The only personage bearing that name is the archbishop of Canterbury 668 – 690.

Queen Æthelswith survived her husband and signed his charters till the year 869; but she does not sign this charter of 868.

This is the fourth charter condemned by H. Wharton.

7. Charter of earl Algar 'Ælfgar' the elder,

Leicester, ...810.

[Kemble no. 1026*, Birch no. 331.]

This charter and the two following ones are dated at 'Legecestria', which ought to mean Chester, but from the circumstance of 'Wonwona episcopus Legecestrensis' being mentioned, the place can only be Leicester. In the C. C. C. Oxf. MS. of Fl. Wig., which is of the 12th century, are many notices of bishops inserted in the margin, 'in another and of course later hand'. There the bishop of Leicester who died 796, is called 'episcopus Legecestrensis'; the adjectives 'Legerecensis' and 'Legerensis' are also found (Fl. Wig. Thorpe j. 63³, 79¹, 72¹). Fl. Wig. himself (d. 1118) however calls Leicester 'Leogereceastra' (a. 914, 918, 919), 'Legereceastra' (a. 942); Chester he calls 'Legeceastre' (a. 908) or 'Legionum civitas' (a. 973). Leicestershire is called 'Legrecestrescira' in Hunter Magnus Rotulus Scaccarii 31 H. 1. p. 81. In his account of the return in 1056 of the outlawed earl Algar (Fulm. p. 66), Ingulf says:

'...... comitatum suum recepit, classisque sua Legecestriam deducta est, et a patre suo largissime praemiata recessit'. This Riley wonderfully translates: 'and so [he] recovered his earldom; while his fleet was taken up to Leicester, and after being most bountifully rewarded by his father took its departure'. It was a Norwegian piratical fleet ('xviij piraticis navibus acquisitis' Fl. Wig.), and would much more easily be paid off at Chester on the Dee (Fl. Wig. a. 973), than at Leicester on the Soar (Fl. Wig. s. a. 1055).

Ælfgar is called 'consul Cestriae' by H. Hunt. (R. S. p. 195).

This charter has, besides the signature of Wulfred, the archbishop of Canterbury, only that of Unwona bishop of Leicester c. 783 – c. 800, who is therefore wrong, Werenberht subscribing 803 – 814; he occurs, wrongly also, in no. 3 (a. 806).

The lay signataries are: king Kenulph, Ceolwulf brother of the king and himself king of Mercia 819 – 821 as in no. 3, and 'Algar the son of Algar'. If the latter is the benefactor of 833 mentioned in no. 4, Algar the younger must have been quite a child, when this charter was witnessed by him, as he was killed in battle with the Danes in 870. Leland (De Scriptt. p. 132) mentions 'Fremundus nobilissimi Algari nobilior filius', who was murdered by the Danes 11 May 866; his life was written by Burghard his friend. Bale (cent. 2, p. 125) calls Algar 'occidentalium Anglorum dux'. But according to Capgrave (1516 fo. 150 ff.) Fremund was the son of a certain king Offa (Hardy D. C. j. 521). The name Algar occurs also in Domesday (Ellis j. 368). Earl Ælfgar son of earl Leofric was the father of the two earls Eadwine and Morkere in the time of Eadward the Confessor (A.S.Chr.). The abbat spoken of is Siward (see no. 3).

8. Charter of Fregist the knight,   **394**
Leicester, Festival of St James 25 July 819.
[Kemble no. 213*, Birch no. 365.]

This charter, which is given by Gough, is wrong throughout.

The king is Withlaph 'Withlafius' (Will. Malm.) Wiglaf 825 – 838; the archbishop of Canterbury is Athelard Æthelheard 793 – 805, Wulfred subscribing 805 – 832. We find besides two bishops as witnesses: 1. Egbald of Winchester c. 772 – c. 782, Wigthen subscribing 811 – 828, and 2. Adulph 'Ealdwulf' of Lichfield c. 802 – 814, Ethelwald, who was consecrated 818 (Stubbs), subscribing 822 – 825.

Turstan priest of king Wiglaf also subscribes, besides Siward abbat of Croyland, and Fregist himself.

Fregist is spoken of by king Kenulph in no. 3 of 806 as

'quondam magister meus', and as having bestowed land, not further described, at Langtoft on the monastery before the year 806. The lands mentioned in this charter and in no. 4 (833) are the same.

The name Fregist is probably the same as Frithegist, which appears in the A.S.Chr., but at a much later date.

395   9.   Charter of Algar, Ælfgar the knight,
                                       Leicester, ...825.
[Kemble no. 221*, Birch no. 383.]

In Fulm. p. 10 we read 'Item donum Algari militis [filii Northlang] scilicet Northland in Baston', in Fulm. p. 14 'de dono Algari militis filii Northlang', in Fulm. p. 19 'de dono Algari militis filii Northlang, in Baston'. In this charter Gough prints: 'Algarus miles filius Vorthangiæ'. In the Guthlac scroll he is thus spoken of: 'Ego Algar*us* filius Norlang do tibi [pater Guthlace] Bastune *et* Teford *cum* pertinent*iis*'.

This charter, printed by Gough as of the year DCCXXV, though bearing the name of king Withlaph Wiglaf 825 – 838, has only one bishop subscribing and that wrongly: Osmund of London 802 – c. 809, Ceolbert subscribing 824 – 839; he is also given a. 833 in no. 4.

The remaining witnesses are: Osbert (see no. 6) 'abbas Ripadii', abbat of Repton (no. 4), duke 'Athelin', perhaps Æthelm, who was killed in 837 (no. 4).

The abbat referred to in this charter is Siward (no. 3).

396   10.   Charter of Edred, Eadred king of 'Great Britain',
                                       London, ...948.
[Kemble no. 420*, Birch no. 872.]

Here three out of the four bishops are wrongly dated; they are: 1. Alfred of Sherburn 933 – 943, Wulfsy sitting 943 – c. 958; 2. Kinsy of Lichfield, whose predecessor Wulfgar subscribes in 948, but who, as he was previously bishop of Berkshire (Stubbs Regist.) signing 931 – 934, might succeed without delay, so as to make his signature a possible one. 3. Ceolwulph [so also Stubbs, but Coenwulf Fl. Wig. see § 155, 284] of Dorchester 909 – ..., his successor Winsy subscribing 926 – 934.

Of the lay witnesses: 'duke' Oslac did not become an ealdorman till 966 (A.S.Chr. E); duke Brithnod ealdorman of the East Saxons 962, is mentioned in Eadgar's charter to Medeshamsted (A.S.Chr. E) in 972, signed a charter of Æthelred II. (Earle p. 200) in 987, and was killed at Maldon in 991 (Fl. Wig.).

The names of the earls 'comites', who sign are: Alcin Ealhwine?; Aigulf Ecgwulf Ecgulf?; and Radbod. Radbod prior or provost of Dol c. 925 is mentioned by Will. Malm. Gesta Pontificum [R. S.] p. 399; Radbod bishop of Séez 1025 – 32 occurs in Ord. Vit. ij. 64.

The sheriffs are: Byngulph (vicedominus) and Alfer (vicecomes). Byngulf is probably a mistake for Ryngulf or Hringulf (no. 11); Alfer may be the ealdorman Ælfhere, who died in 983 (A.S.Chr. A E, Fl. Wig.).

Three thanes sign: Farceus ('Harceus' Sav.); Sigeus; and Ethelward. 'Æthelward minister' signs the Malmesbury charter of Eadgar of 974 as given in Reg. Malm. [R. S.] i. 316, but does not appear in the Ingulfine form of it (no. 13). The other two names do not seem to occur elsewhere.

Two abbats sign: Athelwold of Abingdon bishop of Winchester 963 – 984, who in that capacity signs nos. 11, 13, 23; and Dunstan of Glastonbury 942 – 957 (Fl. Wig.).

Queen Eadgifu widow of king Eadward the elder and mother of king Eadred signs with her son in 947 – 9 (Earle, Genuine records p. 182 ff.), but does not sign this charter of 948.

Though this charter is of great importance in the Ingulfine history of the monastery, and is referred to in the later Ingulfine charters of Eadgar, Cnut, William I., Henry I. and elsewhere, yet it is not mentioned by Ord. Vit.

This charter is regarded as spurious by Dr Hickes (Thes. pref. p. xxviii).

11. The charter of Eadgar king of 'Great Britain' or of 'Albion' to Croyland, ...966.
 [Kemble no. 520*, Birch no. 1178.]

The two archbishops and three bishops sign this charter; they are all rightly placed.

The abbats, who sign, are: Ælfstan of Glastonbury, mentioned by Fl. Wig. a. 970; Æthelgar of Hyde (the New Minster), Winchester, 964-980; and Wulfsy 'Wulfsige' of Westminster (Dugd. j. 265 ff.).

Merwenna abbess of Romsey was appointed in 967 (Fl. Wig.). The five caldormen 'duces' are: Ordgar d. 971 (Fl. Wig.); Elphege Ælfheah, duke of Southampton, 'Suthamtonensis dux' (Ingulf), 'Suthamtunensium dux' (Fl. Wig.) d. 971; Brithnod caldorman of Essex (no. 10) killed 991; Alwine, Æthelwine 'Dei amicus', caldorman of the East Angles, killed 992 (Fl. Wig.); Alfer Ælfhere caldorman of the Mercians, d. 983 (Fl. Wig.); these seem all right (Freeman j. ed. III. note AA. pp. 633 ff.); Oslac the sixth caldorman was appointed caldorman in 966 (A.S.Chr. E).

The thanes 'ministri' mentioned are: Ernulph; Rynguhus (Ringulph Riley); Ethelward; and Veif.

In Liber Eliensis Vol. I. pp. 113, 156 (Kemble no. 563*) is found 'Hringulf miles' of the year 970, HRINGVLF occurs among the moneyers of Eadward the Confessor (Journ. Archæol. Ass. 1880, p. 313), and Riggulfus in Sym. Dun. (Hist. Dunelm. eccl. [R. S.] j. 79). Veif (Fulm.), Veisi in Birch, and Vif in Fulm. marg., might be Ulf (Vlf), who appears in Domesday Linc. XXXIIII. 'Terra Gisleberti de Gand' (Photozincograph p. XL. b).

398   12. Charter of Eadgar king of 'Great Britain' or of 'Albion' to Peterborough, ...970.

[Kemble no. 575* a. 972.]

This charter is given, but as of the year 972, in much more concise form, and with fewer attestations, in A.S.Chr. E; it is also given in Dugd. Mon. Vol. I. (1657) p. 65, and in Gunton, History of Peterborough App. p. 135 ff. In the Ingulfine charter the king speaks in the first person plural, wherein Dugdale's and Gunton's transcript agree with it, but in the A.S.Chr. E king Eadgar speaks in the first person singular, as he does also in no. 11; 'Richard I. is the first king, who regularly uses the plural 'we' in the granting of Charters' (Stubbs Const. Hist. j. 631).

With the date 970 an archbishop is wrong: Oswald of York

972 – 992, whose predecessor Oskytel died 1 Nov. 971 (A.S.Chr. B C). Archbishop Oswald signs this charter in A.S.Chr. E (s. a. 963) also, but there the date is 972, 16 Eadgar, i.e. the 16th year since his election as king of Mercia.

The bishops, who subscribe, but to whose names their sees are not appended (see Earle, pp. 195 ff.), are the following: 1. Æthelwold [of Winchester, 963 – 984]; 2. Ælfstan [of London, 961 – 995] who may be right; 3. Adulph, who is called 'Apulf b.' in A.S.Chr. E; Athulf bishop of Hereford subscribes 973 – 1012, the date of his consecration not being given and his predecessor Ælfric subscribing 941 – 951; he also therefore may be right.

Three abbats subscribe: Aswi Æscwig, who signs a charter 968 – 999 in Hist. Mon. de Abingdon [R.S.] j. 275; Osgar of Abingdon d. 978; and Æthelgar of Hyde Winchester (no. 11).

The caldormen are: Alfer Ælfhere; Alwin Æthelwine; Brithnod; Oslac; all found in no. 11.

So far the signataries of no. 12 agree with those recorded in the A.S.Chr. E; in this latter charter the words 'and many other great men' then follow, corresponding to which Ingulf adds 5 thanes and 14 other undescribed witnesses.

The thanes are: Æthelward (no. 11); Arsnulph Ersnulf (Dugd.) Ernulf (Gunton); Alfsy 'Ælfsige mīs' minister (Earle, p. 195 a. 956, p. 197 a. 960, p. 209 a. 987); Elfward, Ælfweard minister (Earle, p. 207 a. 969); Frithegist.

The remaining undescribed witnesses are: Thured Thored earl (Fl. Wig. a. 992); Veif, Veisi (Birch) Vlf (Dugd.) Vif (Gunton) (no. 11); Olfric, Wulfric minister, (Earle, p. 195 a. 956); Offord, Offerd, Osferth minister (Earle, p. 192 n. 949), miles (Liber Eliensis, p. 113 a. 970); Wulstan, Wulfstan miles (Liber Eliensis, p. 113 a. 970), minister (Earle, p. 207 a. 969); Ringulf (no. 11); Elfstan, Ælfstan minister (Earle, p. 182 a. 946); Athelfis, Æthelfys Fulm. marg. Athelsis (Dugd.) Æthelsige? minister (Earle, p. 199 a. 961, p. 208 a. 984); Wulfeah Wulfheah (in Riley misprinted Wulfear) dux Fl. Wig. 1006; Ethelmund, Æthelmund minister (Earle, p. 207 a. 969); Thureferd miles (Liber Eliensis, p. 113 a. 970), a moneyer of Cnut at Norwich c. 1025 [Thurefcrth], and a Danish jarl [Thurferth], who submitted to Eadward the elder in 921 (A.S.Chr. A); Alfhelm, Ælfhelm minister (Earle, p. 199 a. 961), and a moneyer of Æthelred II. and Cnut; Frava [Frana] and Frethegist, possibly two of the three thanes of Lindsey Linc. mentioned in 993 (A.S.Chr. Fl. Wig.), who being 'ex paterno genere Danici' betrayed their trust as commanders of the English army and caused its defeat; both these names occur in Eadgar's charter to Ely Monastery of 970 (Liber Eliensis, p. 113; Kemble no. 563*).

In Gunton's Peterborough the same witnesses are found, but with many variations or misspellings in their names.

The signataries to this charter are nearly identical with those to Eadgar's charter to Thorney in 973 (Red Book of Thorney, MS. Lib. Univ. Camb.; Dugd. Mon.). The fantastical formulæ of subscription (§ 420) also are in most cases the same.

This charter Dr Hickes considers most highly suspicious (Præf. p. xxix).

399 13. Charter of Eadgar king 'basileus' of 'Albion' to Malmesbury, ...974.

[Kemble no. 584*.]

This charter is also given in the Registrum Malmesb. [R. S.] j. 316 – 8, in Will. Malm. Gesta regum [R. S.] j. 173 (without any list of signataries), and in his Gesta pontificum [R. S.] pp. 404 – 5. Here the king calls himself 'Anglici orbis basileus', basileus being equivalent to emperor.

Besides the two archbishops, three bishops sign; of two the dates are right, but Ingulf adds Leofwin of Dorchester 958 – ..., who is not in the Reg. Malm., and whose successor signs in 975.

Three abbats sign, who are not mentioned in Reg. Malm., one is Turketul of Croyland, the others being: Æthelgar of Hyde Winchester (no. 11) and Adulph of Burgh.

The three 'duces' are: Alfer, Athelwin, Brithnod, who occur in no. 11; they are right as to date, and are the only laymen who subscribe.

The differences between the Ingulfine charter and that of the Reg. Malm. are very great. The Reg. Malm. has 18 witnesses, Ingulf 12 'et alii'; of these only 8 including the three 'duces' are the same. The Eadulf, who signs the Reg. Malm. charter, was not an abbat, and was therefore not abbat Adulph of Peterborough, who signs the Ingulfine charter. His name may, however, have reminded the writer of that of the abbat of Burgh.

This charter is recited by Ingulf, because, 'among those who set their signatures to the royal charter, after the bishops, the signature consignatio of ...abbat Turketul occupies the first place'. Of Turketul abbat of Croyland, however, there is no trace in the Registrum Malmesb. or in the two recitals in Will. Malm. that in the G. R. having no list of witnesses, and that in G. P. only mentioning the two Archbishops, Æthelwold bishop of Winchester and the three bishops Ælfstan of London, of Rochester, and of Wiltshire.

14. Charter of Cnut king of England, ...1032. **400**
[Kemble no. 748*.]

Here one bishop out of three is wrongly dated: Elfward of London 1035 – 44, unless this name is a mistake for Elfwy his predecessor, who sat 1014 – 35.

The three abbats are possibly right: Brihtege of Pershore, bishop of Worcester 1133 – 38; Wulnoth Wulfnoth of Westminster 1017 – 49 (Fl. Wig. Dugd. Mon.) and Oswy of Thorney.

Of the laymen, Godwine signs as earl; he was certainly earl in 1018 (Freeman j. ed. III. p. 409); Eadwine the brother of earl Leofric, and the 'king's thanes' Thurkill and Ælfgeat were slain in 1039 (A.S.Chr. A [not E] Fl. Wig.); Harold (II.) the son of earl Godwine signs, being then about 10 years of age (Freeman ij. ed. III. p. 541). Earl Leofric (d. 1057) and his son Ælfgar (d. 1059) also sign.

15. Charter of Eadward the Confessor king of England, **401**
..........[1048].
[Kemble no. 794*.]

Only the two archbishops sign, and sign rightly.

The three earls, Godwine, Leofric and Siward, of Wessex, Mercia and Northumberland, who were earls in 1043 (A.S.Chr. D) are the only other witnesses, who are mentioned by name. The archbishops and earls are all mentioned in Fl. Wig. 1043. This charter is signed also by queen Egitha 'Eadgyth' (§ 362).

402 16. Charter of Thorold of Bukenhale [Bucknall],
Leicester, 19 May 1051.
[Kemble no. 795*.]

Thorold, who is spoken of as sheriff 'vicecomes' of Lincoln and as of the race and kindred of Thorold sheriff 'vicedominus' of Lincoln mentioned in n°s. 3, 4, 5 (Fulm. p. 65), describes himself (Fulm. p. 86) as brother of Godiva 'Godgifu' wife of Leofric earl of 'Leicester'; he is also so described in Joh. Petrib. a. 1052. The statement of Domesday concerning some land at 'Buchehale': 'Hanc terram dedit Turoldus vicecomes sancto Guthlaco pro anima sua', strangely omitted by Ingulf in his version of Domesday, probably refers to the second Thorold. The name in the Guthlac Scroll (§ 82) 'Toroldus vicecomes' may also be that of the later benefactor. The property at Bucknall continued with the abbey till the Dissolution.

The only bishop, who signs, is Wulfin of Dorchester; Ulf sat 1050 – 52, Wulfwy Wulfwige Wlfwius (Fl. Wig.) 1053 – 67; the latter may be meant.

The two abbats are Wulgat Wulfgeat of Croyland, and Lefwine Leofwine of Thorney 1048 – 66.

Besides these, the 'comitissa' Godiva signs (§ 375), as do also 'Turnerus', 'Wulnarus' (Fulm. marg. Wlmarus 'Wulfmær'), and Sihtric, chaplains to the bishop; and Stanard (Stanhardus, Domesday, Ellis, j. 487; Inquis. Com. Cantabr. ed. Hamilton), servant to earl Leofric; Fulco a monk of Croyland (a name, which occurs again in 1109, and which is found in the series of the earls of Anjou 888 – 1129); Pigot a monk of Thorney; and Living the clerk, who was also the scribe.

The rev. R. H. Warner in his history of Thorney Abbey says: 'In some printed records [abbat Lefwine] appears as Leofric', and he conjectures, that these two names belong to the same personage, the great abbat Leofric of Peterborough, who ruled also over Croyland, Thorney, Coventry and Burton (A.S.Chr. E a. 1066); but he did not become abbat of Peterborough till 1052 (A.S.Chr. E), and the date of his obtaining the rule over Thorney and the other abbeys is not recorded.

'Turnerus' may be a misreading of the name 'Turner', which occurs in Domesday, Linc. XXII. 'Terra Willelmi de Perci' (Photozincograph, p. XXXVII. a), LVI. 'Terra Juditæ comitissæ' (pp. LXVII., LXIII.), and elsewhere.

The only other persons signing are: Thorold himself, earl Leofric (Freeman ij. ed. III. note KK p. 679 ff. The family of Leofric), and carl Algar 'Ælfgar' his son.

This charter is considered spurious by Dr Hickes (Præf. p. xxviij).

17. Charter of king William I. (1066 – 1087),   **403**

.... c. 1086.

[Rymer, Fœdera j. 1 from Fulman.]

This charter, which is not dated, is signed by the archbishops, of whom Lanfranc died 1086, by Walkelin bishop of Winchester 1070 – 98 and William de S. Carilefs or de Saint Calais 1081 – 96.

It is also signed by William Malet; of this name there were two men: the one fought at Senlac and was killed in the Isle of Ely probably in 1071 (Freeman), the other was deprived of his lands in 1110 (A.S.Chr. E, H. Hunt., Dugd. Bar. i. 111 a). A third of the same name of later date is mentioned in 1215 (Matth. Paris, Chronica Majora R. S. ij. 585, 643). William Malet is also frequently mentioned in Stapleton's 'Magni Rotuli Scacc. Normanniæ' (Index).

Besides the above, carl William, carl Alfred, and Alfred the son of Topi sign. Earl William might be the count of Eu (killed 1096 Ord. Vit. iij. 411), or William de Warenne earl of Surrey (d. 1088 Ord. Vit. iij. 317), 'Willelmus comes' is mentioned as a tenant in capite in Oxfordshire, and Ellis (Introd. j. 511) says, that William Fitz Osbern earl of Hereford is the person there alluded to; he died however in 1071 (Ord. Vit. ij. 235), and so cannot be the 'earl William' of this charter. There is no earl Alfred in Ord. Vit. 'Topi sochemannus' occurs in 'Inquisitio Eliensis', ed. Hamilton; a man named Topc is found c. 930 in Liber Eliensis Vol. I. pp. 138 – 9, and 'Vif (no. 11) filius Topi' in a charter of William I. given in Gunton Peterb. p. 142.

404 18. Charter of king Henry I.

Oxford,......14 Henry I. 1114.

In this charter given in the Pet. Bles. the two bishops of Lincoln and Ely are right. The other witnesses are: 'Warnerus de Lusors' and 'Hugo de Essartis'; Clarenbaldus de Lisors, Lusoriæ (dep. Eure) East of Rouen, and Guarinus and Gislebertus des Essarts, Sartensis, occur in Ord. Vit. (Index). Warnerus de Lusor is found in Mr Hunter's Magnus Rotulus Scaccarii 31 H. I. (8º Lond. 1833) pp. 23 (Wilts), 57 (Essex). Fulco de Lusoriis occurs in Domesday (Ellis j. 448).

This charter is not given in Rymer j.

405 19. Charter of king Henry I.
to Spalding.   ....c. 1114.

The text of this charter is not given in the Pet. Bles. All that is found is 'Henricus etc. ...'

406 20. Charter of Alan de Creoun, ...c. 1114.

No witnesses are mentioned in the text of this charter in the Pet. Bles.

This charter is wrongly placed in 1114. As printed in Fulm. p. 126, it is a reduction from the charter given in Dugdale of Alan de Croun to the priory of Freston (Monast. 1657, j. 443); in this the donor speaks of having made the grant 'post liberationem regis Stephani [1141], præsente domino Godfrido abbate' [1138 – 53], and the writer of the Pet. Bles. may have missed the allusion to king Stephen, and have mistaken abbat Godfrey of St Albans for abbat Joffrid of Orleans (1109 – 24), Joffrid being spoken of by Ord. Vit. as Godifredus. In addition to the wrong dating, the whole charter is much disfigured; a donation of the church of Claxeby has been introduced, other minor matters have been added, and the names of the tenants of the land at Burton in Kesteven, and that of the 'parson' of Toft omitted. Alan de Croun belongs to a later period than that [1114] indicated by the Pet. Bles., as besides the above charter Dugdale has another of his, to which Edward abbat of Croyland (1153 – 73), the successor of the above abbat Godfrey, was witness.

21. The statute of Æthelbald king of Mercia 719 or 749. **407**
[Kemble no. 70, Birch no. 140.]
In Ingulf this document has no signatures appended to it. As printed in Fulman, Ingulf puts 'in the third year of his reign', but probably the word 'tricesimo' has dropped out, for it was really granted at Godmundesleah in 749. Ingulf's form is a shortened form of the document given in Earle p. 42 ff., which also has many witnesses.

22. Donation of Æthelwulf king of Wessex, **408**
Winchester 5 Nov. 855.
[Kemble no. 275*, Birch no. 484.]
Witnesses to this document are mentioned, though not by name: 'all the archbishops and bishops', abbats and abbesses, dukes, earls, 'comites', nobles, 'proceres', and 'others of the faithful'.

This is the famous Donation of Æthelwulf, which is referred to and quoted by most of our mediaeval historians. Different forms of it are given in Birch, Cast. Sax. nos. 468 – 9 – 70 – 1 – 2, 483 – 484 – 5, no. 484 being the Ingulfine form. See Hallam Middle Ages Suppl. notes 1848, p. 180 ff.

23. The ecclesiastical censure for the protection of Croyland, **409**
London, 10 June 966.
[Kemble no. 528*, Birch no. 1179.]
The two archbishops sign, the archbishop of York styling himself 'archiepiscopus Eboracae' (§ 378), and ten bishops, of whom three or four are wrong: 1. Kynsy of Lichfield 949 – 963, Winsy signing 964 – 73; 2. Alfric of East Anglia or Elmham, otherwise known only by Fl. Wig. Cat.; 3. Godwin of Rochester, mentioned also in nos. 4 and 5, 995 – ...; 4. Æthelstan of Cornwall 909 – ... (Fulm. p. 36), his successor Conan subscribing 931 – 934.

Besides the king and the bishops, there are of ecclesiastical signataries: the abbats Elfstan of Glastonbury (see no. 11); Ethelgar of Hyde Winchester (no. 11); 'Wulfinus', 'Wulfwig' of Westminster (Fulm. marg. Wlſinus) 958 – c. 970; and Osward of Evesham c. 960 – c. 980; and the abbesses Merwenna of Romsey (no. 11), appointed 967 (Fl. Wig.), Herleva Herelufu of

Shaftesbury and Wulwina Wulfwin of Wareham, who both died in 982 (A.S.Chr. A, Fl. Wig.).

The ealdormen 'duces' Ailwin, Brithnod, Oslac, Alfer, Elphege are the same as in no. 11, though in different order; the thanes Frithegist and Ethelward occur also in no. 11, and Ethelmund in no. 12.

410 24. The decree of Whitsunday, 27 May 1072.

The signataries are all ecclesiastics: the two archbishops, eleven English and two Norman bishops, Odo bishop of Bayeux and Goisfrid Geoffrey de Montbrai bishop of Coutances, and twelve abbats, among whom however the abbats of Croyland and of Thorney are not found, although the abbats of Peterborough and Romsey sign.

In this charter and elsewhere Ingulf writes the name of the East Anglian see 'Helmham'. This spelling is found also in Fl. Wig., who s. a. 1038 calls Arfast 'Helmhamnensis episcopus', and in Matth. Paris Chron. Majora [R. S.] i. 345, 503. This document is given also by Will. Malm. Gesta regum [R. S.] ii. 349 - 52 with the same signataries, and in Gesta pontificum [R. S.] p. 42 without the attestations.

411 Besides these charters, the Ingulf presents us with five short documents, being leases granted in 1091 by the monastery 1. to Eustace sheriff 'vicecomes' of Huntingdon, who is mentioned in Domesday, of the manor of Thyrnyng Thurning Hunts, near Oundle; 2. to Oger priest of Repyngale Rippingale (near Bourn) Linc. of all their lands there; an Oger is mentioned in Domesday at Repyngale, but not with the designation of 'presbyter'; 3. to Robert the servant 'homo' (a frequent designation in Domesday) of Simon of Baston near Market Deeping of 36 acres of land at Baston; 4. to William the miller and Agge of Newton his partner of some land and fishing rights at Croyland; the name Age, one of many variations of Ako, is found in Langebek (Index); and 5. to Gunter Siword of Spalding of 200 acres of land near Croyland. Among the witnesses to this last deed are: Aldieta the wife of Gunter, Wulmer 'Wulfmer' his son, and Fareman his brother. In the mortuary roll of abbess Matilda 1113 (§ 477) we find at Werwell 'Aldita monacha' (Delish p. 188); an earlier Wulmaer and an earlier Farman were moneyers of king Æthelred II.

These charters are signed (except the last) by (among others) Sigwata the steward 'provisor', a name which is well known among Scandinavian names (Langebek, Scriptt. rerum Danic. Vol. IX. fo. Copenh. 1878 p. 644) as borne by several Icelanders, one being Sighvatr the brother of Snorro, another a 'poeta Islandicus' etc. In Hunter's Magnus Rotulus Scaccarii 31 H. I. p. 112 (Linc.) is found mentioned 'Siwatus de Hollanda'. It is curious to find, among the persons connected with Croyland so many bearing Norse names: Thurcytel, Ulfcytel, Ascytel, Grimcytel, Ingulf, Sigwata, Torfi (Thorwy, Fulm. p. 114); Croyland is however only just south of the Danish district of Lincolnshire, the nearest villages, whose names end in -by, Careby and Carlby between Stamford and Bourn, being only about 12 miles distant to the west from Croyland.

Haco of Multon in 1091 (Fulm. p. 99), Sihtric chaplain of bishop Ulf of Dorchester in 1051, and Harold in 1109 and Sweyn in 940, also bear Danish names.

Three 'procuratores' sign these leases: 'Trigus', 'Asius', and Ægelmer. The name 'Triggus' is found as that of a monk of Croyland in the mortuary roll of the abbess of the Trinity at Caen, Matilda the daughter of William the Conqueror f. 1113 (§ 477). It may be the norse name Tryggvi (Langebek, Index). Willelmus Trig is found Cartul. Rames. [R. S.] j. 417.

xxxj. The dating of the Ingulfine charters.

These charters run from 716 to c. 1114, and are as follows:

1. Æthelbald of Mercia 716
2. Offa 793
3. Kenulph, Coenwulf 806
4. Wiglaf 833 Feast of St Augustine of England, 26 May.
5. Bertulph, Beorhtwulf 851 Friday after Easter, 27 March.

6.	Beorred, Burgred	868	Kal. Aug. 1 Aug.
7.	Earl Algar	810	
8.	Fregist the Knight	819	Feast of St James, 25 July.
9.	Algar the Knight	825	
10.	Eadred of England	948	
11.	Eadgar	966	
12.	Eadgar to Peterborough	970	'anno regni 10°'.
13.	Eadgar to Malmesbury	974	'anno consecrationis primo'.
14.	Cnut	1032	
15.	Eadward the Confessor	[1048]	
16.	Thorold of Bukenhale	1051	Pentecost, 19 May.
17.	William I.	c. 1086	
18.	Henry I.	1114	
19.	Henry I. to Spalding	—	
20.	Alan de Creoun	—	
21.	Æthelbald of Mercia	749	
22.	Æthelwulf of Wessex	855	Nonis Nov. 5 Nov.
23.	Ecclesiastical censure	966	'in octavis Pentecostes', 10 June.
24.	Ecclesiastical decree	1072	

415 According to Earle (p. xxxiij ff.), dating by our present era began with Beda, and a council held at Chelsea 27 July 816 ordered its practice with regard to the acts of the Synod, 'genuine records' being rarely dated by the A.D. before 735 the year of Beda's death (cf. Earle p. 4, 674?; p. 15, 701; p. 15, 704; p. 20, 718; p. 21, 723?; p. 22, 725; p. 23, 727).

416 In Earle the 'genuine records' after 735 are generally dated by the A.D.; the Indiction also is nearly always given, the year of the Indiction beginning 1 Sept. More rarely are the day and month of the execution of the charter added. Thus we find in Earle:

Eadric, king of Kent [686], — June Indictione xiij
Swaebraed, king of Essex [704], 13 June (Id. Jun.) Indictione xiiij

Æthelberht, king of Kent   732 , 20 Feb. Indictione xv
Æthelbald, king of Mercia [734], — Sept. Indictione ij
Ceolwulf, king of Mercia   811 , 1 Aug. (Kal. Aug.) Indictione iiij
„   „   „   822 , 17 Sept. (xv Cal. Oct.) Indictione xv
Æthelwulf, king of Wessex 847 , 26 Dec. Indictione x

The Ingulfine Mercian charters which record the day of the month are, therefore, so far in accordance with the practice of genuine documents.

One charter, no. 5, a. 851, gives the day of the week, 'feria sexta in hebdomada Paschæ', and is on this ground condemned by Dr Hickes (Præf. p. xxviij), 'siquidem *feriæ* rara aut nulla mentio in designatiouibus Temporum, quibus saltem vetustiores *Anglo-Saxonum* chartæ confectæ esse notantur'. Earle gives however (p. 26) a charter of Æthelbald king of Mercia a. 723 or 734 dated 'quarta feria viij kal. Decembris'.

In later times, notices of the day and month are no longer common, and of Eadred and Eadgar no charters so dated are given by Earle.

None of the Croyland charters mention the Indiction, which is very commonly found in Earle, although there also there are a few cases of charters of Eadred and Eadgar, where the Indiction does not appear. It is however found in no. 22, the Donation of Æthelwulf king of Wessex of 855, a document which is found dated in the same manner in other works, as in Roger of Wendover (E.H.S. j. 290, not in R. S., which begins in 1154) and Will. Malm. Gesta regum [R. S.] j. 119.

In the earliest times the Indiction is sometimes the only date, e.g.

Æthelbert king of Kent [604] iv. kal. Mai. 28 Apr. Indict. vij.
Eadric   king of Kent [687] — June   Indict. xiij.

The regnal year, which is occasionally found in Earle, occurs in no. 12 Eadgar's charter to Peterborough a. 970, 'anno regni decimo', as given in Ingulf dating from his accession to the throne of England in 959; this charter is also found in

A.S.Chr. E, where it is however dated a. 972 'anno regni xvj ', dating from his rule over Mercia in 957. Other instances in Earle's 'Genuine Records' are :

Æthelberht king of Kent [732] a. r. 7°
Æthelbald king of Mercia 742 a. r. 27°
„ „ „ 749 a. r. 33°
Coenwulf „ „ 811 a. r. 15°
„ „ „ 812 a. r. 16°
„ „ „ 814 a. r. 18°
Wiglaf „ „ 836 a. r. 7°
Eadwig king of England 956 a. r. 1°

although, according to Thorpe, a charter of Coenwulf of 798 (Kemble C.D. no. 175) is the earliest one so dated.

There are in Earle none of later times, and so also none of Eadgar, dated by the regnal year.

In Pet. Bles. we find

Henry I. king of England 1114 a. r. 14° (Jan.-Aug. 1114).

xxxij. Formulæ of Subscription in the Ingulfine charters.

419 In the 'Genuine Records dated' printed by Prof. Earle, many different formulæ of subscription occur, one single one being mostly used by all the signataries, though often also the greater personages allow themselves some latitude herein. The following are some of the principal styles:

The name alone ('Totta ep'): a. 674 - 803 - 933,
'Ego (Wilfredus episcopus)': a. 676 - 803 - 1058,
'Signum manus (Osrici regis)': a. 679 - 774 - 847,
'Ego (Eddi episcopus) subscripsi': a. 680 - 736,
'Ego (Eadberht) consensi': a. 718 - 831,
'Ego (Eadwald) consensi et subscripsi': a. 676-863 - 889, the king using such forms as:
'Crucis xp̄i signo munio' a. 725,
'Signum crucis xp̄i inpressi' a. 833,
'Signo sanctæ crucis roboravi' a. 785,
'Cum sigillo sanctæ crucis confirmavi' a. 939;

while in addition we find used now and then: 'confirmavi' for 'sigillo sanctæ crucis confirmavi', 'roboravi' for 'signo sanctæ crucis roboravi', 'consignavi' for 'cum tropæo agiæ crucis consignavi'.

It is only in the short time from Æthelstan to Eadgar **420** (c. 925 - 975), that the style, which is used uniformly in the Ingulfine charters (716 - 966) is found; if anything is added to the name in early times, it is 'consensi et subscripsi' most commonly. The additions to the names are mostly the same in each charter. Varied and fanciful additions begin after Ælfred (Earle p. 171 ff.). The charter of Eadred to Christ Church Canterbury of 949 (Earle, Genuine Records p. 185 ff., Kemble no. 425, Birch no. 880), is even more fantastical in its signatures than most of those in Ingulf; in it we find: '.... agiæ crucis .... notamine perstrinxi', 'signo crucis fixi', 'signum crucis depinxi', 'signo salubri adnotavi', 'patibuli confirmatu addidi', 'crucis xp̄i constipulatu munivi', 'corroborationem contuli', 'unamitatem (sic) præbui', 'permissionem perfudi', 'prompto animo consensi'.

The form 'signum manus N', so common in genuine records of the Mercian period, is not found in Ingulfine charters, nor do the expressions: 'roboravi', 'consolidavi', 'depinxi' occur there.

The forms used in the Croyland charters are here tabulated, **421** those marked with a star occurring also in charters regarded as genuine (Earle pp. 188, 191, 195, 197, 210, 211), those marked with two stars occurring in Earle's Secondary Documents (pp. 324, 326, 384, 404, 433). Possibly others might be found in the larger collections of charters.

Many other verbal forms (mostly referring to the Cross) are found in Earle (a. 940 - 960), but not in Ingulf: 'conclusi' (pp. 191, 194), 'consolidavi' (p. 197), 'roboravi' (pp. 177, 194), 'addidi' (p. 187), 'adhibui consensum' (p. 187), 'adnotavi' (p. 187), 'ascripsi' (p. 187), 'impressi' (p. 194), 'depinxi' (pp. 191, 197).

*confirmavi	716 - 1051	approbavi	716 - 1032
ratificavi	716 - 1051	collaudavi	716 - 1051

*corroboravi	716 – 974	adjuvi	868
constabilivi	966 – 1032	illud fieri rogavi	716
stabilivi	868, 948	**consilium dedi	716 – 966
*concessi	793 – 1051	—— præbui	966
**constitui	966	consului	806 – 948
*consensi	716 – 1072	commendavi	806 – 966
consensum dedi	833 – 966	communivi	966 – 1032
* —— præbui	851 – 966	fulminavi	966
assensum dedi	806 – 833	audivi	716 – 1032
** —— præbui	833 – 868	auscultavi	948 – 1053
affirmavi	1032	vidi	966
ratum habui	966	aspexi	868 – 1051
adoptavi	716 – 948	**conspexi	1051
gratum habui	810 – 833	afflui	806 – 1051
*acquievi	966	interfui	825 – 1051
applausi	1051	*astiti	833, 974
**annui	833 – 970	præsens fui	825, 833
*non renui	970	consessi	1032
**favi	833 – 970	*subscripsi	793 – 1072
acceptavi	833 – 1051	conscripsi	868
affectavi	716 – 948	signavi	1032
aspiravi	793 – 833	*consignavi	793 – 1032
desideravi	948 – 1051	subnotavi	793 – 1072
consideravi	868	crucem feci	868, 966
procuravi	806 – 966	signum feci	851
impetravi	868	scripsi	793

xxxiij. Norman words and expressions found in Ingulf.

422 'The Norman phraseology, in which [the Ingulfine] charters are clothed, though it shews at once that Ingulphus only presents the reader with *modernized* paraphrases, is not entirely inconsistent with the existence of Saxon originals' (Palgrave, Qu. Rev. 1826 p. 292).

This 'Norman phraseology' is pointed out by Dr Hickes (Pref. p. xxix and Dissert. Epist. p. 67), and his observations Mr Riley repeats and supplements.

423 A. In the early charters, i.e. those of the Mercian period, we find the following words and expressions:

a. 716, § 387, no. 1.   'hoc chirographo patenti'
  'separalis piscaria'
  'communis sewera'

a. 806, § 389, no. 3,

a. 833, § 380, no. 4.

a. 851, § 381, no. 5.

'leuca
'omnibus scisonis'
'nigri monachi'
'libras legalis monetæ'
'passagium'
'miles meus'
'ballivus monasterii'
'advocatio'
'manerium'
'feodum'
'quarentena'
'feria sexta'.

B. In the later Ingulfine charters, i.e. those after 948, we **424** find:

a. 948, § 385, no. 10.

a. 966, § 386, no. 11.

a. 970, § 387, no. 12.

'manerium'
'catalla'
'secta in schyris'
'affidare suos nativos'
'advocatio ecclesiæ'
'separalis piscaria'
'tenentes suos'
'commune pasturæ'
'meremium'
'Christianitas attinentium parochiarum'
'telonium'.

C. In the historical part of Ingulf's work, professedly **425** belonging, by authorship or revision, to c. 1095, we find:

*'armiger' (Fulm. p. 53) 'an esquire'
'bracinum' (Fulm. p. 53) 'a brewery'
'campanile' (Fulm. p. 101) 'a belfry'
'carcosium' (Fulm. p. 99) 'a carcase'
'cariare' (Fulm. p. 52) 'to carry'
'catalla' (Fulm. p. 4) 'chattels'
'conquassare' (Fulm. p. 97) 'to crush'
'copia' (Fulm. p. 92) 'a copy'
'corium coctum' (Fulm. p. 68) 'cuir bouilli' §§ 311, 312

'corrodiarius' (Fulm. p. 97) 'a pensioner'
'fiscus' (Fulm. p. 25) 'treasury'
*'froccus' (Fulm. p. 49) 'a monk's frock'
*'garcio' (Fulm. p. 49) 'a servant'
'indentura' (Fulm. p. 51). According to Spelman this word does not occur in genuine records before the time of Henry III. 1216–72 (Hickes, Præf. p. xxix).

'justitiarius' (Fulm. pp. 28, 63) 'a justiciar'
'latomus' (Fulm. p. 4) 'a mason'
'libra argenti' (Fulm. p. 4)
'loquutorium' (Fulm. p. 23) 'the parlour of a convent'
'manerium' (Fulm. p. 68) 'a manor'
'matricularium' (Fulm. p. 101) 'an inventory'
'miles' (Fulm. p. 63) § 367, 'knight'
'nativus' (Fulm. p. 101) 'a serf'; fem. 'a neife'
'parliamentum publicum' (Fulm. pp. 103, 131)
'persona' (Fulm. p. 79)
'pitantiarius' (Fulm. p. 49) 'the pittancer'
'portiforium' (Fulm. p. 79) 'a breviary'
'prebenda pinguissima' (Fulm. p. 30) 'a very fat prebend'
'quindena' (Fulm. p. 95) 'a fortnight'
'restaurare' (Fulm. p. 29 [Ord. Vit.])
'restaurator' (Fulm. pp. 25, 83)
'secta' (Fulm. p. 54)
'secundarius panis' (Fulm. p. 65) 'second bread' [Suet.]
'separalia facere' (Fulm. p. 78)
'serjantia' (Fulm. p. 103) 'serjeantship'
'serviens cissor' (Fulm. p. 103) 'a serjeant-tailor'
'serviens sutor' (Fulm. p. 103) 'a serjeant-shoemaker'
'sewera' (Fulm. p. 107) 'a drain'
'in tabulis' (Fulm. p. 104) '[bound] in boards'
'theoricum verbum' (Fulm. p. 31), § 286
'vastum' (Fulm. p. 4)
'vicarius' (Fulm. p. 105)

xxxiv. Authors quoted or incorporated by Ingulf.

426 Direct extracts from other authors are not found in the Ingulf, except three words from Ovid Met. iij. 218 (Fulm. p. 82), a line from Lucan (Phars. x. 407): 'Nulla fides pietasque viris qui castra sequuntur' (Fulm. p. 21), and a passage (Fulm. p. 94) from a hymn of St Ambrose, Hymn V 'Illuminans Altissimus' in the Benedictine edition of his works (fo. Paris 1686 – 90) ii. 1221; Daniel Thes. hymnol. (1841) i. 19. no. xiv. He also refers (Fulm. pp. 82, 83) to Ovid Met. iv. 192 ff. and to Isidori Etymologica (lib. xv. c. xvi. 3 in the edition 4° Rom. 1801).

Lucan is quoted also by Æthelweard the historian.

427 The writer however very frequently incorporates the language of other writers into his own narrative. Besides a passage from Statius (Thebais viii. 398 – 9) used in Fulm. p. 37,

'Jam clipeus clipeis, *umbone repellitur umbo*,

Ense minax ensis, *pede pes et cuspide cuspis*,'

which is quoted also by John of Salisbury in his Policraticus

(vj. 6), and the line: 'Sicut rosa spinam, genuit Godwinus Editham', which is found in Ailred of Rievaulx' Life of Eadward the Confessor in Twysden (Scriptores Decem) p. 377, he incorporates passages, which have been enumerated already, from the following writers:
Florence of Worcester,
Ordericus Vitalis,
Will. Malm. De gestis regum, and Gesta pontificum,
'John of Peterborough' (MS. Cott. Claud. A. v.),
Vita S. Guthlaci by Felix the monk.

The passage from John of Salisbury mentioned above, which is given by Freeman (ij. Ed. III. 480), seems to have been known to the Ingulfine writer.

These extracts refer exclusively to the life and doings of **428** St Guthlac, and to the general history of the country; by their date they may be presumed to be fatal to the authorship of abbat Ingulf, who is stated to have brought his history down to the year 1092 and to have died 17 Dec. 1108. For these authors are mostly later than that date, as Ord. Vit. brings his history down to 1142, Fl. Wig. to 1117, Will. Malm. to 1128, while Ailred of Rievaulx died in 1166, and John of Salisbury in 1182. 'John of Peterborough' (MS. Cott. Claud. A. v.) is still later.

In the course of the prose history of Ingulf, we find (Fulm. **429** p. 94) the following lines:
'Prosperitatis iter gaudens huc usque cucurri,
  Jam labor et luctus funera tanta strepunt'.

In like manner in a charter of Eadward the Martyr dated 977 (Earle 'Secondary Documents' p. 295) are the lines:
'Nunc velut umbra cito sic corpore[a] fugiunt res,
  Sed decus æternum hoc visu stat certius omni'.

Ingulf gives 24 hexameter lines on the foundation of the **430** abbey. They are thus introduced: 'Hinc quidam poeta sic dixit', while Riley translates 'On this occasion it was that a certain poet wrote the following lines', and observes elsewhere, that 'we may safely say', that such expressions as 'vastum', 'catalla', 'latomus', 'argenti trecentas libras', which occur in them, 'were never used, as asserted, by a poet of the 8th century'. It does not, however, appear to be so 'asserted'.

431 Ingulf also gives the beginning of a poem on the destruction of Croyland in 870 by 'dominus Bricstanus', the chanter of the monastery, which, he says, was to be found 'in multis locis'. The name of Bricstan of Chatteris c. 1115 is found in Ord. Vit. (iij. 123), and it also occurs in H. Hunt. Lib. ix. (R. S. p. xxv).

432 Some lines on the death of archbishop Lanfranc in 1089, given in Fulm. p. 96, are stated to be the beginning of an 'Epitaphium elegantissimum' written by 'quidam monachus noster'.

xxxv. Abbat Ingulf.

433 Ingulf is a name which is found frequently in England and Normandy in the 10th and 11th centuries.

INGOLF occurs as a moneyer of Eadgar and of Eadward the Martyr.

Ingulf the brother of Siverth is mentioned as of c. 975 in Liber Eliensis lib. ij. c. 35.

Ingulf the son of Slepe was a benefactor to Ramsey c. 1125 (Chron. Abb. Rames. [R. S.] p. 242).

The name occurs in the Exon and Winton Domesday (Vol. iij. 174, 476 ; 535, 556).

Ingulf prior of Winchester was elected abbat of Abingdon in 1130 (Fl. Wig. Cont.); he died 19 Sept. 1158 (Chron. Monast. de Abingdon [R. S.]).

William and Alice Ingulf occur in 1282 in the Hist. Mon. S. Petri. Glouc. (R. S. iij. 118, 126).

Robert Ingulf is mentioned at Dunstable in 1282 (Ann. Monast. [R. S.] iij. 289).

434 Ingólfr Arnarson was an early settler in Iceland c. 850, and several localities, such as Ingolfshöfði, are named after him (Landnámabók 8°. Copenh. 1843, Index).

The name is found also many times in Stapleton's Magni Rotuli Scaccarii Normanniæ 1180-1203, e.g. Vol. I. p. 48 'Ingulfus Florien.', p. 79 'Ingulfus de Chemino', p. 159

'Ingulfus de Sancto Albiñ', 'Ingulfus de Campis', p. 175
'Ingulfus Freel', Vol. II. p. 347 'Ingulfus de Maisnillo', p. 369
'Radulfus filius Ingulfi', p. 418 'Robertus filius Ingulfi'.

No Ingulf, however, occurs in the extensive indices to Ord. Vit., to Matthew Paris, and to 'Matth. Westm.' [R. S.].

The name is found as that of a bishop of London in MS. Arundel 178 (Birch) by a mistake for Ingwald, which is found in Savile and Fulm. (p. 4), and similarly in H. Hunt. 'de contemptu mundi' (R. S. p. 215) for Gundulf bishop of Rochester 1077 – 1108.

He is called 'Indulphus' by Arn. Wion in his Lignum Vitæ (4to. Ven. 1595) j. 429.

Ingulf was born in England c. 1030 (Fulm. 'Lectori'), his **435** parents being Londoners. He began his studies at Westminster, where he attracted the attention of queen Eadgyth (Egitha), and continued them at Oxford, 'pro literis addiscendis in teneriori ætate constitutus, primum *Westmonasterio*, postmodum *Oxoniensi* studio (§ 322) traditus eram'.

Being desirous of rising in the world, he attached himself to duke ('comes') William of Normandy during his visit to England in 1051 (Fl. Wig.) or 1052 (A.S.Chr. D. only), and returning with him into Normandy became his secretary.

With the duke's leave he went on a pilgrimage to the **436** Holy Land, together with the archbishop of Mentz, several other bishops, and a large company of about 7000 persons. This pilgrimage is placed by Fl. Wig. (1601) and Joh. Petrib. in 1064. Fl. Wig., or rather Marianus Scotus, says: 'Multi divites et pauperes cum Maguntino archiepiscopo, Trajectensi quoque, nec non Babbenbergensi, atque Ratisponensi Episcopis .. plus vij millibus hominum Hierusalem perrexerunt.... Ita autem omnis multitudo Christianorum consumpta est, ut vix [de] septem vel amplius millibus duo millia sint reversa'. Joh. Petrib. writes: 'Multi ex regno imperatoris Alemanniæ cum Maguntino aliisque tribus episcopis Jerusolymam peregre adeuntes, adversa multa... perpessi sunt, in tantum ut vix de septem millibus duo millia reverterentur'. Mr Riley thinks, that 'the notion of the pilgrimage of Ingulf to Jerusalem (Fulm. p. 74) is probably borrowed from the account of that of Theodoric, first abbat of Saint Évroult (sic) [in 1056], in the *History* of [Ordericus] Vitalis (B. iii. c. 4 [ed. Le Prévost ii. 63 – 66])'. There is however no resemblance between the two narratives; the abbat of Saint-Évroul never touched the Holy Land, but, having reached Antioch, took ship for Cyprus, and there died.

437 At Constantinople the pilgrims saw the emperor 'Alexis' 1081 – 1118 (§ 319), and passed on through Asia Minor, 'divertentesque inde per Lyciam, in manus Arabicorum latronum incidimus', but at length reached Jerusalem. Swegen the brother of Harold II., returning from Jerusalem, 'mortuus est in Licia' (Fl. Wig. a. 1052), and Lycia is mentioned in connexion with Syria in the Pet. Bles. (Fulm. p. 112) and in Will. Malm. Gesta Regum (R. S. j. 276). H. Hunt. (R. S. p. 22) says: '[Vespasianus] vicit Judæam, Achaiam, Lyciam, Rhodum....', but this is merely a variation from a quotation from Eutropius (vij. 19): 'Achaiam, Lyciam, Rhodum,.... quæ liberæ ante hoc tempus fuerant,.... in provinciarum formam redegit'.

438 At Jerusalem the pilgrims were received by Sophronius the patriarch, who certainly occupied that see in 1053 – 59, though the dates of his accession and of his death are not known; Riley is wrong in stating, that he died in 1059 (L'art de vérifier les dates j. 265, 267).

439 Having visited the Holy Places they returned from Joppa to Brundisium and thence to Rome, where the party divided, the German pilgrims 'archiepiscopi ceterique principes imperii' going to their own land, while Ingulf and his immediate companions returned to 'Francia' ['*Francia*. La France, distinguée de la Normandie, de la Gascogne, de la Bretagne, et de la Flandre' (Ord. Vit. v. 498 'Dict. Geog.')]. 'Principes Imperii' seem to be mentioned in early times; Ducange ([1734] v. 845) has the reference: '1189 Charta Henrici VI. Imperatoris'.

440 On his return Ingulf renounced the world, becoming a monk in the monastery of Saint-Wandrille (Wandragesilus) or Fontenelle, in Normandy near Caudebec on the Seine, under abbat Gerbert 1062 – 89. 'Non paucis interlabentibus annis' (Fulm. p. 74) Ingulf became prior (see § 457); he brought some assistance in men and money to duke William for his expedition in 1066, and when Wulfcytel abbat of Croyland, formerly a monk of Peterborough, was deposed in 1075, Ingulf was appointed his successor. He kept up his acquaintance with people about the king, especially with archbishop Lanfranc and Odo bishop of Bayeux the king's half brother, and so was able to procure permission for his predecessor to return to his old home at Peterborough, where he died in 1085.

During the time of his abbacy the new abbat exerted him- 441
self strenuously to retain the property of the abbey, and to regain what had been taken from it. In 1076, Ingulf had, he says, especial trouble with Asford of Helieston, the steward of abbat Wulfcytel, who knew the whole state of the monastic property, but refused to give the information that he possessed. At length he gave way as to other estates, but was obstinate with regard to Helieston, insisting that the estate belonged to him. However, through the death of Asford the convent recovered possession of its property there, and this part of it, being some meadow land, it held at the time of the composition of Ingulf's history (Fulm. p. 76, 77). Asford is a name found in Domesday in Lindsey (Photozincograph LXI. a) in the 'Terra Will*elmi* Blundi', at Croxby, and in the 'Clamores de Chetsteven' (Photozinc. LXXVIII. b): 'Terram Asford [Asford's land] in Bercham hundred dicit Wapentak non habuisse Herewardum die qua aufugiit'. Helieston (Fulm.) is probably Helpeston (Birch) Northants. near Market Deeping; but no Croyland estate at Helpeston is mentioned in Ingulf's version of Domesday, and the manor of Helpeston, spoken of Fulm. p. 63, was part of the property of Pegeland monastery and had been seized by 'Hugolin the treasurer' in c. 1048. Hugolinus is a norman name; 'Hugolinus de Escalfou' occurs at Saint-Évroul before 1093 (Ord. Vit. v. 183), and in Domesday (Ellis i. 233 Berkshire, 438 Somersetsh.). What the charter and the documents were, which the monks brought forward to prove their ownership, does not appear, as Helpeston is not referred to in any Ingulfine charter. Helpeston is not mentioned in Domesday (Bridges Northants ii. 514 ff.).

442 In the year 1091, a date also given by Joh. Petrib. and the Ann. de Wintonia, the monastery was nearly consumed by fire, and Ingulf erected as good a substitute as he could. The church was replaced by a better one in the years following 1114 by abbat Joffrid, but this too was burnt in 1146 (Joh. Petrib.) in the time of abbat Edward 1142-72 (Fulm. p. 452). Ordericus mentions the fire in Ingulf's time: 'Pars ecclesiæ cum officinis et vestibus et libris multisque aliis rebus necessariis repentino igne combusta est'.

443 In the year 1092, or soon after, Ingulf completed his history of the abbey (Fulm. p. 107); this he had put together

1. from the older history of the monastery up to c. 970, written by brother Swetman from information furnished him by the five Sempects in abbat Turketul's time (§ 196 ff.),

2. from the life of abbat Turketul written by abbat Egelric II. his kinsman and one of his immediate successors 984-992, supplemented by

3. his own account of the house from 975 to his own times.

444 Of the remaining 16 years of his life we are only told, that they were spent in restoring, as far as possible, the losses caused by the fire (Fulm. p. 112). His numerous ailments 'multiplices morbi' (including gout) hindered him in his later years from continuing the history of the abbey 'historiam sui monasterii' to the end of his life. He died on 16 kal. Jan. 1109, 9 Hen. I. i.e. on 17 Dec. 1108.

He is only thus mentioned at the beginning of Pet. Bles. in the letter of the archdeacon to the convent and in his account of the abbat's death, and not again till the end of the First Anonymous Continuation c. 1471 (Fulm. p. 545).

445 Dugdale in his Monasticon (ed. 1655 i. 383 ff., ed. 1816 iij. 544) makes use of a Bodl. MS. 'authore Simone Warwicensi [8. W. 46] 92. a', 'De fundatione abbatiæ sanctæ Mariæ virginis Eboraci anno ab incarnatione Domini Mlxxxviij', which professes to be the composition of abbat Stephen Whitby (d. 1112). It gives an account of the foundation of the abbey, and goes on to mention a claim made by archbishop Thomas on four acres of land, which was settled by king William II.; it then adds:

'Actum est hoc in concilio apud *Glocestriam*, audientibus istis... quorum nomina hic inserta sunt: *Anselmus Cantuar.* archiepiscopus, *Thomas Eboraci* archiepiscopus...*Robertus Herefordiæ* episcopus (1079 – 26 Jun. 1095)...*Robertus Lincoln.* episcopus (12 Feb. 1093/4 – 1123)...*Thorstanus Glestoniæ* abbas (§ 452)...*Ingolfus Croilandiæ* abbas...'. From the dates above given the council at Gloucester was held between 12 Feb. 1093¾ and 26 June 1095.

A further trace of Ingulf during this period is furnished us **446** in 'Annales Monasterii de Thorney' in the Isle of Ely from 961 to 1421, in MS. Cott. Nero C. vij. nᵒ. 13 fo. 79:

'A.D. MXCVIII. Hoc anno intravimus in novam ecclesiam nos Thornenses Id. Nov. [13 Nov.] primo. Postea Kal. Decemb. [1 Dec.] reliquias sanctorum transtulimus, presbiterio et duabus porticibus et turre solummodo perfectis: accersitis vicinis nostris, scilicet domino abbate Aldeuuino de Ramesie [1091 – 1112] et Ingulfo de Cruland, et priore de Burch, domino Alwaldo, quia sine abbate erat Burch tunc, et Rogero Bigod et multis aliis quorum nomina non recordor' (printed in Dugd. Mon. ij. 611. a).

Abbat Thurold died a. 1098 (Joh. Petrib.); after an election by the monks, which was not confirmed by archbishop Anselm, the abbey of Peterborough was vacant for five years.

'The whole story of the birth, education, promotion, fortunes **447** and deeds of abbat Ingulf there can be little doubt, with the exception of the slight' (?) 'foundation afforded by the pages of Vitalis, is as unsubstantial and fictitious as the narrative in reference to Turketul' (Riley).

Ingulf makes some display of classical lore. He speaks of Ovid's Metamorphoses and Isidorus' Etymologica; he mentions the planets Saturn, Jupiter, Mars, Mercury, and Venus; he uses several words of Greek origin (§ 324). The writer of the first part of the history of Croyland up to 870 has some classical allusions, if they be not Ingulf's additions; he quotes a line from Lucan and a passage from Statius, mentions the Amazons, Diana, Helen; the biographer of Turketul in like manner refers to Atropos and Alecto.

The charter of king Wiglaf of 833 has many classical names of the winds: Vulturnus, Subsolanus, Africus, Corus,

Favonius, and speaks of the destruction of Troy 'excidium Troiæ' (Fulm. p. 9).

448 The existence of Ingulf is vouched for by Ordericus Vitalis, the MS. Cott. Vesp. B. xj. and the MS. Cott. Claud. A. v. (Joh. Petrib.), besides the York charter and the Thorney chronicler mentioned above. His successor Joffrid was appointed in 1109 (Ord. Vit.); the date of Ingulf's death as given by Pet. Bles. 17 Dec. 1108 is therefore probably correct, the same day and month being also given by Ord. Vit.

449 The correctness of the year of Ingulf's succession to the abbacy given by himself as 1075 is more than doubtful. Ulfcytel Wulketul his predecessor was really deposed at a council held at Gloucester in the midwinter of 1085 – 86, when also three bishops, Maurice of London, William de Beaufeu of Thetford or Elmham, and Robert de Limesey of Chester or Lichfield were appointed. The latin App. of A.S.Chr. A. (A.S.Chr. [R. S.] j. 386 ff.) speaks thus: 'Sexto decimo anno [after the accession of Lanfranc to the primacy, i.e. in 1086] apud Cleucestriam concilium celebravit, in quo Wulfecetulum, Crulandensis coenobii abbatem deposuit'. To the same effect is the statement of Gervase of Canterbury (actus pontificum Cantuar. [R. S.] ii. 367): 'Sextum (concilium tenuit Lanfrancus) apud Glocestriam, in quo deposuit Wlfcetulum abbatem de Cruland'.

450 In Domesday also we find among the Tenants in capite in Surrey (Ellis i. 439):

'Terra Sancti Wandregisili. Abbas S. Wandregisili tenet Wandesorde per Ingulfum monachum'.

The Survey was ordered to be taken at Christmas 1085 and was rapidly completed in the course of the following year 1086. At Christmas 1085 also Ulfcytel was deposed by archbishop Lanfranc, and Ingulf was appointed abbat of Croyland soon after, being then a monk of the monastery of Saint Wandragesilus or Wandrille. If the Wandsworth monk is not the abbat of Croyland, we have here at all events a very curious coincidence in name, monastery and date. Otherwise, living at Wandsworth as representative of the monastery, Ingulf might easily keep up, or renew, his acquaintance with the Court, and his speedy appointment would be not unlikely. The monastery of Saint-Wandrille possessed, besides, lands in Dorsetshire and in Cambridgeshire at Dullingham (Ellis i. 506). In like manner his successor Joffrid of Orleans was sent over to England, when prior of Saint-Évroul, by his abbat in 1097 (Ord. Vit. iij. 453). Between Croyland and Saint-Wandrille there was the indirect connexion that Judith the widow of earl Waltheof (§ 231) bestowed on the Norman monastery 3½ hides at Buchidone (Buckden) in Northants 'concessu Regis' (Ellis j. 330).

Moreover Wulketul was still abbat in 1080, as he is mentioned **451** under that date in MS. Cott. Tib. A. vj. (Hamilton, Inquisit. Comit. Cantabr. 4°. Lond. 1876, pref. p. xvij) the year being given 'Anno ab Incarnatione Domini millesimo octogesimo, Indictione xj, epactæ xxvj', this paragraph being also given in identical terms in Liber Eliensis Vol. I. p. 251. There is, however, this difficulty, that in the year 1080 the Indiction was iij.

There is again another difficulty with regard to Wulketul. **452** Ingulf states, that that abbat, after being deposed in 1075, was committed to the custody of Thurstan abbat of Glastonbury; but Ord. Vit. says only: 'Glestoniæ claustro deputatus est' (ij. 285), without mentioning Thurstan; and Thurstan or Turstin of Caen, who was appointed in 1081 (Ord. Vit. ij. 226¹, iij. 266¹), was by the king sent back to Normandy in 1083 on account of his sanguinary treatment of his monks; so that he was abbat neither in 1075 nor in 1085. By bribery he recovered his abbey in England early in the reign of William Rufus, and died in 1110 (Fl. Wig. a. 1083, Ord. Vit. iij. 310 note). The MS. Cott. Vesp. B. xj. 'Vitæ abbatum Croylandiæ' and Leland's account of the abbats of Croyland agree with Ord. Vit. in not mentioning Thurstan, and in fixing the beginning of Ingulf's abbacy at 24 years before Dec. 1108, or in 1085.

Wulketul sat for 24 years according to Ord. Vit. (ij. 285); **453** this would make his appointment date from 1062; indeed Freeman (iv. 598, 805) accepts this year as that of the accession of Wulketul; but the dates and other details given by Ord. Vit. are not too trustworthy. The accession of

Wulketul is placed by Ingulf in 1052, between the visit of duke William to England in 1051 and the deaths of queen Ælfgifu-Emma in 1052 (Freeman) and of earl Godwine in 1053. Ord. Vit. says, that he was appointed to Croyland 'jubente Leofrico abbate [Burgensi]', who sat 1052 – 1066; this unfortunately decides neither for 1052 nor for 1062.

454 Joh. Petrib. s. a. 1075 speaks of that year as the 20th year of abbat Wulfketul's rule, 'vicesimo anno regiminis sui'. In 1075 he speaks of, or places, both the decollation and burial of earl Waltheof and the deposition of abbat Wulfcytel. The abbat would then have been appointed in 1055. With regard to the death of abbat Wulfcytel he says: 'post paucos dies morbo correptus in Domino requievit', which might well enough be correct of his deposition in 1085.

455 Wulketul's predecessor Wulget 'Wulfgeat' was abbat in 1052 or even in 1051 (Cartul. Mon. de Rameseia [R. S.] j. 188 ff., ij. 79). In the Cartul. Rames. j. 188 ff. is an undated charter of Eadward the Confessor referring to an exchange of lands between the monasteries of Ramsey and of Burgh [Peterborough]; it is witnessed by abbat Wulget. Harold, who succeeded his father as earl of Wessex in Apr. 1053, but who before that was earl of the East-Angles in 1045? (Freeman ij. Ed. III. p. 37), is mentioned as 'earl' in that charter. The latin translation states: 'Notificaverunt...mihi, quod hæc compositio facta fuit inter eos sub testimonio Lefsii abbatis de Ely, et Wlfgeti abbatis Croylandiæ...'. But from the Liber Eliensis (Vol. I. pp. 200 ff. 215 ff.) it would appear, that Leofsy was appointed by king Cnut in 1029, and dying 26 Nov. 1044 (Anglia Sacra j. 609) was succeeded by Wulfric in 1045. According to this, Leofsy 1029 – 1044 could not have been the contemporary of either Leofric abbat of Peterborough 1052 – 66 or of Wlfgeat of Croyland 1048 – ....., as represented in this document.

456 A correction of ten years does not get over the difficulties in the chronology of the appointment of Wulketul and of his deposition and the subsequent appointment of Ingulf, for the following reasons:

1. Ingulf (Fulm. p. 65) recounts the death of abbat Wulget

'Nonis Junii' [5 June] 1052; Ord. Vit. says 'Nonas Julii' 7 July, without specifying the year; Ingulf then mentions the succession of abbat Wulketul, and a series of events belonging to the years 1053 – 6 – 5 – 7 – 8 – 9 – 1060 – 1 – 2 – 3 – 5 – 6. He clearly seems then to intend to fix 1052 as the date of the accession of Wulketul. This would also give Wulget only four years of rule at Croyland, although Ord. Vit. says of him: 'Vulfgeatus.... postquam longo tempore Crulandiae curam gessit.... obiit' (ij. 285);

2. The deposition of Wulketul is stated to have taken place 'cito post sancti martyris [Waldevi] sepulturam' (§ 232); and

3. Wulketul is said to have survived his deposition for 10 years, dying on St Jerome's day 30 Sept. 1085, while Ord. Vit. says: 'post aliquot annos vii°. Idus Junii [7 June] obiit', again without specifying the year.

The fact of king William I. sending for Ingulf in abbat **457** Gerbert's time presents no difficulty, as Gerbert lived to 1089.

The words 'non paucis interlabentibus annis' (Fulm. p. 74) referring to the time between Ingulf's entering the monastery of Fontenelle and his promotion to be prior, seem to belong wholly to the period before the Conquest; but perhaps they were inserted where they stand only in order to complete Ingulf's history before he became abbat of Croyland, and the date of his becoming prior might then fall some years after the Conquest, and not before it, as the position of those words might seem to imply (see § 440); Joffrid of Orleans had been monk of Saint-Évroul for 15 years, before he became prior of the monastery.

There is a further troublesome circumstance, that Ingulf **458** (Fulm. p. 78) speaks of his making use at London of the intercession of (among others) Odo bishop of Bayeux. Now Odo was in prison at Rouen from 1082 (A.S.Chr. E., Fl. Wig.) to king William's death in Sept. 1087. Ingulf might therefore have interceded for his deposed predecessor, if Wulketul's deposition had been in 1076, but not if it happened in 1086.

François Michel in his Chroniques Anglo-Normandes prints **459** (ij. 99 ff.), from the Douai MS. n°. 801, the 'Vita et passio Waldevi comitis', by William of Ramsey, a monk of Croyland (§ 80). This mentions the execution of Waltheof and the removal of his body to Croyland a fortnight after by abbat Wulketul 'Ulketellus', but says nothing of that abbat's deposition; it then relates the translation of his remains from the chapter house to the church near the altar 'sexto decimo anno suae dormitionis', under abbat Ingulf, no notice being taken of the great fire. After mentioning the miracles wrought at Waltheof's tomb, the writer finishes his account by relating the blasphemy and death of Audin the monk of St Alban's in the days of abbat Joffrid, Ingulf's successor, and that abbat's vision of St Guthlac and St Bartholomew. This story is also told by Ord. Vit. (ij. 288 – 9), and from this in Pet. Bles. (Fulm. pp. 116 – 7). St Neot being in this latter place added to the other two Saints.

460 Dr Lingard in the Index to his History of England (5th ed. 1849, Vol. x. p. 490) styles Ingulf 'bishop and historian'! He accepts his history generally, although considering it to be 'much interpolated'. He has however not stated, what passages he considered interpolations. Mr Riley also says: 'it cannot be denied that the work is full of interpolations'; the chief interpolations, that he suspects, are in:

the notice of Turketul as 'chancellor' to the king,

the account of Turketul's influence in the matter of the seven bishops of 905,

the mention of Oxford as a place of education in the 11th century, and (in Pet. Bles.)

the allusion to the writings of Averroes.

461 In Gunton's History of Peterborough [1686] App. pp. 253 ff. we find mentioned, among certain witnesses of the time of abbat Joffrid 1109 – 1124, 'Robertus nepos abbatis Ingulphi' with the reference 'Swaph. fo. cxviij'.

462 Names belonging to the time of Ingulf after 1075 (?) besides those already mentioned (§ 329, 400), are:

Jocelyn, priest of Cappelade (Whaplode),

Fulcard, priest (intruded) [moneyer of Æthelred II.],

Grimketul, corrodier [§ 132],
Fulmar, cantor of the monastery,
Haco of Multon [§ 412],
Elsin (Ælfsige) of Pinchbeck,
Ardnot (Eardnoth) of Spalding,
Juliana a widow [Hunter pp. 16, 58, 59, 102 etc.],
Fergus, coppersmith of Boston, a Scotch name [Bened. Abbas R. S. j. 67],
Trig, procurator of the monastery [§ 413],
Wulsin (Wulfsige), barber of the monastery,
'Seniannus' de Lek [Andreas de Leck Fulm. p. 484 a. 1390; Johannes Leck de Grantham, Fuller Worthies Linc. Names of the gentry 1434],
Asius, procurator of the monastery,
Ægelmer (Æthelmær), procurator of the monastery.

In the charter of Thorold of Bukenhale no. 16 (§ 402) we find a series of names of his serfs, which may be inserted here, as they are mostly found in Domesday:

Colgrin, [moneyer at Lincoln and York, Æthelred II. and Cnut. Domesday Linc. no. LXVII. no. XI. (Croyland)],
Hardyng, § 133,
Lefstan, Leofstan [moneyer of Æthelstan II. and Cnut],
Ryngulf, § 397,
Elstan, Ælfstan, [bishop of London 961 – 996],
Gunter Liniet,
Outi Grimkelson, [Outi Domesday Linc. VII. Outi de Lincoln 31 H. 1. Hunter Mag. Rot. Scacc.],
Turstan Dubbe,
Algar (Ælfgar), niger, the swarthy,
Edric, Eadric son of Siward. Siward and Edric. Domesday Linc. no. III. at Fulletby,
Osmund, [bishop of London 802 – c. 808, of Salisbury 1078 – 1099],
Besi Tuk, [Bese moneyer at Reading, Eadred. Domesday Linc. LVI],
Elmer (Ælfmær), of Pyncebek,
Goose Gamelson; Gamel was a tenant of Croyland. Domesday Linc. no. XI.

The object of the author of this present investigation into the History of Ingulf, which is the first part of the Historia Croylandensis, is rather to enable a more competent student to arrive at a definite conclusion respecting its date, than to speak himself decidedly on that matter.

The Ingulf has been the subject of much controversy, the result being, that, whereas in the sixteenth and seventeenth centuries it was looked upon by Caius, Parker, Savile, Camden, Dugdale and other antiquaries as a most important and trustworthy authority on early English history, it has sunk down to a position of almost contempt and is treated as a mere forgery (F. Liebermann, Ostenglische Geschichtsquellen. Neues Arch. xviii. 1892).

But even then, Ingulf is a forgery of mediæval times, and since it has gained admission into 'our elementary books, nay' into 'more than elementary books' (Stubbs), it must surely be interesting to trace out, on the one hand, how far its statements, which are said to have done so much mischief, are derived or copied from statements of contemporary writers, how far they may have originated in misunderstandings of those historians, how far they are shared by mediæval writers, and, on the other hand, how far they are the result of the imagination and invention of the author.

With regard to the statement, that Ingulf is a forgery, 'a mere monkish invention', 'little better than a historical novel' (Palgrave, Qu. Rev. 1826, p. 294), critics who accept it differ very much as to the date of the forgery. While Hickes was willing to some extent to believe, that Ingulf forged only the charters, the history being then of the assumed date of c. 1095, Sir Francis Palgrave (Qu. Rev. 1826, pp. 295, 296) was of opinion (from Spelman's misreading of *Euestres* for *Euesges*, a mistake consequent on the peculiar handwriting of the Croyland 'autograph') that the whole was compiled 'during the reign of Edward I. and II.' (1272 - 1327), 'about the end of the thirteenth, or the first half of the fourteenth, century' (c. 1280 - 1350), or (Doc. and Records, p. cvj) in the reign of Edward II. (1307 - 1327); but Mr Riley considered that the charters were forged c. 1415, 'the manuscript long preserved at Croyland as the *autograph* of Ingulph' being then 'first compiled', and he thus describes the doings of the monks: 'Finding among their archives a Chronicle of the convent from the earliest times, (said to have been composed by the Sempects by order of abbat Turketul) the monks made it the vehicle of their fictitious Charters, added to it the histories which had been written by Egelric and Ingulph, had the whole copied afresh, and deposited the manuscript in the Sacristy as corroborative proof of their title to their lands. It was for this reason, perhaps, that so few copies of the manuscript were allowed to circulate; as the forgers must have been conscious that to the scrutinizing view of the scholar, the anachronisms and contradictions with which the Charters were filled would be too evident' (Ingulph's Chronicle, Introd. p. x).

Mr Riley thus, in 1854, accepted Ingulf's statements respecting the materials of the Historia Croylandensis, and only charged the monks with forging the charters. But the notion, that the monks should forge the charters with conscious ignorance and carelessness, and copy them into the Historia Croylandensis, and then store the manuscript away for fear of the fifteenth century scholars detecting the anachronisms in them, is a somewhat strange one.

But in 1861 his views had become more sweeping, and he boldly rejected the whole of the Ingulf, both history and charters. Of course with the Ingulf the later work, the continuation by Petrus Blesensis must also fall, for it seems scarcely imaginable, that a genuine Ingulf should have been replaced by a forged Ingulf, while the genuine Pet. Bles. remained untouched.

Why the author of the Ingulf should have been at the trouble to compile his work, is not clear. Hickes thinks, that it was found necessary to forge the Golden Charter of Æthelbald, that the convent might preserve from Norman spoilers lands, which it had held undisturbed without deeds, or lands of which the deeds had been lost. But there is nothing more in the restoration-charter of Eadred than is registered in Domesday, —indeed Domesday has the record of certain pieces of property as belonging to the monastery, of which no notice is taken in the Ingulf,—and what else was in the earlier Mercian charters was totally lost, and acknowledged as lost, while there is no charter recited in the Historia Croylandensis, which might have acted as a protection to any property acquired after c. 1095.

The date of the compilation of the Ingulf it seems at present difficult to fix. Ingulf borrows expressions from Florence of Worcester (d. 1117), from William of Malmesbury (c. 1128), from Ordericus Vitalis (c. 1141), and from John of Salisbury (c. 1182). This at all events fixes the compilation to about a century later than Ingulf's date of c. 1095. If we further allow, that John of Peterborough (MS. Cott. Claudius A. v) supplies materials for the Ingulf, this would bring the compilation of the work down later than 1368, when the above MS. abruptly closes.

But furthermore, a MS. in the British Museum (MS. Cott. Vitell. B. xj) contains a history of the abbots of Croyland extending to the year 1427, a work which must have been written by a person interested in Croyland, extracted as to the Anglo-Saxon part of the Croyland history from Ordericus Vitalis only, with total disregard of Ingulf, while the Ingulf itself exists in another MS. (MS. Cott. Otho B. xiij) written about 1490. The date of the composition of the Ingulf seems then necessarily to fall between those two periods, or somewhere about 1450. The author there seems no possibility of even guessing at.

The charters of Æthelbald king of Mercia of 716 and of Eadred king of England of 948 were, however, in existence in 1393, as in that year they were recited in a charter of Inspeximus and Confirmation (§ 192); indeed the former is mentioned by Ordericus Vitalis, who wrote c. 1140.

Sir Francis Palgrave says (Doc. and Records, p. cvj), that Ingulf was 'in after times' (i.e. later than c. 1290) 'considered as the peculiar treasure and pride of the abbey'. Unfortunately he has given no references to corroborate this assertion, but it may be derived from a passage at the end of the First Anonymous Continuation (Fulm. p. 545).

If the Chronicle of Sir John Harrington belongs really (as Sir Thomas Lambert its translator says) to 'the beginning of Henry the Eighth's time', then both the Ingulf and the Pet. Bles. its continuation were in existence in c. 1510, as he says : 'This is to be redd in Ingulphus' (Gough II. App. p. 225), and 'Soe it appeareth by Petrus Blessensis' (p. 236). The latter work he may have known in a more complete form than that exhibited by Fulman's edition of 1684.

But these two parts of the Historia Croylandensis were quite unknown to John Bale in 1557, while only the Ingulf as printed by the first editor Sir Henry Savile was known to Dr Caius in 1574.

The fact of the Ingulf being a mediæval forgery increases the difficulty of working at it. Unlike the small but mischievous work of Richard of Cirencester, which Prof. Mayor was able to dissect and resolve into its easily recognized and identified atoms, the Ingulf is of considerable length, 107 large and closely printed folio pages, and is derived from the writings of many not very familiar authors, which have to be searched very closely to find the passages, and even the words, which have been borrowed. A systematic study of the whole book has been attempted, but it is quite possible that a still more minute investigation would reveal points that would betray the date of its composition.

Many mistakes made by the Ingulfine compiler have been noticed, but also some curious points of accuracy; some of the mistakes have arisen through the ignorance of the copiers of the Marsham MS. (§ 105 ff.) or of the MS. Cott. Otho B. xiij (§ 111 ff.); the recognized historians, however, are not without errors of the grossest kind.

If an excuse is needed for this investigation into the Historia Croylandensis, it may be found in the fact, that the author's mediæval predecessors in the vicarage of Hockington were monks of Croyland, the manor and advowson having been in the possession of that abbey till the dissolution of the monasteries in 1539, after which revolution they became in 1557, in the reign of queen Mary I, the possession of Queens' College, Cambridge. They were held by the monastery certainly in 1086, being mentioned in Domesday among the possessions of Croyland, but how much earlier cannot be determined, unless we accept the statement of Ingulf and of Ordericus Vitalis respecting Turketul and his gift to the monastery of six manors, of which Hockington was one. A desire to explore the history of Hockington led to a desire to explore the history of Croyland, when the Historia Croylandensis offered itself as matter for investigation, which has resulted in the foregoing pages.

CORRIGENDA AND ADDENDA.

p. 7, l. 28, *read:* possessions
p. 9, l. 17, *read:* elucubratiuncula
p. 14, l. 2, *read:* 673
p. 21, l. 22, *read:* His
p. 22, l. 19, *read:* ædificato
p. 24, l. 9, *read:* [R.S.], and so elsewhere.
p. 25, l. 4, *read:* Policraticus
p. 28, l. 36, *read:* Priore
p. 30, l. 12, *read:* anglorum regi dedicavit
p. 33, l. 21, *read:* vita
p. 34, l. 2, *read:* miraculis
p. 36, l. 14, *add:* (Wright [Thos.] Biogr. Brit. Lit. ij. 424.)
p. 38, l. 20. This work has since come to light, having been discovered by M. Paul Meyer, professor at the École des Chartes at Paris, in the MS. Trin. Coll. Dubl. B. 2. 7. It is simply a re-writing, in an abridged form, of Felix' life of the saint. Few expressions, indeed, derived immediately from the original, are to be found in it, but the chapters follow on in exactly the same order. It is introduced by an undated letter of 'Petrus Blesensis Bathoniensis archidiaconus' to Henry de Longchamp, abbat of Croyland, and is followed by a chapter 'De munificentia Aethelbaldi,' which seems re-written from the account given by Ord. Vit. of the building and endowment of the monastery, though with a difference in the extent of land given to the monks.

This life of St Guthlac, with its continuations, is certainly the composition of the writer of the Opera Petri Blesensis, for in it we find repetitions of passages taken from the Epp., and from the following opuscula: In depravatorem, Compendium in Job, and Passio Reginaldi, and also from Sermo 62.

p. 42, l. 8, *read:* virginis

p. 42, l. 14, *read:* Ménard
p. 44, l. 1, *read:* MS
p. 53, l. 32, *read:* Twysden
p. 59, l. 21, *read:* defensione regis ligea debent esse,...
p. 61, l. 17, *read:* Ingulfine
p. 61, l. 30, *read:* (Ascytel), ...
p. 62, l. 2, *read:* 833 :
p. 68, l. 18, *read:* horse thane
p. 69, l. 16, *read:* and
p. 73, l. 23, *read:* Brunanburh
p. 75, l. 23, *read:* expectabant,
p. 78, l. 21, *add:* In Birch's Cartularium Saxonicum are notices of several persons of King Eadgar's time named Thurkytel:

1. B.C.S. 1017–1020 K.C.D. 960, 961, —, 959 are undated charters of the Thurkytel Heyng referred to in § 167.
2. B.C.S. 1044 K.C.D.— a grant of Eadgar of A.D. 958 to Oscytel archb. of York, and B.C.S. 1052 K.C.D. 480 a grant of the king of A.D. 959 to Quen, a matron, of land in Yorkshire, which contain some northern and norse names among the signatures, have both the name: 'Thurkytel minister.'
3. B.C.S. 1266 K.C.D. 563* a royal charter of A.D. 970 to Ely monastery has the signatures of two persons named Thurcytel referred to in § 167. They are described by Kemble as 'm.,' by Stewart in the Liber Eliensis, where the charter is also found, as 'miles,' and by Birch from the Stowe Charter 31 in the British Mus. as 'minister.' The original charter is mentioned by Birch as 'doubtful if authentic.'
4. B.C.S. 1220 K.C.D. 598* a royal charter of A.D. 968 to Winchester Cathedral of lands in Somerset is witnessed among others by 'Thyrcytel abbas.'

B.C.S. 1230 K.C.D. 556 a royal grant of A.D. 969 to the thegn Ælfhelm of lands in Oxfordshire has among its signataries 'Thurcytel abbas.'

B.C.S. 1266 K.C.D. 563* the royal charter of A.D. 970 to Ely monastery above referred to has in addition the name of 'Thurcytel abbas.'

Several other charters, which contain long lists of abbats, and might in consequence have been expected to have supplied us with the name of an abbat Thurcytel, do not do so; e.g. B.C.S. 1228, 1268 K.C.D. —, 483*, forged charters to Westminster of A.D. 969 ;
B.C.S. 1269 K.C.D. 1270, a charter to Ely of A.D. 970 ;
B.C.S. 1303 K.C.D. —, a charter to the thegn Ælfhere of Devon of the year 974.

It would seem, then, that there was a real abbat Thurcytel of an unrecorded abbey in the west of England, whose name appears in K.C.D. 598* and 556, and who is different from the abbat of Bedford and of Ramsey referred to in § 166.

Another charter pertaining to Wilton Nunnery printed in the 'Registrum Wiltonense' (fo. Lond. 1827) by sir R. C. Hoare from MS. Harl. 436, contains the name of this western abbat.

Strangely, this charter has been overlooked by both Kemble and Birch, who print every other one of the 36 charters contained in the MS. and the folio of 1827.

It is here given from the MS., having enjoyed the advantage of Mr Birch's collation and the careful supervision of Prof. Skeat.

Grant by King Eadgar to Wilton Nunnery of land at South Newton, Sherrington, Deverill, Watchingwell (I. W.), Frustfield and Baverstock formerly held by Wulfthryth A.D. 968.

SUÐ NIWETUNE.

Ðis his þare landa boc þe Eadgar cyng geboeode Gode and Se'a Marian into Wiltune, swa he hy ær forlet to Wulfðriðe, him to ecere alysednesse.

Omnium jura regnorum celestium atque terrestrium, claustra quoque infernalium, dumtaxat divinis Dei nutibus subiecta sunt. Quapropter cunctis sanum sapientibus satagendum est toto mentis conamine, ut prævideant qualiter tormenta valeant evadere infernalia et celestis vitæ gaudia concedente Christo Jesu concendere. Hoc EADGAR rex Anglorum cum Norþhymbra regimine, ac progenie Paganorum Brettonumque prosapia sublimiter roboratus, sagaciter intelligens secum tractat, concedens largiflue lucrum cosmi, Christicolis ut choris angelicis feliciter collocetur. Huius rei gratia Rex præfatus rura quæ olim WULF-DRYDE temporaliter concesserat, Domino nostro Jesu Christo ejusque genitrici Mariæ, ad usus sanctimonialium in Wiltune degentium, eterna largitus est dapsilitate, uti ecclesiæ Mariæ genetricis Domini nostri Jesu Christi consecratæ cum omnibus utensilibus, pratis videlicet, pascuis, silvis, perpetuo deserviant.

Prædictæ telluris nomina hæc sunt: NIWANTUN, SCEARN-TUN, DEFEREAL, BABBANSTOC, FRYSTESFELD, HWÆTINC.

Sint autem hæc rura omni terrenæ servitutis iugo libera, tribus exceptis, rata videlicet expeditione, pontis arcisve restauratione. Si quis igitur hanc nostram donationem in aliud quam constituimus transferre voluerit, privatus consortio sanctæ Dei ecclesiæ, in æternis barathi incendiis lugubris iugiter cum Iuda Christi proditore eiusque complicibus puniatur, si non satisfactione emendaverit congrua quod contra nostrum deliquit decretum.

His autem metis præfata rura hinc inde girantur.

Þis sint þare ·x· hida land-gemære to Niwantune. Ærest, of ðare lace, up andlang Wilig on Stanford; þanon up andlang þæs hwitan weges; of þan weige on þa die, andlang die east on þone caldan her-paðe; of þone caldan her-paþe ut on Afene, andlang Afene on þas poles heafod; þanon on Ættandenes norð hyldan swa seo calda furh scæt up to þam stænenan stapole, and swa west to þære caldan hline-rewe, and swa be þære yrð-mearce nyþer to Higforda; of þan forda est ofer Wilig on otores hol; of þam hole up andlang Wilig; of Wilig on þa fulan lace; of þare lace ðwires ofer þa die west; be þære die-heafde on Winding ford ufeweardne; þanon up andlang þære westemyste lace; swa eft on Wilig.

Dis synt þara x hida land-gemæra to Scearntune. Ærest, on Odenford; þanon on heandunsweoran easteweardan, and swa up andlang wille weges; þanon on Grimes-die andlang die on Leofheres garan west-weardan; of þam garan on Bradanleage westeweardan; þonon andlang hlinces to þam caldan elebeme, and swa forð to Wurdeslea middeweardne; and þonne on Mædenbeorge, and swa ut on Wilig.

Dis synt þare ·xx· hida land-gemæra to Defereal. Ærest, of Defereal on þa caldan die, and swa andlang die to Langan beorge; þonon on þone her-pað, andlang paþes on Pudelan ham; þonon on Hean leage; þonon on Peocesham : of þam hamme on laudes(?)wege; of þam wege on þa caldan die; of þære die on þone her-paþ; andlang paþes on Efer beorhe; of ðam beorge þanon eft on Defereal.

Dis sint þare ·x· hida land-gemæra to Hwæt ineg le þe hyræð into Niwantune. Ærest, of þære sie, andlang stiðes fleotes heafod ; of þam heafde on þa ge-clyppedan treowa ; of þam treowan on Heort-lege; þanon on þa wylle; þanon on þa ræwe on ðane haliganstan; þanon on þære caldan heorte heges (sic) ræwe on Mot-beorh; þanon on Hreces cumbes heafde on

þanc lim-pyt; þanon on Hrece-lenge middewcardre; þonon on Æsc-stede; of Æsc-stede þonon eft on þa sæ.
Dys synt þare ·iii· hida land-gemære to Fyrstes felda. Ærest, of þam secundan hweole, andlang hemede weges on þone caldan mapoldre; þonne on þa ruwan þirnan; þanon on þa oðre on þæs heges byht; of þæs heges byhte on Fox-hylle; þonne west in on ðone crundel; þanon on ðene caldan orcheard eal swa þe hege bylþ swa on ðaere her-pæð; andlang paðes on Dyre broc; of þam broce on þone wylman on þitan wille; þanon on Hæsyl oran; þonne ut þurh þane holt on þæt secunde hweol.
Dis synt þære ·iii· hida land-gemære to Babanstoce. Ærest, of die on Huna weg, andlang Huna weges on Æsc-wylle; andlang Acscwylles ut on Nodre; up on Noddre on Luing lace oð ðone ford; þanan norð andlang dic on þa readan hane; þonon on caldan þorn; of þam þorne on haran wic westwearde; þonon on haran apuldre; þanon on þa caldan gemotewil(l)e; þanon andlang dic; þanon eft on Huna weg.
þonne scalde Eadgar cing twa mylna on Wiltune into þære stowe swa swa he hy aer Wulfþryþe geseald hæfde.

Anno Dominicæ incarnationis DCCCCLXVIIJ scripta est hæc carta, his testibus consentientibus, quorum inferius nomina notantur:

    Ego Eadgar, rex Anglorum, corroboravi.
    Ego Dunstan archiepiscopus concessi.
    Ego Oscytel archiepiscopus confirmavi.
Ego Aðelwold ep's consolidavi.   Ego Bryhthelm ep's concessi.
Ego Aelfstan ep's consignavi.   Ego Oswold ep's adquievi.
Ego Osulf ep's consensi.   Ego Alfwold ep's confirmavi.
    Aelfðryð regina.

Acscwig		Aeþelgar		Ealdred	
Osgar	abbas.	Cynewcard	abbas.	Siferð	abbas.
Aelfstan		Þurcytel			
Aeþelstan		Oslac		Eadulf	
Aelfeah	dux.	Aeþelwine	dux.	Beorhtnoð	dux.
Ordgar					
Byrhtferð		Wulfstan		Leofsige	
Eanulf	miles.	Aelfsige	miles.	Aelfhelm	miles.
Aelfwine		Alfwold		Leofwine	
Aeþelweard					

MS. Harl. 436, f. 24.   Registrum Wiltunense [R. C. Hoare, fº. Lond. 1827] p. 12 ff.   Dugd. Mon. [1816] ij. 324.

p. 83, l. 33, *read:* la petite Bretaigne

p. 80, l. 33. In B.C.S. 720 K.C.D. 1128* 'the original charter to the burgesses of Malmesbury' (a spurious charter) we find king Æthelstan (925 – 940) speaking of Wolsinus his chancellor and Odo his treasurer. This was in Thurkytel's time.

p. 83, l. 37, *read :* fo.

p. 103, l. 9, *read :* valida manu,

p. 119, l. 7, *read :* Riley copies Thorpe, who translates......

p. 123, l. 12, *read :* æmulari

p. 126, l. 1, *read :* Stubbs'

p. 133, l. 20, according to Rob. de Torigni, archbishop Robert of Jumiéges died between 1055 and 1060 [R.S. Chron. of the reigns of Stephen, Henry II and Richard I] iv. 34.

p. 134, l. 18, *read :* ...Anglorum (l. ij. c. 2).'

p. 134, l. 31, *read :* Tocsny

p. 137, l. 34, *read :* Ingulf has...

p. 151, l. 3, *add :* by Rev. J. B. Mackinlay O.S.B. in his St Edmund king and martyr (1893)

p. 158, l. 20, *read :* Cynethryth

p. 161, l. 22, *read :* Records; and so elsewhere.

p. 178, l. 26, *read :* 'basileus'

p. 181, l. 12, *read :* Fœdera (1816)...

p. 182, l. 6, *read :* east

p. 183, l. 4, *read :* puts it

p. 183, l. 18, *read :* Cart. Sax.

p. 185, l. 2, *read :* Delisle

p. 185, l. 4. The mortuary roll of c. 1113 is printed in 'Rouleaux des morts du ixe au xve siècle' by Léopold Delisle (8vo. Paris 1866). Matilda was the daughter of William the Conqueror, and abbess of the Trinity at Caen. News of her death and requests for prayers for the repose of her soul were sent to 253 monastic establishments in France and England, and in return many of these houses begged for the prayers of the nunnery at Caen on behalf of their own members, sometimes in general terms, but often with mention of the persons, for whom intercession was requested. Of this latter kind was the reply of Croyland abbey, which is here transcribed (Delisle, p. 200):

44. TITULUS SANCTI BARTHOLOMEI ET SANCTI GUTHLACI
CRULANDIE.

Anima ejus et animae omnium fidelium in Christi nomine requiescant in pace. Amen.

Orate pro nostris, Thurkytelo abbate [948—975], Oskytelo abbate, Ulskytelo (l. Ullkytelo) abbate [1052—1075], Godrico abbate [1005—1018], Algerico (l. Egelrico) abbate [975—984 or 984—992], Ingulfo abbate, Wlfgeto abbate [1048—1052], Suivato (l. Siwato) priore, Afgaro (l. Algaro ?) priore, Feggo monacho, Leofwino monacho, Bristano monacho, Askyllo monacho, Thurgislo monacho, Triggo monacho, Ulfo monacho.

p. 185. l. 25, *read*: of 1113
p. 192, l. 19, *read*: § 288

Only one charter, besides the forged charters of the Ingulf, has come down to us from Anglo Saxon times with a reference to Croyland abbey, viz. K.C.D. 953, printed with a translation in Thorpe, Diplomatarium pp. 594—596. The translation of part of the charter is thence transcribed.

ULF AND WIFE. ABOUT MLXVI.

✠ This is the agreement that Ulf and Madselm his consort made with God and St Peter, when they went to Jerusalem.

Þat is þat land æt Carlatune into Burh æfter heora dæge heora saule to alysednesse, and þat land æt Bytham into Sēe Guthlace.

That is, [they give] the land at Carlton to Peterborough after their day, for the redemption of their souls; and the land at Bytham to St Guthlac's [at Crowland];

and the land at Sempringham to St Benedict's at Ramsey, and the land at Lofington and at Hardwick to bishop Ealdred (bishop of Worcester 1044—1061, archbishop of York 1061—1069), at full price; and the land at Shillington, and at Hoby, and at Morton, whereon are due to the bishop eight marks of gold. And if they come home, let the bishop be paid his gold; and if neither of them come, let the bishop do for their souls as much as the land is better than the gold is. And if it betide the bishop other than all good, let the abbot Brand (abbot of Peterborough 1066—1069) enter on the same agreement...

......And if I come not home, let Ingemund have the land at Carrington; and the land at Claxby I have given to Healdene my brother; and the land at Ormsby and all that I there possessed, to St Mary's convent. And let my pages have the land at Linbeorh, if I come not home; and let the land that she has at Loughton be given to Thorney.

There is among Kemble's charters an extract referring to Earl Waltheof (§ 228 ff.) from the Register of Peterborough Abbey (MS. Soc. Ant. No. 60) thus given as no. 927:

WÆLDEOF, 1066—1069.

✠ Godgive uidua dedit sancto Petro in loco qui dicitur Burch duas uillas Righale et Beolmesthorp, pro redemptione animæ suae per consensum regis Eaduuardi. Postea accepit eam Siwardus comes in conjugio; post tempus non multum mortua est, et deprecatus est Siuuardas comes abbatem Leofricum et fratres, ut quamdiu uiueret posset habere supradictas uillas; et post illius decessum reuerterentur ad monasterium. Mortuoque Siwardo comite, facta est conuentio ante regem Eaduuardam inter Waltheof filium supradicti comitis et Leofricum abbatem, et accepit ipse Waltheof .v. marcas auri, tali tenore, ut ipse Waltheof haberet Righale in uita sua, et Beolmesthorp quieta remansit in monasterio sancti Petri per iussionem regis Eaduuardi. Hoc actum est ante regem publice; sed post mortem regis fracta est conuentio ab ipso Waltheofo. Sed postea, pœnitentia ductus, ueniente ipso ad monasterium præfatum, concessit ambas terras sancto Petro, eo tenore, ut ipse quamdiu uiueret teneret; et post obitum illius ambas simul in monasterio dimitteret; nec ipse aliquomodo istam conuentionem frangere, nec terras proprio reatu perdere, potest. Sed si quis istud instinctu diabolico euertere cupit, sciat se excommunicatum cum ipso diabolo in inferno mercedem accipere. Fiat! Fiat!

www.ingramcontent.com/pod-product-compliance
Lightning Source LLC
Chambersburg PA
CBHW021834230426
43669CB00008B/971